Church and Society in England: Henry VIII to James I

Each volume in the 'Problems in Focus' series is designed to make available to students important new work on key historical problems and periods that they encounter in their courses. Each volume is devoted to a central topic or theme, and the most important aspects of this are dealt with by specially commissioned studies from scholars in the relevant field. The editorial Introduction reviews the problem or period as a whole, and each chapter provides an assessment of the particular aspect, pointing out the areas of development and controversy, and indicating where conclusions can be drawn or where further work is necessary. An annotated bibliography serves as a guide to further reading.

PROBLEMS IN FOCUS SERIES

PUBLISHED

The Hundred Years War
edited by Kenneth Fowler

Church and Society in England: Henry VIII to James I
edited by Felicity Heal and Rosemary O'Day

The Reign of James VI and I
edited by Alan G. R. Smith

The Origins of the English Civil War
edited by Conrad Russell

The Interregnum: The Quest for Settlement 1646–1660
edited by G. E. Aylmer

Britain after the Glorious Revolution 1689–1714
edited by Geoffrey Holmes

Popular Movements, c. 1830–1850
edited by J. T. Ward

The New Poor Law in the Nineteenth Century
edited by Derek Fraser

Britain Pre-eminent: Studies of British World Influence in the Nineteenth Century
edited by C. J. Bartlett

The Conservative Leadership 1832–1932
edited by Donald Southgate

Perspectives in English Urban History
edited by Alan Everitt

Sweden's Age of Greatness 1632–1718
edited by Michael M. Roberts

The Republic and the Civil War in Spain
edited by Raymond Carr

VOLUMES IN PREPARATION INCLUDE

The Restored Monarchy
edited by James R. Jones

Church and Society in England:

Henry VIII to James I

EDITED BY **WITHDRAWN**

FELICITY HEAL
and
ROSEMARY O'DAY

M

First published 1977 by
THE MACMILLAN PRESS LTD
London and Basingstoke
Associated companies in New York Dublin
Melbourne Johannesburg and Madras

ISBN 0 333 18524 2 (hard cover)
0 333 18525 0 (paper cover)

Printed in Great Britain
at The Spottiswoode Ballantyne Press by
WILLIAM CLOWES & SONS LTD
London, Colchester and Beccles

Contents

Preface

THE editors regret that in a volume of this size it has not been possible to treat every problem with which the church was faced during the post-Reformation period. As a matter of policy, it was decided to prefer treatments of problems not dealt with in other general works (such as changes in popular culture or the effects of the redistribution of ecclesiastical patronage) over straight treatments of more usual subjects (such as puritanism). Taken together, the studies present a survey of the effects of the Reformation changes on English society at a variety of levels. Taken separately, each chapter presents an individual interpretation of current research in a given field and points to fresh avenues of thought and study. While the chapters complement one another, there has been no editorial attempt to impose a general view of the Reformation on the component parts of the volume.

Spelling and punctuation have been modernised in quotations. Place of publication is only cited for works published outside the United Kingdom. A brief Glossary has been included to help the student with technical terms. A Select List of Theses has been provided as a companion to the Bibliographical Notes, but this list is in no sense intended to be comprehensive.

The editors would like to thank Mr Derick Mirfin of Macmillan for his co-operation in devising the book and, also, their contributors, with whom it has been a pleasure to work. Heartfelt thanks go also to their respective husbands and children, without whose patience and tolerance this work would never have been completed.

FELICITY HEAL
ROSEMARY O'DAY

Introduction

FELICITY HEAL and
ROSEMARY O'DAY

I

'OUR estate', wrote the judicious Mr Hooker, 'is according to the pattern of God's own ancient elect people, which people was not part of them the commonwealth, and part of them the church of God, but the selfsame people whole and entire were both under the chief governor, on whose supreme authority they did all depend'.[1] Although Hooker is arguing specifically here against the puritan desire to divide church from state, he is also expressing a wider idea of the deep links between spiritual and secular society. Since church and state ministered respectively to the needs of the souls and bodies of the same group of men, they could not be torn asunder in the arbitrary manner recommended by papists and puritans. In those societies peculiarly chosen by God (which many sixteenth-century Englishmen believed to be ancient Israel and modern England) there existed an excellent harmony within the commonwealth, exemplified by the control of the supreme head over clergy and laity alike. This was to be contrasted with the pre-Reformation situation, or that in lands still obedient to Rome, where 'one society is both the church and the commonwealth; but the bishop of Rome doth divide the body into two diverse bodies, and doth not suffer the church to depend upon the power of any civil prince or potentate'.[2] Even this situation is to be preferred to one in which the church is in direct conflict with a heathen ruler, but the divisions between spiritual and lay authority impede the evangelisation of society, and lead to unseemly disputes between church and state which bring the former into disrepute with the laity. Of course, Hooker argued that the Church of England was also armed with the correct theological weapons to preach the gospel, while the Roman church was fundamentally erroneous in its doctrinal beliefs. This being so, the English church was doubly blessed with spiritual insight and an institutional structure conforming to the principles of natural law and

For Notes to the Introduction, see p. 188.

the best ancient models. In these circumstances, the attempts by the puritans to challenge the structure of the church were an offence not only against the ecclesiastical hierarchy, but also against the monarch and the whole society which could best be guided into godly behaviour by the existing arrangements of church and state.

Thus the great Anglican apologist defended the church that had been constructed during the first half-century of the Reformation. The theory of the English church and its relations with lay society was formalised in his work in a manner which was not entirely unassailable but which served as a framework of reference for centuries after his death. Yet Hooker was well aware that the realities of church and state often fell far short of his idealised picture. What reality lies behind the lucid expositions of the defenders of English religion between Bishop Gardiner and his *De Vera Obedientia* in the 1530s and Hooker, Bancroft and Lancelot Andrewes towards the end of our period?

The interaction between church and lay society has always fascinated English historians of the Reformation, while continental historians have given due attention to this theme only in recent years. This is partly because the royal supremacy was such an obtrusive fact of English life and the moments of tension between church and state, such as the dissolution of the monasteries, so dramatic. It is also because, with all due deference to Cranmer, the greatest theological ideas of the Reformation were not English in origin and England's distinctive contribution was a form of religious polity that combined the power of Calvinist theology with a traditional form of organisation and discipline. Historians have therefore always been interested to ask how effective was the power of the monarchy within the church; what was the reaction of churchmen to a lay overlord; and how strong was puritan opposition, both lay and clerical, to the arrangements of the 1559 settlement. In recent years questions of a more strictly social nature have been added to these enquiries about relationships between church and state. Which groups proved most receptive to Protestant doctrine and which resisted it most strongly? Are these groups to be seen as reacting purely to the stimulus of preaching and religious instruction or were they influenced also by political and economic considerations? What role did the laity play in the church, especially in patronage and economic arrangements? What was the effect of the Reformation upon the church's hold over popular culture and education? These and similar questions are still the subject of active research, some of which has been published in specialist monographs but little of which has yet reached the general accounts of Reformation history upon which most students must depend. Even such an excellent account as that of A. G. Dickens on *The English Reformation* has now been available for some years and it may be worthwhile to re-examine some of the themes which he treated in the light of more recent research. So this volume is designed not to analyse one historical problem or controversy but rather to investigate a series of changes of profound importance which are still ill-understood by modern historians.

The central issues concerning most of the contributors to this volume are firstly, what effect had religious thought and teaching upon society during the sixteenth century and, secondly, what was the behaviour and attitude of the laity towards the embodiment of those religious values, the clerical hierarchy? This second question could be even more boldly phrased: who controlled the church?

The first question is concerned with such issues as the role of religion in the cultural life of the people; the enthusiasm with which the Reformation was received in various communities; and the popularity of preaching. These are immensely difficult issues to disentangle and none of the essays pretends to provide definitive answers to the question, how dominant and significant was religious ideology in the century of the Reformation? Imogen Luxton does show, however, in her study of popular culture that the dominant form of communal expression in the early sixteenth century was still religious. The liturgy of the Roman church and the cycle of the ecclesiastical year provided the main focus for social activity within ordinary English communities.[3] Even the minority of the literate within lay society continued to depend upon a culture which was primarily religious and pietistic: the output of the early printing press, with its immense concentration upon works of devotion, is evidence of this. Moreover, those areas of cultural activity which were beginning to free themselves from the direct influence of the church, such as the writing of history chronicles, still bore the marks of their origin in the monastic scriptorium. The humanist movement, which in the later sixteenth century was to help to develop a secular culture largely uninfluenced by religious values, was in its early years in England strongly orientated towards the Christian humanism of Erasmus. It might be assumed, therefore, that the cultural and social aspirations of the English people were still strongly religious in orientation on the eve of the Reformation. Caution must be exercised in drawing such a conclusion, however: Keith Thomas's work has suggested that even before the great upheaval many Englishmen had little contact with the church, except through the crucial rites of passage (baptism, marriage and burial), and were, therefore, presumably indifferent towards the teaching of its clerics.[4] Moreover, much of the cultural manifestation of religious belief, such as the miracle and mystery plays, was concerned to examine secular behaviour and mores beneath the legitimate 'cover' of biblical and hagiographical stories. Religious values were always invoked but did not always inform the whole of the cultural activity in question. This is perhaps characteristic in a wider sense of late medieval church and society: the church penetrated lay society very deeply, so deeply that it was not easy to draw the distinction, so simple for a modern mind, between a spiritual and a secular action. Most activities had a religious content and sanction, from the waging of a just war to the labour of the villein. Yet not all activities had a profoundly spiritual meaning for contemporaries and, indeed, the full spiritual and biblical significance of activities which we would classify as religious – the performance of a mystery play; participation in some part of the liturgy – were only imperfectly understood by many of those involved.

This imperfect understanding extended, of course, to the leaders of the community, the parochial clergy. This is not the place to review in detail the continuing debate among historians upon the merits and learning of the pre-Reformation parish priest but it may be noted that the humanist generation of bishops was acutely aware that many clergy had a very limited knowledge of the Bible and the basic theological assumptions of the Christian faith. Recent studies have shown that the clergy had plenty of aids to preaching and instruction at their disposal and, indeed, that a reasonable percentage of them owned such volumes, but the content of these books was heavily biased towards edifying stories and moral precepts.[5] Such homiletic literature was not of itself misleading or useless but it conveyed a different concept of the Christian faith to one centred on biblical teaching. For the priesthood as for the people the liturgical round of the religious calendar and especially the crucial sacrifice of the mass was the focus of spiritual life, although in urban communities sermons were already rivalling the mass in claiming the attention of the populace. The parish priest continued to play a vital role in the community, especially in rural areas where his literacy was at a premium. In law disputes, in the settlement of minor grievances and in the preparation of wills, the learning of the priest was often of great value to the community, even though his economic and social status was frequently little better than that of other village worthies.

The effect of religious teaching and ideology upon the community of the realm after the breach with Rome is discussed in depth in this volume. The changes are difficult to categorise simply because each locality, each social group, even each individual, responded slightly differently to the challenge of religious upheaval. David Palliser (in Chapter 2) pleads for even more detailed local studies than those which have already been conducted so as to avoid the errors of geographical or social determinism. Few students of Tudor religion would disagree – especially the contributors to this volume, most of whom have themselves conducted regional studies – but there is also a need to try to identify the general characteristics of religious change in the society. Imogen Luxton provides some important clues to these in her essay. The Protestant faith preached by the early reformers, by the Elizabethan bishops and by the clerical puritans had this in common: it was a religion of the word; a bibliocentric faith not necessarily excluding other forms of knowledge or activity, but subordinating them to the guidance of the New Testament. This religion of the word, which had already been foreshadowed in the English humanist emphasis upon a life patterned on the gospels, demanded a more positive individual commitment and under-standing than the ritual-centred Catholicism of the late Middle Ages. It was also austere in its visual expression: English Protestantism, notably under Edward VI and during the early years of Elizabeth's reign, sought to simplify the appearance of churches, for example, so that they became functional buildings for the administration of the word and not for the consecration of the elements in the eucharistic ritual. Keith Thomas has suggested that the disappearance of the mass, with its semi-magical transformation of the elements into the body and blood of Christ, took magical practices outside the sphere of the church because they were no longer condoned, or rather ritualised, in its liturgy. Undoubtedly the disappearance of the mass, and the slower removal of other manifestations of popular culture such as the religious plays, created a significant gap in the cultural life of the community. This Protestantism sought to fill partly with preaching to increase men's understanding of their faith, and partly with a stress upon the study of the Bible and a providential philosophy.

As Imogen Luxton suggests (in Chapter 3), this philosophy did, in time, generate a popular literature of its own, a literature often produced by laymen who had been liberated by improved educational facilities and by the Protestant emphasis upon the right of every man to read and understand the Scriptures. Moreover, sermons did become an immensely popular form of urban entertainment, quite as much appreciated as the rival secular activities of theatre and bear-baiting. Nevertheless, cultural expression could no longer be forced to conform almost exclusively to religious patterns. Renaissance influence, in particular, brought to aristocratic and, later, to popular culture a new framework of reference. Humanism brought not only an interest in classical secular culture but also an emphasis upon education which dovetailed happily with the social aspirations of large sections of the laity. These developments were largely independent of changes in religion but they were reinforced by the decline of church-orientated culture and by the deliberate rejection by Protestant clergy of many elements in popular behaviour. The fulminations of the early seventeenth-century puritans against drama, dance and sabbath-breaking sports, were the logical outcome of the withdrawal of the church from the attempt to assimilate these activities which were characteristic of late medieval Catholicism. An extremely vital culture founded upon the Bible and the godly puritan household or community had, as William Haller reminds us, arisen by this date but it was no longer synonymous with the whole society.[6] There was a strain in Calvinist theology which encouraged this withdrawal into a small godly community – the unregenerate were the mass of mankind, who could not be expected to value the religious behaviour of the godly minority.

Even more important was the fact that after the theological bonds of medieval Catholicism had been shattered it was virtually impossible to re-establish unanimity of religious belief. Hooker's ideal vision of the Church of England ministering to the needs of every soul within the kingdom was scarcely grounded in reality. Even at the end of our period, when the English church – Calvinist in doctrine but traditional in organisation – seemed fully established, there was active dissent both within and without. Parts of the north, especially Lancashire, clung tenaciously to the Roman allegiance in spite of half a century of efforts to draw them into the established church. There was a small but significant group of sectaries who equally rejected the authority of the hierarchy and, most important of all, there were wide divergences of opinion within the church, from the still vocal puritans to the growing group of high-church ecclesiastics.

The laity were of great importance in all these movements, with the possible exception of the clerical revivalism of men such as Bancroft and Neile: half a century of encouraging independent thought on the Bible and the great doctrinal truths of Christianity had had a profound effect upon the habits of mind of the more articulate lay members of the Church. Crucial in this context were the years of upheaval and changing policy between 1530 and the late 1560s, discussed by David Palliser in this volume. The laity were almost forced to think for themselves, regardless of whether they had any leanings towards Protestantism, by the very rapid changes in religious observance and by the drastic alterations in the structure of their worship. One familiar reaction to the upheavals was cynicism and mistrust of all forms of observance, although this more often seems to have taken the form of withdrawal from the church than active criticism. The church courts, for example, were gravely weakened by the changes of the mid-sixteenth century, not merely because they lost power to the laity, but also because many of those summoned before them had ceased to have respect for the old sanctions and power of the church. In some cases this found both cause and expression in positive hostility towards ecclesiastical jurisdiction by puritans or recusants but more often in sheer indifference. Although this is a subject which requires yet more research, as only a few pre-Reformation dioceses have been studied, it would seem that this indifference to the courts began after the 1530s and that it continued even after the Church of England was strongly established in the late sixteenth century.[7]

The decisions which men took about their religious beliefs, as David Palliser points out, owed something to their social position as well as to the power of doctrinal arguments. Loyalty to the Tudor dynasty; a general conviction that it was powerful enough to control the religious destinies of the nation; and a desire to retain office, all worked strongly to keep a majority of the influential on the side of the Crown, regardless of its religious policy. Conversely, absence from the centre of political power, expecially in areas where the leaders of society were hostile to new ideas, often meant the survival of traditional practices and beliefs which could merge into positive support for Rome on occasion. Local rivalries sometimes meant that religious divisions followed lines which were already well-established. In some cases social and educational circumstances guaranteed access to new ideas: the mercantile communities of London and some of the east-coast ports are a limited example of this; a more general one is the exposure of many of the young leaders of society to the Protestant atmosphere of Cambridge.

The response of the leaders of the church to the problems of disunity created in the mid-Tudor decades is discussed by Ralph Houlbrooke in Chapter 4. The early Elizabethan bishops were convinced of the power of preaching to convert all who listened to the new way. The key element in the programme of the bishops was, therefore, the recruitment of an effective ministry, of men who could truly preach the Protestant gospel. To this end the universities had to produce more graduates. By the end of the period this ambition of the early Elizabethan episcopate was achieved although it certainly did not guarantee the uniformity of belief for which they had longed. The bishops themselves were active as preachers and teachers, although in some cases a disproportionate number of their sermons were addressed to the court, with promotion as well as the inculcation of godly behaviour in mind. Although the point is rarely articulated in the writings and teaching of these Elizabethan Protestants, they followed earlier evangelists in believing that once the gospel had been rightly expounded, God would incline the hearts of men to hear and follow its message. Not all, of course, were saved and regenerate, but only men such as the papists, whose hearts had been hardened to withstand the truth, could fail to benefit from the word of the gospel. At least, this was the optimistic aspect of Protestant belief: a conviction that the word of God truly preached had the power to join together the nation. In practice, the Elizabethan bishops frequently wrung their hands and lamented the perilous state of the church in an ungodly generation. Enemies of the gospel, complained Richard Cox in a characteristic passage, 'swarm in all corners saying and doing almost what they lyst . . .'.[8] Later bishops, under both Elizabeth and James, questioned the stress placed upon preaching in the early stages of the English Reformation. Unbridled preaching, in their opinion, was as likely to make enemies of established religion as friends. Conformity and discipline became the cry in the face of the puritan opposition, and too often the task of guiding the laity was lost in the struggle between the various clerical factions.

Even before preaching fell under the suspicion of the leaders of the church, one aspect of early Protestant teaching and instruction had been lost. The Elizabethan preachers concerned themselves largely with two themes: the key ideas and consequences of Protestant theology; and the royal supremacy. What was missing from their sermons was the strain of social commentary that had marked the teaching of Latimer and a number of the other early reformers. Concern for the secular good of the commonwealth was a vital part of the programme of those who clustered around Cromwell in the 1530s and who again in the 1540s enjoyed a certain influence under Protector Somerset. Of course, not all the 'commonwealth men' were clerics – many indeed were sharp critics of the ecclesiastical establishment – but most endeavoured to apply their new religious values to solving the problems of society. In some ways they drew upon the well-established medieval pattern of concern for the realm: the sense of close identity between spiritual and secular activity which has already been discussed. But they also drew upon the humanist and Protestant notion that the life of the individual should be lived according to the standards of the gospel and they applied this to the wider social relationships. Latimer not only castigated greed as a vice in the mighty, but adduced specific evidence of the harmful effect which this greed had upon co-operation between social groups. The spiritual and social ferment of the 1530s and 40s offered, in the opinion of the 'commonwealth men', the ideal opportunity for the true enactment within society of Christian ethical precepts. While change should come from the very heart of every individual, they looked to the government to promote and further their schemes: both Cromwell and Somerset seemed, at least in their early years in power, to be ideally suited to be instruments of regeneration. The optimistic projectors completely ignored, of course, the political constraints upon their heroes and the economic realities of mid-Tudor England. After the accession of Elizabeth such optimism was rarely revived and hardly ever by the clergy, who adhered to that division described by Hooker and concerned themselves with the souls of Englishmen. However, it can be argued that the mid-Tudor concern with social justice did bear fruit in the behaviour of individual benefactors whose support of learning and the poor has been so tirelessly chronicled by W. K. Jordan.[9]

In his chapter, William Sheils shows well that preaching during the Elizabethan and Jacobean periods was not a puritan preserve but part of the life of the church. Elizabeth's reaction to the emphasis upon preaching in her new church was emotional and ill informed and, moreover, it has misled successive generations of ecclesiastical historians.

II

To return to the second question posed early in this introduction: what attitude and behaviour was adopted by the laity towards the clerical hierarchy? What was their place in church and society? The fortunes of the church as an institution, and of its individual members, are somewhat easier to identify precisely than the spread of religious ideas. We enter here upon a well-documented field, where both land and livings can be quantified and analysed. Even so, there are considerable problems in understanding the full significance of the laity's role in patronage, for example, or in preventing the clergy from taking a full economic profit from their lands and tithes. The latter subject, in particular, has been the centre of considerable historical debate: were the clergy growing poorer during the sixteenth and early seventeenth centuries? If so should this be laid at the door of rapacious laymen? Another related theme has been accorded some attention, especially in the work of Christopher Hill, and that is the link between puritan ideology and the lay demands upon church property.[10] Did some of the leaders of society espouse puritanism, which had during the Elizabethan age constructed a virulent critique of ecclesiastical wealth, in order to profit from church estates? Of course, many of the gentry and aristocracy had by this time improved their holdings at the expense of the church in the wake of the great dissolutions of monasteries and chantries which Christopher Kitching discusses in this volume. This process did not, however, end lay demands upon church wealth: indeed, it may be argued to have stimulated continued involvement both indirectly and directly. There is an explicit link; once the taboos upon the invasion of church wealth characteristic of the pre-Reformation period had been broken, it was difficult to convince influential laymen that they could not follow the Crown's example and take a little from the weakened and vulnerable clergy. Indirectly, the dispersal of monastic lands may have had some effect, as they helped to stimulate an already lively land market; to reinforce growing legal concepts of private property; and to place such possessions as advowsons and impropriated tithes on the same proprietorial level as land.

It is necessary to return to Hooker and to the contrast between church and state under Rome and under the English King to place these arguments within a more formal framework. The divisions between state and ecclesiastical hierarchy before the Reformation were rarely as sharp as Hooker implied or as might have been wished by the papacy. The English monarchy had established a very strong right in practice to tax the clergy when also taxing the laity; to make most senior clerical appointments; and to control the right of appeal to Rome in certain circumstances. The close links between church and state were reinforced by the policy of using churchmen as ministers and diplomats, and rewarding them with promotion to the episcopal bench. The inevitability of the Crown depending upon ecclesiastics for the more complex tasks of government should not be exaggerated: by the early sixteenth century in particular men trained in the common law provided a good alternative and played an important part in the governments of both Henry VII and Henry VIII. Nevertheless, churchmen were valued both for their loyalty to the Tudor regime and for their skill in civil law and international diplomacy. Laymen also had close relationships with the church at the lower levels of society: as farmers of ecclesiastical land; as secular officers to the bishops and monasteries; as patrons of benefices. Yet all these close ties between church and society did not obscure the fundamental distinction that the clergy owed a loyalty to two masters and that in all spiritual matters this loyalty was to the Pope as Christ's representative on earth. In every way that it could the church stressed its separation from lay society: the priest was consecrated to the task of offering the sacrifice of the mass, of mediating between man and God, and separation was, therefore, in the nature of his office. The property of this separate order was inviolate once it had been endowed by pious laymen for the work of the church. The lay authorities had no control over the spiritual activity of the priesthood. Since the church was universal its laws had a general application and were wholly independent of the laws of a particular state or polity. On the whole the English church was able to maintain this basic position until the very eve of the Reformation, although there were contested areas, such as the liberties of the clergy, which the common lawyers, sometimes with the active support of the Crown, were trying to limit.

The enunciation by Henry VIII of his supreme headship over the English church involved a dramatic alteration of pre-Reformation assumptions. The institutional consequences were more immediately obvious than the religious ones. As an apology for the Reformation expressed it in 1539: 'The clergy have submitted to the King, from whom they have immediately jurisdiction and goods, except mere spiritualities granted by the gospels and Scripture, and have acknowledged that without his assent and confirmation they could pretend none other.'[11] As Claire Cross shows (in Chapter 1), the clergy spent several generations trying to assimilate the theoretical and practical fact of the royal supremacy. By the time of Hooker the theoretical justification for the rule of the English monarch was well-developed, but the practical consequences of her authority were still sometimes unpalatable. A succession of churchmen whose religious sensibilities were directly opposed to those of the ruler were willing to suffer deprivation and even death for their beliefs. The agonies of conscience that this could cause are clearly shown in the case of Cranmer, one of the earliest and most fervent believers in the right of the monarch to lead the church, who almost surrendered deeply Protestant beliefs when the monarchy returned to Rome. A calmer commitment to the royal supremacy was possible for the Protestant bishops under Elizabeth, though even then there was a constant undercurrent of anxiety that a change of rulers or a marriage might mean another official change in religious policy. Elizabeth was able to take advantage of her bishop's fervent belief that she alone could protect the Protestant faith: a variety of unpalatable policies were accepted by them as *adiaphora*, things indifferent. Only in the very last years of the century, and particularly under the more sympathetic James I, did some leading churchmen come to see that the royal supremacy might have positive advantages for the church if the monarchy could be persuaded to shelter the clergy from the aggressive demands of the laity and the puritans. The success of their struggle to influence the Crown really belongs outside our period to the reign of Charles I, as it has now been convincingly argued that James I was careful not to involve himself too deeply in the plans of the bishops.[12]

The social and economic consequences of the royal supremacy for the church were equally far-reaching. Taxation of the clergy immediately became much heavier than lay taxation with the introduction of first fruits and tenths and this remained a major problem throughout the sixteenth century. Even more significant was the dissolution of first the monasteries and then the chantries, which gradually placed a great deal of former ecclesiastical wealth and present ecclesiastical patronage in the hands of the laity. As Christopher Kitching points out (in Chapter 6), it can no longer be assumed that all the monastic land and patronage was rapidly dispersed by the

Crown: enough land was retained into the late sixteenth century to make a difference to the pattern of royal landholding and greatly to enhance the monarch's patronage. Rosemary O'Day shows (in Chapter 7) that the Lord Keeper's administration of Crown patronage worth less than £20 per annum was of considerable importance, and many of these livings derived from the monasteries. The Crown also acquired, and sometimes retained, control over more of the senior positions in the church when it established a number of the monastic cathedrals as secular foundations. Under Elizabeth the monarchy further enhanced its powers as patron by legislation which allowed the bishops to make long leases of land only through the Crown. This became a very attractive way of rewarding deserving servants of the Crown without drawing on royal property or capital resources. Nevertheless, it is perhaps more surprising that the church managed to retain as much as it did of its desirable property than that part had to be surrendered directly or indirectly to the laity. Both Henry VIII and Elizabeth needed a hierarchy which preserved the semblance of independence and authority because they wished to maintain the traditional structure of the English church. Both were divided between their desire to profit from the church and their interest in conserving the *status quo*. Elizabeth, in particular, tried the devotion of her senior clergy to the limit by her wish to have the best of both worlds and it was in recognition of the strains which she had imposed upon the hierarchy that James I, very early in his reign, enacted legislation to prevent the alienation of church land.

Where the Crown led, the laity was naturally eager to follow. As Christopher Kitching shows, much monastic land did pass to the laity and, on the whole, it seems to have served to reinforce the existing social structure, most of it ending up in the hands of the local aristocracy and gentry. This had considerable, although as yet imperfectly understood, influence upon the local political élites, but for the church its most important consequence was that the laity acquired an economic interest in the parishes through the ownership of tithes and advowsons, and a religious interest through their rights of patronage. Rosemary O'Day suggests that patronage rights were even more fragmented than before the Reformation but that the shift was away from ecclesiastical to lay control. Advowsons were usually sold with the manors and not many laymen, with the exception of a few great nobles, consolidated blocks of patronage. Later in the century advowsons were certainly bought and sold and a few convinced puritans took advantage of this to promote men of their own persuasion. However, these collections of livings acquired to advance a religious policy appear to have been the exception rather than the rule. A much more general problem was that the bishops could less easily influence the quality of men presented by lay patrons – a problem accentuated by the changed patronage balance after the Reformation. Both advowsons and the right to collect tithes were regarded as forms of property after the 1530s and it is not necessary to posit any great hostility to established religion or even wealthy clergy to explain the behaviour of lay tithe owners, lessees or patrons. Lay financial rights within the parishes certainly inhibited the clergy from making their full profit from tithe but, as Felicity Heal points out (in Chapter 5), many of the parochial clergy were improving their economic situation in the late sixteenth and early seventeenth centuries, even including a percentage of those who held vicarages and were losing part of their tithe to an impropriator.

It may be worth emphasising in conclusion that not all the problems of the sixteenth-century church arose from its struggle to enforce religious conformity or from its relations with Crown and society. The clergy were as susceptible as any other group to changes in the economy and society at large. In the sixteenth century undoubtedly the greatest of these was price inflation. The rising price of agricultural products encouraged major changes in society, improving the situation of many large tenant farmers and efficient landlords, while creating serious difficulties for the conservative landowner and the landless. Similarly, certain sections of the church benefited greatly from the change, especially parish clergy with adequate glebe for food production. Others, from the bishops and cathedral clergy who were disadvantaged by beneficial leases granted to their tenants, to the landless parish clergy and curates, suffered from inflation as much as or more than from the intrusion of the laity. Rising prices and the escalating costs of warfare forced the Crown to demand more from the church than it could reasonably bear and probably made the economic attitude of the laity more aggressive. Such tensions contributed greatly to the arguments between clergy and laity and made the already delicate problem of enforcing religious change much more difficult. Only after the Civil War did the social and economic arrangements of the English church become acceptable to a majority of the clergy and laity in a period of greater stability for the society at large.

1. Churchmen and the Royal Supremacy

CLAIRE CROSS

IN 1525 the English clergy, as in centuries past, still thought of themselves as in temporal matters subjects of the English King but in spiritual matters subjects of the overlord of western christendom, the Pope. Within ten years their standing in society had been totally transformed. In a series of statutes Parliament recognised that England was and always had been an empire, independent of all external jurisdiction, and the monarch supreme over all his subjects, clerical and lay. The Crown forced the clergy to acknowledge its powers within the church, and the clergy had then to work out the implications of this momentous change upon their own authority. Clerics and laymen propounded many theories about the royal supremacy between 1525 and 1625 and ideas on the form of the supremacy did to some degree alter over the century. For the greater part of the period the fundamental issue concerning the powers of the lay monarch or of the laity in general within the church continued to challenge the consciences of conservative and radical churchmen alike: some died for their principles, others preferred disgrace to compromise. Towards the end of the sixteenth century, however, a new group of ecclesiastics began to emerge who looked upon the royal supremacy not as a possible source of conflict between the sacred and secular spheres but as a means of protection against an ever more intrusive English laity. Elizabeth and James I both recognised an incipient threat to their prerogative in increasing clerical assertiveness but Charles I did not. In his reign certain churchmen, by capturing the support of the King, succeeded in using the royal supremacy to re-establish a new clerical control in the church. For a section of the clergy the royal supremacy seemed to have become a source of strength, not a hindrance, and they appeared to be on the point of regaining authority their predecessors had enjoyed in the late medieval church.

Even before Henry VIII embarked upon the proceedings which ultimately led to the break with Rome some of the earliest English

For Notes to Chapter 1, see pp. 188–9; for Bibliographical Notes, see pp. 180–1.

Protestants had raised issues which materially influenced relations between monarch and churchmen throughout the following century. Tyndale and his fellow theologians turned to the godly prince as the agent for the introduction of true religion into England but also assumed that once papal dominion had been renounced the King and kingdom would be ruled by the word of God as interpreted by God's ministers. While increasingly perceiving that the present power of ecclesiastics must be curbed if he were ever to achieve the annulment of his marriage, Henry never contemplated overthrowing the authority of clergy loyal to the papacy merely to replace them with equally powerful Protestant churchmen. In *The Obedience of a Christian Man*, published in 1528, Tyndale did not preach unlimited obedience to the secular monarch, though on a superficial reading the King may have reached a different conclusion. In phrases which may have sounded conventional, but which later events showed had still the ability to inspire action, Tyndale stressed the limits as well as the extent of the powers of Christian Kings. 'As God maketh the King head over his realm, even so giveth he him commandment to execute the laws upon all men indifferently. For the law is God's, and not the King's. The King is but a servant, to execute the law of God, and not to rule after his own imagination.' Subjects must obey their monarch, but the monarch in his turn had the overriding duty of obeying the Scriptures.[1]

The process of the political measures which eventually resulted in the separation of the English church from the jurisdiction of Rome at times seemed far from the idealism of the early Protestants but they had this virtue that by their very gradualness they could always be seen as steps towards the creation of a fully reformed church: the usurped authority of the Pope had first to be cast off before the church could be free to begin a total reformation; the godly prince must first be restored to his full powers before the word of God could gain its rightful sway. In the early 1530s the overwhelming majority of the English clergy had little sympathy for these Protestant arguments yet they also were brought to make the revolutionary admission that their loyalty to their monarch came before their age-old loyalty to the Pope. From the first meeting of the Reformation Parliament in 1529, the clergy had experienced the hostility of the leading laymen who sought to impose new restraints upon ecclesiastical courts and remedy the traditional abuses of clerical pluralism and non-residence. They cannot, in consequence, have been entirely unprepared when early in 1531 the King accused them of having infringed the Statutes of Provisors, Provisions and Praemunire by exercising an independent clerical jurisdiction in England. In the forlorn hope of safeguarding their privileges for the future, the clergy bought their pardon from the King but they did not in 1531 recognise without qualification Henry's supremacy over the church. At the suggestion of Bishop Fisher, Convocation acknowledged the King to be supreme head, but only 'as far as the law of Christ allows'. Though the anticlerical feeling in Parliament had in no way abated and though by this resistance the churchmen had increased the antagonism of the King, Convocation, when it next met in 1532, still refused to accept that its legislation in the future required the royal assent. Archbishop Warham even dared to remind the King of the confrontation between Henry II and Becket. The defiance of Convocation merely intensified the King's determination to secure its defeat. Opportunely discovering that 'We thought that the clergy of our realm had been our subjects wholly, but now we have well perceived that they be but half our subjects, yea, and scarce our subjects', he obtained his victory. A depleted Convocation conceded that, in future, no Convocation could meet except by royal summons, no new cannons be made except with royal approval. An act passed in the first session of Parliament in 1534 confirmed this Submission of the Clergy and in the second session of the year in the Act of Supremacy, Parliament required clergy and laity alike to acknowledge the King as 'the only supreme head in earth of the Church of England'. From 1532 English churchmen had to grant that the monarch under God had the final responsibility for the spiritual and temporal welfare of his subjects, that he was their final overlord and that neither he nor they owed any allegiance to the bishop of Rome.[2]

Sir Thomas More resigned from royal service the day after the clergy surrendered to the Crown and his subsequent refusal to disown papal authority in England led to his execution in July 1535. Bishop Fisher, also, refused to deny his allegiance to the papacy and he, too, was executed. Others, like Bishop Gardiner, who had a scarcely less strong attachment to traditional Catholic theology than had More and Fisher, strove at this time to account for their recognition of the royal supremacy. Only three years previously in Convocation, Gardiner had vehemently opposed the Crown's demand to participate in ecclesiastical legislation, but in 1535 he wrote *The Ora-*

tion of True Obedience to justify the right of 'the most victorious and most noble prince Henry the Eight ... to be in earth the supreme head of the Church of England'. 'Surely, I see no cause why any man should be offended that the King is called the head of [the] Church of England rather than the head of the realm of England.' Anticipating an argument later employed to much effect by Hooker, he asked, 'Seeing the Church of England consisteth of the same sorts of people as this day that are comprised in this word realm of whom the King is called the head: shall he not, being called the head of the realm of England, be also the head of the same men when they are named the Church of England?' For Gardiner, it seems, the King had assumed in England the powers of the Pope in their entirety: Henry VIII had now become the guardian of English Catholic orthodoxy.[3]

Yet despite the views of Gardiner and his allies, more advanced churchmen in England continued to look upon the royal supremacy as an agency of reform. This attitude appears most forcibly in *The Institution of a Christian Man* brought out by a commission of bishops and other clerics in 1537. Having denied that Christ ever conferred upon the bishop of Rome supremacy over all bishops and clergy, or that the Pope ever had authority to depose monarchs from their realms, the English bishops declared that God had committed to Christian princes 'the cure and oversight of all the people which be within their realms and dominions without any exception'. The powers of princes, they went on to add, included superintendence 'over ... priests and bishops, to cause them to administer their office and power committed unto them purely and sincerely'. 'And God hath also commanded the said priests and bishops to obey, with all humbleness and reverence all the laws made by the said princes, being not contrary to the laws of God, whatsoever they be; and that not only *propter iram*, but also *propter conscientiam*.'[4]

Cranmer certainly believed with his whole being in the mission of the godly prince to institute true religion in England. He saw Henry VIII undertaking responsibilities such as had been entrusted by God to the Kings of Israel in Old Testament times or to the Emperor Constantine in the Christian dispensation. His writings display an idealised erastianism reached perhaps by no other of his contemporaries; to Cranmer the needs of the church and of the state had become fused and could only be supplied by the prince. 'All Christian princes', he explained, 'have committed unto them immediately of God the whole cure of all their subjects, as well concerning the administration of God's word for the cure of souls, as concerning the ministration of things political and civil governance. And in both these ministrations they must have sundry ministers under them, to supply that which is appointed to their several offices.' From this he drew the stark conclusion that 'there is no more promise of God, that grace is given in the committing of the ecclesiastical office, than it is in the committing of the civil office'.[5]

In the latter part of Henry VIII's reign both Gardiner and Cranmer had some reason to regard the supreme governor, despite his imperfections, as the guarantee of their very different aspirations for the church. Henry had given his consent to the passing of the Act of Six Articles in 1539 and the conservatives could, without too much straining of the imagination, look upon him as the defender of Catholic orthodoxy. Cranmer could no less clearly see that he and the surviving reforming clerics owed their offices in the church, indeed their lives, to royal protection. While Henry remained King neither party in the church had the temerity to explore the limits of the royal supremacy. Yet that there were limits few articulate churchmen had any doubt and in the successive reigns of Edward VI and Mary conservative and radical clergy in turn felt constrained by conscience to make explicit the extent to which they thought the law of Christ restricted the authority of the royal governor. When the future duke of Somerset took control over the regency council set up by Henry VIII, Gardiner and his sympathisers among the churchmen realised that the supremacy exercised by the Protector in the name of the nine-year-old King would no longer be used to defend Catholic orthodoxy, and suspected that the mass might be abolished. Almost at once Somerset confirmed their fears by proclaiming that all bishops held their offices at the pleasure of the Crown and only during good behaviour, and then by arranging for a visitation of the church by royal commissioners which would automatically suspend any episcopal visitations. In a last ditch attempt to prevent Protestant innovations, Gardiner tried to use the royal supremacy against the Protector, arguing that the religious settlement must be retained exactly as it had been in the last years of Henry VIII until Edward VI came of age and could act in his own right. He failed to prevent the royal visitation in his own diocese and the Council sent him to the Tower. Later, after further refusals to obey new religious regulations, first Bonner and then Gardiner were deprived of their sees. Certain Catholic churchmen who had recognised Henry VIII as supreme head of the English church had now demonstrated where they believed the limits of the royal supremacy lay.

For Cranmer and his reforming colleagues, however, the issue still seemed clouded. On the one side they achieved considerable freedom to implement Protestantism. They altered the mass into a Protestant communion; with the first and then the second prayer book they provided the English church with a partially and then a decidedly Protestant order of service in the English tongue; they had advice on request from some of the leading continental reformers recently brought to live in England. Yet the Protestant churchmen knew that they could procure religious change only so far as their actions conformed to the wishes of the Councils first of Somerset, then of Northumberland. Even as they devised plans for the restoration of the commonwealth, the education of youth in true learning, the care of the sick and the relief of the poor, they saw politicians, their lay supporters and dependants, enriching themselves at the expense of the church. Many Protestant clerics prophesied a judgement of God upon the evil and backsliding generation. When expounding Christ's saying, 'Know ye not that I must do the business of my father' in a sermon he preached during Edward's reign, Latimer did not hesitate to proclaim that there could be limits to the obedience of Protestants even in an avowedly Protestant state.

> We learn here how far forth children are bound to obey their parents; namely, so far as the same may stand with godliness. If they will have us go further, and pluck us from true religion and the serving of God, make them this answer, *Oportet magis obedire Deo quam hominibus*; that is, 'We ought rather to obey God than men; for otherwise we are not bound to obey our parents' etc. Here not only children may learn, but subjects and servants, to obey their King and masters, so far as it may stand with God's pleasure; and further to go we ought not.[6]

On the accession of Mary, churchmen like Latimer knew exactly how far they might go with their new monarch. In the tradition of Tyndale, they felt obliged to obey the royal governor only to the extent that she obeyed the word of God. For Cranmer, with his more exalted view of the royal supremacy, the matter appeared a little less simple. The Protestant churchmen did not stand alone in their crisis of conscience: a Catholic monarch now succeeded to the English throne who rejected the political teaching of the two previous decades and quite positively did not believe that English monarchs enjoyed supremacy in matters both temporal and spiritual. Yet Mary could not legally renounce her title of supreme head of the Church of England except by act of Parliament and this the Parliament which met in the autumn of 1553 refused to allow her to do. Until, therefore, England had been reconciled to the papacy at the end of November 1554, after Mary had married Philip of Spain and after the Pope had confirmed English landowners in their occupancy of monastic lands, the Queen found herself using powers which she did not consider she possessed to advance the return of Catholicism in England. Despite her scruples, Mary as supreme head in the eighteen-month period between her accession and the recognition by Parliament of papal jurisdiction filled vacancies on the episcopal bench and issued royal articles restoring medieval canon law in its entirety. By means of these articles some bishops and many lower clergy were deprived of their livings for having married in the previous reign even though clerical marriage had then been permitted by act of Parliament. The spectacle of the supreme head first using her royal powers against what they regarded as true religion and then, in a solemn public ceremony, admitting that these powers in no way pertained to the office of a monarch but resided exclusively in the Pope tested the loyalty of the Protestant churchmen to the uttermost.

No English Protestants could be tried for heresy before papal jurisdiction had been restored in England or before Parliament in December 1554 had re-enacted late medieval heresy laws and, consequently, the Marian persecutions did not begin until the early months of 1555. Mary could have executed Cranmer for treason for his unwilling support of the attempt to divert the succession to the Protestant Lady Jane Grey on the death of Edward, but it seems that she quite deliberately preferred to condone the political offence in order to proceed against Cranmer and some other leading Protestant clerics on theological grounds. Spending most of their time in prison between Mary's accession and the beginning of 1555, Ridley, Latimer and Cranmer had the opportunity to reconsider at length their attitude to the royal supremacy. Ridley now set out to judge the godliness of the monarch by the Scriptures. King Edward's laws, he maintained, had been valid because they corresponded with scriptural truth; Queen Mary's laws, on the other hand, went against the clear teaching of the Bible and, therefore, placed upon the subject no obligation to obey. The churchmen who until the summer of 1553 had been the chief defenders of the royal supremacy now perforce had to acknowledge an even greater authority. This does not seem to have presented the same intellectual difficulties to Ridley and Latimer as it did to Cranmer. When at his trial Latimer's judges exhorted him to follow the example of the King and Queen and of Parliament and recant his heresies, he repeated Ridley's argument that all power in the church must be exercised according to the will of God, and, if it was not, it had no validity. Ridley and Latimer had been appointed bishops after the renunciation of papal supremacy so they could not be charged with breaking an oath sworn to the Pope. Cranmer's case was different since he had sworn allegiance to the Pope before his consecration. At his trial the prosecution raised the matter of his perjury and so allowed him a greater chance of examining the royal supremacy than Ridley or Latimer. In reply to the medieval theory advanced by the Catholic side that the power of the keys belonged to the Pope, the power of the sword to the King, Cranmer asserted that the King possessed both powers. 'By the scripture the King is chief, and no foreign person in his own realm above him. There is no subject but to a King. I am a subject. I owe my fidelity to the Crown.' As a faithful subject he considered that he was standing against Philip and Mary's illegal repudiation of a spiritual power inherent in their office as Kings.[7]

The Crown could not proceed with the burning for heresy of an archbishop of Canterbury consecrated before the schism without first referring his case to Rome, so Cranmer, unlike Latimer and Ridley, escaped death immediately after the conclusion of the Oxford trials in October 1555. He lived for a further five months until papal commissioners after a second trial had handed him over to the secular power, and that power was ready to act. In these last months, bereft of the support of Ridley and Latimer, he began to think afresh about the royal supremacy. Wavering in his former resolution, he now admitted that perhaps after all his temporal sovereigns knew more of God's truth than he did himself, and that he should no longer withstand their judgement. In January 1556 Cranmer made his first, conditional, recantation, confessing, 'Forasmuch as the King and Queen's majesties, by consent of their Parliament, have received the Pope's authority within this realm, I am content to submit myself to their laws herein, and to take the Pope for chief head of this Church of England, so far as God's laws and the laws and customs of this realm permit.' After this he went on to recognise the Pope without any reservation as the supreme head of the English church. For a time his belief in the royal supremacy appeared to have triumphed over his Protestant convictions. Yet before he died Cranmer began to see again that the royal supremacy was only an instrument for the establishment of the true church: it could never be an end in itself. He returned to his belief in the Protestant church as the only true church and, immediately before his burning, renounced his recantations, denied the supremacy of the Pope, and reaffirmed the validity of his own writings on the Protestant interpretation of the sacrament of the altar.[8]

Had Mary's reign continued longer, had she not been followed by a Protestant monarch, it is entirely possible that the concept of the godly prince and the special devotion to the supreme governor as the divinely appointed protector of the national church might well have disappeared in England. The accession of Elizabeth, however, the new Deborah, revived the idea and also resurrected the old tension between the supreme governor and her churchmen. The theoretical position seemed about to revert to that prevailing in the last years of Henry VIII, but this did not happen in practice. The Marian persecution had caused attitudes to change towards the royal supremacy and may even, to a certain extent, have changed the royal supremacy itself. In 1559 Elizabeth had no choice but to appoint Protestant clergy to bishoprics since almost to a man the Marian bishops refused to serve in a Protestant church, and these clergy, after their experiences of the previous five years, stood in rather less awe of their royal overlord than their Henrician precedessors had done. In addition, the nature of the royal supremacy seems to have been regarded in a subtly different way, perhaps by the Queen and certainly by some of her lay subjects. Henry VIII had claimed to hold his headship direct from God. He considered himself a lay bishop such as Constantine had been and believed he could delegate his powers to whomsoever he wished. In the Act of Supremacy of 1534 Parliament had merely confirmed that the royal headship had always belonged to the English crown and in no sense conferred this authority upon the King. Nevertheless, even Henry had had to have recourse to Parliament for this declaration and for statutes to enforce his supremacy and, during the minority of Edward VI, the passing of further supremacy acts strengthened the supposition that the essence of the supremacy lay in the King in Parliament rather than in the

King alone. Elizabeth continued to maintain that her supremacy was inherent in her office as monarch, as her father's had been, but increasingly from 1558 it became possible for parliamentarians to argue that Parliament had some right to participate together with the Queen in the supremacy. Overriding the dissenting voice of the Catholic bishops in the Lords, Parliament, not Convocation, in 1559 in the Act of Uniformity transformed the English church once more into a Protestant church. In the Act of Supremacy for the third time in a century a monarch had had to turn to Parliament to obtain a definition of royal powers within the church. This Parliament went yet further and attempted to define heresy, ordaining that in future royal delegates might only take action against those who held doctrines 'adjudged heresy by the authority of the canonical Scriptures, or by the first four general councils . . . or such as hereafter shall be . . . determined to be heresy by the high court of Parliament of this realm, with the assent of the clergy in their Convocation'.[9]

The Act of Supremacy of 1559 referred to Elizabeth not as 'supreme head', the title both her father and her brother had taken, but as 'supreme governor'. 'The Queen is unwilling to be addressed, either by word of mouth, or in writing, as the head of the Church of England,' Jewel explained to Bullinger in Zurich in a letter which he wrote from London in May 1559. 'For she seriously maintains that this honour is due to Christ alone, and cannot belong to any human being soever; besides which, these titles have been so foully contaminated by antichrist, that they can no longer be adopted by anyone without impiety.' Whether in fact Protestant scruples put to the Queen by Lever affected her decision as Sandys imagined, or whether Elizabeth was making a politic gesture which cost her nothing in terms of actual power as Parkhurst more plausibly suggested, the change in style made it considerably easier for Protestant ecclesiastics to support the Queen's authority in the church. John Jewel, who in his *Apology* wrote the classic defence of the Elizabethan church against the church of Rome, made considerable play with this alteration in the Queen's title in his reply to his Catholic antagonist, Thomas Harding:

> Concerning the title of 'supreme head of the church', we need not to search for Scripture to excuse it. For first, we devised it not; secondly, we use it not; thirdly, our princes at this present claim it not.

He then went on to define the powers of the supreme governor which he had first set out in the *Apology*:

> Howbeit, that the prince is the highest judge and governor over all his subjects whatsoever, as well priests as laymen, without exception, it is most evident by that hath been already said, . . . by the whole course of the Scriptures, and by the undoubted practice or the primitive church. Verily the prince . . . had both the tables of the law of God evermore committed to his charge; as well the first, that pertaineth to religion, as also the second, that pertaineth to civil government.[10]

Whatever the theoretical change in the royal supremacy may have been, in practice the churchmen raised to the bench early in Elizabeth's reign showed a new determination in reminding the supreme governor of the limits of her influence in the church and of their allegiance in the final resort to a yet higher power. In the autumn of 1559 Matthew Parker, archbishop elect of Canterbury, and other clerics wrote to the Queen against retaining images in a reformed English church. After rehearsing at length arguments in the Bible and in the Fathers against images, they explained to the Queen,

> that God's word doth threaten a terrible judgement unto us, if we, being pastors and ministers in his church, should assent to the thing which in our learning and conscience we are persuaded doth tend to the confirmation of error, superstition and idolatry, and finally, to the ruin of the souls committed to our charge, for the which we must give an account to the prince of pastors at the last day. We pray your majesty also not to be offended with this our plainness and liberty, which all good and Christian princes have ever taken in good part at the hands of godly bishops.

Having cited the words and example of St Ambrose before the Emperor Theodosius, they ended their petition, beseeching 'your majesty also in these, and such like controversies of religion, to refer the discussion and deciding of them to a synod of your bishops, and other godly learned men, according to the example of Constantinus Magnus, and other Christian emperors . . .'.[11]

On this occasion more strong-minded colleagues may well have put words into Parker's mouth, but there were times when the primate himself felt that he had no alternative but to remonstrate with Elizabeth over her interpretation of the royal supremacy in

similar vein. At court at Christmas in 1561 the Queen had in no uncertain terms expressed her antipathy to married clergy in Parker's
earshot and on New Year's Day he wrote in great consternation to
Cecil.

> I was in an horror to hear such words to come from her mild
> nature and Christianly learned conscience, as she spake concerning
> God's holy ordinance and institution of matrimony. I marvelled
> that our states in that behalf cannot please her highness, which
> we doubt nothing at all to please God's sacred majesty, and
> trust to stand before God's judgement seat in a good conscience
> therewith, for all the glorious shine of counterfeit chastity.

He piously hoped that the Queen would think again 'and will use
Theodosius' days of deliberation in sentence giving, in matters of
such importance. I would be sorry that the clergy should have cause
to show disobedience, with *oportet Deo obedire magis quam hominibus.*'[12]

Both these expostulations bore some fruit: excepting only the
chapel royal, the Queen sanctioned the removal of images from the
church, and, more grudgingly, permitted the clergy to retain their
wives. During Parker's episcopate Protestant churchmen never
reached the point at which they considered they must place their
obedience to God above their obedience to their royal governor.
These instances of muted protest, nevertheless, help to place in its
context the stand of Archbishop Grindal in the following decade.
Elizabeth's first bishops had not allowed her to suppose that she
possessed unlimited authority as royal governor and Grindal, when
he succeeded as archbishop of Canterbury on Parker's death in 1575,
continued in the tradition which Protestant churchmen had already
endeavoured to establish. In 1576 the Queen again precipitated the
crisis with her archbishop by incautious speaking. Thinking that
clerical exercises, which to the majority of her churchmen seemed a
highly necessary means to improve the capabilities of the ill-educated
lower clergy, might foster political and religious subversion, the
Queen ordered Grindal to dissolve them throughout the southern
province. She then went on to affront Protestant susceptibilities yet
further by asserting that two or three preachers would suffice for an
entire county at a time when committed Protestants were calling for a
preaching minister in every parish. In the clear knowledge that he
might forfeit his position for his disobedience, Grindal refused to
comply and delivered to the royal governor the most unsparing

rebuke any Tudor churchman ever made. '"And what should I win"', he asked the Queen, '"if I gained" (I will not say a bishopric, but) "the whole world, and lose mine own soul?" Bear with me, I beseech you, Madam, if I choose rather to offend your earthly majesty, than to offend the heavenly majesty of God.' Having set before the Queen numerous examples of Christian emperors who accepted guidance from their churchmen, he concluded his disquisition with two requests:

> The first is, that you would refer all these ecclesiastical matters which touch religion, or the doctrine and discipline of the church, unto the bishops and divines of your realm, according to the example of all godly Christian emperors and princes of all ages. . . .
> The second petition I have to make to your majesty is this: that, when you deal in matters of faith and religion, . . . you would not use to pronounce so resolutely and peremptorily, *quasi ex auctoritate*, as ye may do in civil and extern matters; but always remember, that in God's causes the will of God, and not the will of any earthly creature, is to take place. . . .
> Remember, Madam, that you are a mortal creature. . . . And although ye are a mighty prince, yet remember that he which dwelleth in heaven is mightier. . . . Wherefore I do beseech you, Madam, *in visceribus Christi*, when you deal in these religious causes, set the majesty of God before your eyes, laying all earthly majesty aside: determine with yourself to obey his voice, and with all humility say unto him, *Non mea, sed tua voluntas fiat*. . . .[13]

Grindal had fundamentally miscalculated the malleability of his prince: Elizabeth would not accept advice couched in such terms nor would she contemplate delegating her authority in matters ecclesiastical to a synod of her churchmen. The Queen sequestered Grindal from the full exercise of his episcopal duties for the remainder of his life, though she found that she could not depose him from office on account of the extent of the sympathy evoked by his protest among clergy and laity alike. No other Elizabethan churchman dared defy the supreme governor as Grindal had done, and indeed the Queen appears to have taken greater care from this date that no cleric with the known independence of Grindal should be elevated to the episcopate. Grindal's disgrace marks a watershed in the relations between the supreme governor and her churchmen. The Queen had made clear her determination to rule as well as reign as fully in the ecclesiastical sphere as in the secular. While she lived none of her churchmen again tried citing the laws of Christ to counter the will of the prince. From 1583, when Whitgift became archbishop of Canterbury, the churchmen tended to change course and seem to have decided that the interests of the church could best be defended by supporting the Queen's interpretation of the royal supremacy against the interpretation of some of the leading laymen. Very soon these laymen began claiming that this new group of conservative clerics, by exalting their own powers in the church, were seeking to undermine their concept of the royal supremacy as being that of the monarch in Parliament.

Until the late 1580s no Elizabethan churchman had maintained that bishops constituted an inalienable order in a reformed church. In reply to Cartwright's arguments in favour of presbyterianism as the only divinely ordained form of church government, Whitgift had merely stated that God had not prescribed any one form of government and that in consequence ecclesiastical polity fell among the many matters indifferent. A reformed church might retain or abandon episcopacy according to circumstances. In England – a monarchy – the supreme governor had decided to keep bishops and all subjects ought to accept episcopacy as the choice of the monarch. In a further debate with Cartwright, he went on to demonstrate that there had been an inequality, not, as the presbyterians maintained, an equality, of ministers in the primitive church and, therefore, rule by bishops could in addition be justified on historical grounds. The sermon which Bancroft preached at Paul's Cross in February 1589 created a sensation not because he dwelt at some length on the existence of the ministry of bishops, priests and deacons in Christ's church from apostolic times but because he failed to make the by now customary admission that church government constituted one of the many matters indifferent and that the church was not throughout the ages tied to any particular form. To Sir Francis Knollys this omission seemed highly significant and he asserted that Bancroft 'though not by express words, yet by necessary consequence' had insinuated that the superiority of bishops was 'of God's own ordinance', and that those who did not accept this superiority could be considered heretical. If Bancroft established his claim for episcopacy existing by divine appointment, then Knollys feared that the royal supremacy would be found to be a great deal less strong than it had been thought to be.

During the controversy Knollys consulted Dr John Reynolds at Oxford and received a reassurance concerning the position of bishops as erastian as any Cranmer or Whitgift had previously made. He stated unequivocally 'that the supreme civil magistrate, in every country, may appoint under officers, in the execution of that government, which he hath in ecclesiastical causes, as well as he may do in civil matters . . .'. He had no doubt that the charge committed to ministers of the word and sacraments 'is but an human ordinance, and may not be entitled to any greater authority, nor otherwise said to be God's ordinance, than all officers of civil magistrates be'. In a statement which most politically conscious laymen would have endorsed right up to the Civil War, he concluded:

> The bishops of this realm do not . . . nor must not, claim to themselves any greater authority, than is given them by the statute of 25 of King Henry VIII, revived in the first year of her majesty's reign, or by other statutes of this land. Neither is it reasonable that they should make other claims. For if it pleased her majesty, with the wisdom of the realm, to have used no bishops at all, we could not have complained justly of any defect in our church. . . .[14]

The debate on the nature of episcopacy, however, did not end here, and Knollys discovered further occasions on which the royal supremacy appeared in danger from ambitious churchmen. In 1590 Saravia, a Dutch minister who had taken refuge in England, published a Latin treatise, *De Diversis Ministrorum Gradibus,* in which he said without any qualification that the office of bishops had been ordained by God and their retention was indispensable for any true church. In the same year, Anthony Marten included Saravia's arguments in an English book he had written in defence of episcopacy. Immediately Knollys retaliated, accusing Marten of having 'foolishly advanced the said superiority of bishops'. For Knollys, Marten's particular fault lay in the fact

> that he doth justify largely and plentifully the said superiority of bishops to be first from God's own ordinance, and in a second degree he claimeth the same superiority (also for the bishops) from her majesty's grant and allowance. But by claiming the said superiority of government first and principally from God's own ordinance, and not principally and directly from her majesty's grant, nor from her supreme government, therefore Mr Marten aforesaid is fallen into the penalty of *praemunire* . . .[15].

Knollys may have overreacted to works which do not at first seem to
have had much influence outside somewhat restricted clerical circles,
but he did gauge pretty accurately the direction in which some
churchmen's thought was progressing in the latter years of Elizabeth's reign. Another cleric, Matthew Sutcliffe, in 1591 stated that
Christ himself had established episcopacy in his church. In 1593
Thomas Bilson wrote *The Perpetual Government of Christ's Church* to
prove that on account of its divine institution episcopacy must always
be retained, and in the same year Bancroft said in his *Survey of the
Pretended Holy Discipline* what he had only implied in his earlier sermon, that government of the church by bishops had been ordained
by God. It is not surprising that some defenders of episcopacy, in the
face of *de iure* claims for presbyterianism made by some puritans,
eventually proceeded to make similar claims for the traditional
system of church government. Indeed it is only surprising that English
churchmen had not made these claims two decades earlier when the
presbyterians had first mounted their attack. To a certain extent they
were merely defending the existing system of church government
with refurbished weapons, but Knollys quite correctly realised that in
so doing the churchmen were elevating their estate against that of the
laity. The idea of the royal supremacy being government under the
Crown by bishops, which Elizabeth herself quite clearly preferred,
was being advanced at the expense of the concept of the royal
supremacy residing in the Crown in Parliament. Churchmen of
Bancroft's persuasion would acknowledge, without drawing too
precise distinctions, that while their primary calling came from God,
their external jurisdiction derived from the supreme governor. They
would not concede that the laity, in particular the laity as represented
in Parliament, had any control over their activity.

By no means all of the bishops adopted these views in the 1590s
and they remained the opinions of only a tiny minority in the church
at large. In this same decade Hooker could write:

Till it be proved that some special law of Christ hath for ever
annexed unto the clergy alone the power to make ecclesiastical
laws, we are to hold it a thing most consonant with equity and
reason that no ecclesiastical laws be made in a Christian commonwealth without consent as well of the laity as of the clergy, but
least of all without consent of the highest power.[16]

It still continued possible for laymen and churchmen interchangeably to hold two different interpretations of the royal supremacy.

Elizabeth never intervened in the literary controversy over episcopacy and the powers of the laity in the church, perhaps realising that in the 1590s obstreperous laymen rather than her bishops still offered the greatest threat to her idea of her powers as supreme governor. In Scotland James VI acted somewhat differently. Bancroft had, in his Paul's Cross sermon, illustrated the political dangers of presbyterianism by giving examples of the manner in which Scottish presbyterians had thwarted the wishes of their King. Under pressure from his Edinburgh presbytery, James demanded a public retraction, and at one moment it looked as if the sermon might interrupt the harmonious co-operation between England and Scotland. Burghley only succeeded in calming the situation by extracting an apology from Bancroft for seeming to suggest inconsistencies in the church polity of the Scottish King. Elizabeth in 1590 might feel moved to warn her brother in Scotland of the political threat to monarchy inherent in the presbyterian system: James, on the other hand, had thus early become aware of the potential dangers to the exercise of the royal prerogative also contained in divine right episcopacy.

In her last years Elizabeth showed far more concern over quelling present disputes than in anticipating future unrest in her church, and it is in this role of peace keeper that one of her most dramatic interventions as royal governor occurred. It took place against John Whitgift, the authoritarian opponent of puritans and by far the most sympathetic archbishop Elizabeth ever had. In the 1590s a small number of young graduates at Cambridge had begun to question the prevailing Calvinist theological orthodoxy, and some heads of colleges appealed to Whitgift against their presumption. Late in 1595 Whitgift and the heads together drew up articles at Lambeth which stated that:

> God from eternity predestined certain men to life and condemned others to death.
>
> The moving or efficient cause of predestination to life is not forseeing of faith, or of perseverence, or of good works, or of any other thing which is in the person predestined, but the will of the good pleasure of God alone.

As soon as she heard of the articles the Queen acted to prevent their promulgation, commanding Robert Cecil to tell Whitgift 'that she mislikes much that any allowance hath been given by your grace and the rest of any points to be disputed of predestination, being a matter tender and dangerous to weak, ignorant minds, and thereupon requireth your grace to suspend them . . .'. Whitgift, still believing the articles to be 'undoubtedly true', obediently bowed to the Queen's wishes, and forbade their public discussion in the university. When the Arminian Richard Montagu related the incident of the Lambeth Articles to his friend John Cosin in 1625, he described with relish the way in which 'Archbishop Whitgift was soundly chidden and threatened with a *praemunire*, by Queen Elizabeth, for presuming to tender anything contrary to the doctrine of the church'. He does not seem to have understood that if the Queen then had the power to control the discussion of Calvinist theology, a subsequent royal governor would enjoy a similar power to curb the spread of quite different theological innovations.[17]

At the end of her life Elizabeth had the support of her higher churchmen because they saw she would prevent change: they looked with foreboding towards her successor. Bancroft had already incurred James's displeasure; Whitgift feared more generally that the new King might adapt the existing government of the English church to bring it into greater conformity with that in Scotland. In fact their apprehensions were not realised, for James had already grasped the advantages to a monarch of an episcopally governed church in which the supreme governor kept the final control. At the Hampton Court Conference he let it be known that episcopal government would remain unaltered in the English church. James, however, had little regard for prelacy, or for churchmen who questioned Calvinist orthodoxy. At least in theology English Protestants gained in James a godly prince such as Elizabeth had never been. In contrast with Elizabeth, James delighted in the academic discussion of theology, and made no attempt to disguise his Calvinist opinions. 'Predestination and election', he declared in 1604, 'dependeth not upon any qualities, actions or works of man which be mutable, but upon God his eternal and immutable decree and purpose.' He still expressed very similar Calvinist opinions fifteen years later. He also gave scant encouragement to clerical assertiveness: when Convocation in 1606 drafted canons which made reference to priests being created by God's ordinance, and in no sense elected by the people, he refused to allow their enactment.

Bancroft's appointment, therefore, as archbishop of Canterbury on Whitgift's death did not bring any significant difference to the relationship between the churchmen and the royal governor. It meant that episcopal government would continue virtually unchanged but it did not imply that the King shared Bancroft's theological views. Historians are now beginning to question whether Bancroft's episcopate did see a wholesale reconstruction of the English church. The known Calvinism of the King and his antipathy towards clerical pretensions seem to have acted as a very effective check on the school of Arminian churchmen developing around Richard Neile. The King gave the see of Canterbury, when Bancroft died, to George Abbot, an undoubted Calvinist, and most of his key episcopal appointments went to men whose theology and ideas on church government closely resembled those of the early Elizabethan bishops. The Jacobean bishops did not come into conflict on any major issue with their supreme governor, while the laity in Parliament, apart from early hostility towards Bancroft for his deprivation of nonconforming ministers, seems in general to have acquiesced in the government of a church in which Protestantism could be freely expressed. In 1618 James pronounced in favour of the ultra-Calvinist position at the Synod of Dort and he certainly could not be charged with backing a theological movement among his own clergy contrary to the generally received views of the laity. A state of equilibrium seemed to have been reached both between the supreme governor and his churchmen and between the supreme governor and his lay subjects.[18]

| On the accession of Charles I the situation altered dramatically. The new monarch, oblivious of the political niceties of the royal supremacy contested over the previous century, threw in his lot with the clerical Arminians and upset the hardly won balance. From being a debating ground between the royal governor and his churchmen, indeed a possible protection of the laity against a powerful clerical estate, the royal supremacy, because of the actions of this party among the upper clergy, came rapidly to be seen as a permanent barrier against lay participation in ecclesiastical affairs. With Charles concurring in the divine right claims of the bishops, elevating more and more Arminians to the episcopal bench, the laity could no longer regard the monarch in any sense as the upholder of lay rights in the church. Laymen and many of the lower clergy considered that the supreme governor had relinquished his prerogative to ambitious

and unrepresentative clericalists; the King and the bishops appeared as an interest united against the laity, and the very concept of the royal supremacy deriving from King in Parliament seemed lost. Laud and his supporters might applaud the King's devotion to their cause, Charles himself think that he had only the welfare of the English church at heart; but his failure to act towards his churchmen in the way his lay subjects expected a royal governor to act contributed in no small degree to the hostility which led eventually to the Civil War.

2. Popular Reactions to the Reformation during the Years of Uncertainty 1530–70

D. M. PALLISER

THE Reformation provides perhaps the earliest instance in English history of conflicts over beliefs and attitudes in which ordinary people not only took sides in large numbers but also left those choices on record for posterity. Recent researches, especially at regional level, are beginning to show just how complex and fascinating those battles were. Gone is the commonplace assumption of nineteenth- and early twentieth-century historians that the battle was a simple one between 'Catholics' and 'Protestants', in which the 'True Church' was overthrown or revitalised according to one's prejudices; and gone too the assumption that almost everyone was passionately involved in the doctrinal issues at stake. There must have been many, lay and clerical, with the attitude of Vicar Aleyn of Bray, who kept his living from Henry VIII's reign to that of Elizabeth I. 'Being taxed by one for being a turncoat and an unconstant changeling, "Not so", said he, "for I always kept my principle, which is this, to live and die the vicar of Bray"'.[1] Nevertheless, a Christian cosmological framework was accepted (outwardly at least) by almost everyone, despite the massive evidence for semi- or anti-Christian beliefs assembled by Keith Thomas and others. Given that framework, it is not surprising that the various ecclesiastical and doctrinal changes imposed by the Crown provoked strong feelings both of support and of opposition. Historians will always disagree how far the divisions reflected real doctrinal disagreement and how far they were provoked by the social, economic and political changes that were bound up with the successive church settlements; but the fact of a deeply divided country is incontrovertible.

For Notes to Chapter 2, see pp. 189–91; for Bibliographical Notes, see pp. 181–2.

If the 'official' Reformation may be taken for convenience to cover a series of statutes and other measures enacted between 1529 and 1559, the 'popular' Reformation has much vaguer chronological boundaries. But the period considered here is not an entirely arbitrary one. Before about 1530 small though influential groups of Lollards and Lutherans existed clandestinely in an overwhelmingly Catholic country, while after the 1570s a semi-reformed church was accepted, willingly or reluctantly, by the vast majority, and only small minorities openly dissociated themselves from it. Between those dates, however, 'the result was still unsettled and the theological positions not yet sharply and irrevocably defined; the disputants, in England at least, are neither integral Tridentines nor fully Protestant or Calvinist; they are indeed not wholly clear in their own minds where they stand, or whither the world is moving'.[2] The two generations unsure of themselves can be defined by their wills, many of which made provision for religious rites 'if the law will suffer it'. Such bequests can be traced from 1529, immediately after the first statute affecting Catholic ritual, to at least 1572; by then the period of uncertainty was coming to an end.[3]

This chapter considers some of the evidence for the religious divisions of those years, as they are being revealed by recent researches. Older histories, in so far as they were concerned with religious dissent, concentrated heavily on those who became prominent by untypical means – martyrs, conspirators, refugees and rebels. It is now becoming possible, through research in local and diocesan records, to glimpse the opinions of much larger numbers of people, although many conclusions about the social, intellectual or geographical basis of religious disagreements must be very tentative. Much research remains to be done; and in view of the inarticulate nature of the 'silent majority' at all periods, dogmatic generalisations about popular attitudes will never be justified.

I

Since Lutheran books and ideas, and later Zwinglian, Anabaptist, Calvinist and other influences, entered England through London and the east-coast ports, it would be surprising if early Protestantism were not strongest in the south-east. A. G. Dickens has drawn attention to the importance of Lollard survival in the development of Protestantism, but the general pattern of early Protestantism can be explained largely in terms of accessibility to Continental influences. Areas receptive to the new ideas of the 1520s and 30s included London, East Anglia and Cambridge University, and (outside the south-east) districts centred on ports such as Hull and Bristol, which were, of course, in close touch by sea with the capital as well as with Europe. The bishop of Norwich said in 1530 that the gentry and commoners of his diocese were little affected by heresy, except for 'merchants and such as hath their abiding not far from the sea'. There was no geographical determinism in all this; in the south-east, Sussex and Hampshire remained almost unaffected, while Coventry and Yorkshire had their modest share of early Protestants. It may be significant, however, that one of the early Yorkshire heretics had brought back his ideas from contacts in Suffolk as a textile worker, just as the few early Lancashire Protestants can nearly all be shown to have travelled to areas of Protestant influence further south.[4]

Henry VIII's acquisition of control over the church in the 1530s provoked more opposition than was once believed. The royal supremacy was strongly resisted in both southern and northern Convocations and the Act in Restraint of Annates in the House of Lords. It is true that the abolition of papal supremacy provoked no open opposition in the country and that the fifty or so who may be called martyrs to the issue were drawn mostly from eight religious houses of strict observance. There may, however, be some truth in what apologists later said in Mary's reign, that many had consented to the new order only out of fear. G. R. Elton has drawn together evidence from many areas of men arguing in private about the supremacy and other issues and, since the evidence is only of those whose confidence was betrayed, such murmurings may have been even more widespread.

The attack on the religious houses touched more directly on everyday life and one need not take a romantic view of them to see a close connection between their suppression and radical religious attitudes. As Latimer logically pointed out, 'The founding of monasteries argued purgatory to be, so the putting of them down argueth it not to be.' It is therefore not surprising that the first dissolutions in 1536 polarised opinion, and hostility to the suppressions can be taken as an indication of conservatism if not necessarily of articulate Catholicism. There may have been several such incidents as that in Exeter in 1537, where local women attacked the workmen suppressing St Nicholas's Priory. The strongest reaction to the dissolutions, however, occurred in the north.

The Pilgrimage of Grace has become an umbrella term for the five northern risings in the autumn and winter of 1536–7, but is more properly used of the main rising of October 1536, which was ostensibly a protest against royal policies and in defence of the church; the rebels adopted the device of the five wounds of Christ as a banner. The rebellions were complex affairs and some recent writers have emphasised social and economic grievances rather than religious motives and have suggested that the Lincolnshire and Yorkshire risings were instigated by discontented nobles, gentry and senior clergy rather than being, as was once thought, spontaneous mass protests. However, C. S. L. Davies has adduced weighty evidence that popular religious protest was a significant element; and J. J. Scarisbrick's judgement is that the Pilgrimage was an 'essentially religious' movement in 'the widest sense of that adjective'. Certainly contemporaries like John Hales and Robert Parkyn, on opposite sides of the religious fence, agreed that the cause had been the Crown's religious policies and the monastic suppressions. It is surely significant that at least sixteen of the fifty-five northern houses already suppressed were restored by the rebels.[5]

If this view is correct, how can the regional character of the revolt be explained? One of the Pilgrims' ballads exhorted the 'faithful people of the Boreal region' to overthrow the 'Southern heretics' and 'Southern Turks',[6] which must have made good recruiting propaganda, but there is no reason to think that a conservative north was facing a heretical south: the royal general, Norfolk, admitted that his own soldiers thought the Pilgrims' cause 'good and godly'. Without minimising the genuine religious zeal of some Pilgrims, one can agree with R. B. Smith and M. E. James that the crucial factor in the spread of the revolts was the attitude of the local nobles and gentry. For example, the central areas of the West Riding – dominated by the Percies and Lord Darcy – rebelled, whereas Hallamshire, the domain of the loyalist earl of Shrewsbury, did not. Similarly the earl of Derby was able to keep Lancashire quiet, though his authority did collapse north of the Ribble where the threatened monasteries were popular.

After the Pilgrims had been tricked into surrender, Henry encountered no more overt and widespread opposition to his religious policies, though G. R. Elton's evidence from the state papers shows that, in the late thirties at least, discontent from both right and left existed in all regions. The surrenders of the greater monasteries in 1537–40 passed off with the judicial murder of four abbots and one prior, and the Wakefield plot of 1541 was easily nipped in the bud. In the south-east significant numbers were keen to move in a Protestant direction, even after government policy became more conservative. Over 500 Londoners were indicted as hostile to the Act of Six Articles in 1539; at Chelmsford there is a picture of the people flocking to hear the newly installed Bible read out in the church; and a curious incident at Yarmouth in 1541 suggests that four leading merchants had already adopted radical 'sacramentarian' beliefs.[7] On the other hand, there is little sign of Protestantism before 1547 in Devon, Cornwall or Lancashire, though A. G. Dickens has found a number of heresy prosecutions in Yorkshire.

One of the most voluminous sources for information about religious attitudes, if not always the easiest to interpret, is that of wills, which survive for large numbers of Tudor Englishmen (and women). Counting the frequency of bequests for religious purposes can give a rough idea of the relative popularity of a particular practice. W. K. Jordan's researches have shown, for instance, a decline in endowed prayers for the dead by the 1530s in Hampshire and Buckinghamshire, and their tenacious maintenance in Somerset, Kent, Norfolk, Lancashire and Yorkshire. Not all wills have bequests suitable for such analysis but one feature of almost all Tudor wills, on which interest has more recently focused, is the 'bequest' of the soul to God as a first clause. Many such bequests are in a simple form which reveals nothing of doctrinal belief but some testators made clearly traditional bequests – associating Our Lady and All Saints with God – or firmly Protestant statements, expecting salvation through faith in Christ alone. From the later 1530s such bequests vary socially and regionally in sufficient numbers to be worth using as evidence of religious change. Unfortunately the problems raised by analyses of will formulae are also considerable.[8] The most obvious difficulty lies in differentiating between personal statements of faith and those suggested to the dying man by the writer of the will, often a parish priest or clerk; though even in those cases local variations in will formulae still reflect differences of belief.

Analyses of wills of the later years of Henry VIII are not numerous enough to reveal a clear pattern. Published samples of wills from London and the north for 1537–47 are not dissimilar: the proportion of testators omitting the traditional mention of Mary and the saints was 24 per cent among Londoners and 22 per cent in Yorkshire and Nottinghamshire. In a comprehensive count of York citizens' wills in the same period, however, the proportion was only 4 per cent. The difference between the county and city figures may be due partly to a bias of the county sample towards wills of gentry, who included several early Protestants, and partly to early Protestantism among the textile workers of the West Riding; but in any case A. G. Dickens has rightly warned against presenting such results in a 'spirit of statistical pedantry'. Firmer guides to the growth of Protestantism are perhaps the wills of those who made bequests in solefideian form before this became common and who were plainly making personal declarations of faith. Such a man was Alderman Monmouth of London, who had been in trouble for heresy in 1528 and who in his will (November 1537) trusted in his salvation solely through the merits of Christ's passion. As if to make his views crystal clear, he also left money for thirty-one sermons supporting the royal supremacy. A Bristol merchant's widow also made a Protestant will in 1537, and two men of Halifax (Yorkshire) in 1538, while several parishioners of Thornbury (Gloucestershire) did so in the 1540s, apparently influenced by their parish priest. On the other hand, no such will was made by any York citizen until 1547, and of five Cambridgeshire villages only one shows such wills as early as the 1540s.[9]

With the removal of Henry VIII's heavy hand in 1547, a Protestant party could emerge into the open and begin, with government support, to take the initiative. Thomas Hancock, preaching in Poole, Dorset, in 1548, found keen supporters: 'they were the first that in that part of England were called Protestants'. One indicator of religious radicalism was the destruction of images and stained glass, which was widespread in London, Essex and Norwich from the beginning of Edward's reign. Less radical areas took no action until the general order for removal of images in February 1548, while very conservative communities like Oxford and York seem to have made only a token compliance even then. Unfortunately the most recent study of iconoclasm raises the question of regional variations without answering it, and much local research is needed before it can be assessed.[10]

A partial, although not entirely satisfactory, picture of the most conservative areas can be drawn from the extent of the rebellions in 1549. Protector Somerset wrote on 11 June that rebels had assembled 'in the most parts of the realm . . . and first seeking redress of enclosures, have in some places by seditious priests and other evil people set forth to seek restitution of the old bloody laws'. In fact one revolt, in Norfolk, had almost purely economic motives but that in the west country was in the main a protest against the first Edwardian prayer book. It engulfed much of Devon and Cornwall, besides attracting sympathy in Somerset and Dorset. The rebels, marching like the Pilgrims of Grace behind a banner of the five wounds of Christ, issued fifteen demands including the restoration of 'our old service' in Latin and the execution of heretics and including only one non-religious clause. No other Tudor rebels made such overwhelmingly religious demands and the hostile eyewitness Hooker admitted that 'the cause thereof . . . was only concerning religion'. The same summer saw a serious Catholic rising in Oxfordshire as well as a limited revolt in East Yorkshire against the suppression of chantries. The Venetian ambassador referred obscurely to other rebels in 'Arvaschier' (Warwickshire or Derbyshire?) demanding the restoration of Henry VIII's religious settlement, and it may be that other local revolts have yet to be identified; one contemporary spoke of 'many more shires' rebelling in July 1549 'for maintenance of Christ's church'. The rebel areas were not solidly Catholic, as will be seen, and other areas which did not take the extreme step of rebellion were just as conservative as the west country. A Privy Councillor admitted that same year that 'the old religion is forbidden by a law, and the use of the new is not yet printed in the stomachs of eleven of twelve parts in the realm'.

There is abundant evidence of the strength of conservatism in Hampshire, Sussex and the Welsh marches in Edward's reign and well into that of Elizabeth. The north also remained generally conservative, despite pockets of Protestantism in the textile areas of Lancashire and the West Riding. The lack of a serious northern revolt in 1549 can be attributed partly to the savage repression of the Pilgrimage and partly to a subordination of religious to civic loyalties, but it does not indicate active support for the Edwardian reforms. A south Yorkshire priest testified that in 1550 the region 'from Trent northwards' was lagging behind 'the south parts' in abolishing stone altars and Catholic ceremonial. A scheme for itinerant government preachers in 1551 shows clearly the unreliable areas — Devon, Hampshire, Wales, Lancashire, Yorkshire and the Scottish borders. At the other end of the religious spectrum, it is a fair assumption that in those towns which displayed zealous Protestantism almost as soon as Elizabeth ascended the throne – Coventry, Colchester, Ipswich, Leicester and others – Protestantism must have been firmly established before 1553.

Another rough index of religious sympathies is the incidence of clerical marriage. It was legalised in February 1549, though some early Protestant clergy in Suffolk had married as early as 1536–7. The numbers who took advantage of it between 1549 and 1553 can be approximately established by the deprivations of married clergy in Mary's reign. At one extreme was London, where nearly a third of the parish clergy married, followed closely by Essex, Suffolk and Norfolk with a quarter or more, and Cambridgeshire with one in five. In Lincolnshire and the diocese of York the proportion was only one in ten, and in Lancashire less than one in twenty.[11] As with will formulae, the figures should not be treated with too much respect, for the correlation between the religious outlook of the clergy and their propensity to marriage was not a close one. Nevertheless, conservative laymen were generally hostile to clerical marriage both in Edward's reign and later. In Cornwall and Lancashire married ministers were cold-shouldered throughout Elizabeth's reign, though such hostility was traditionalist rather than Catholic and was, of course, shared by the Queen herself.

The ease with which the Catholic Mary I succeeded to the throne in 1553 was, it is now accepted, owing to her legitimate hereditary claim and not to her religion. Early in the reign there was popular agitation in Kent and Essex for the restoration of Protestant worship; and Wyatt's rebellion in early 1554, though ostensibly a political protest, had a covertly Protestant aim if some of his own remarks can be believed. He received strong support in Kent – though even there Canterbury, under a Catholic mayor, fortified itself against him – and his success was also said to be 'joyous to the Londoners', though he failed to take the capital. More important, his fellow conspirators completely failed to raise Devon, Herefordshire and the Midlands.[12] That may reflect loyalism rather than religious feeling but studies of Lancashire and York suggest positive enthusiasm for the Queen's restoration of Catholicism. The York corporation hailed the accession of Mary as a 'godly' ruler – a term they did not repeat for her sister in 1558 – and there was even a rumour after the defeat of Wyatt that Mary would move her capital from London to York 'to be among Catholic people'.[13] After a generation of uncertainty, however, no area was homogeneous in its religious sympathies; Lancashire and Yorkshire both numbered small but dedicated Protestant minorities, like the 'busy fellows of the new sort' prosecuted at Leeds, and a large minority of A. G. Dickens's Yorkshire wills sample was non-traditional.

The best-remembered dissidents in Mary's reign are, of course, the exiles and the martyrs. Both were tiny minorities in a population of some three million, but they were highly influential and their geographical distribution is likely to be similar to that of the larger body of Protestants who did not carry their opposition so far. Christina Garrett counted 472 men, nearly all gentlemen, clergy or merchants, who fled to the Continent; of 350 whose residence she fairly firmly established, two out of five came from London and Middlesex, Kent, Sussex, Essex, Suffolk and Norfolk.[14] The 300 heretics burned between 1555 and 1558, mainly humbler folk, were even more concentrated; over three-quarters were burned in those six counties, through not all the victims suffered in their home county. The chief difference between the two groups, apart from their social composition, is that the exiles were drawn from a wider catchment area. There was no sizeable body of martyrs outside East Anglia and the Home Counties except at Bristol, where Foxe names seven but where recent research can confirm only four.[15] Devon and Cornwall, which contributed about thirty-five exiles, witnessed only one martyrdom; Lancashire and Yorkshire provided only one martyr but nearly forty exiles. The excessive concentration of martyrs in the south-east probably reflects not so much the distribution of heresy as the zeal of the ecclesiastical authorities. Pole of Canterbury and Bonner of London were proverbial for their hunting down of heretics, whereas other bishops like Tunstall of Durham and Heath of York were averse to persecution. Margaret Spufford, speaking of 'the depth of the reception of Protestant feeling' in Cambridgeshire, suspects that 'lenient administration of the diocese' was responsible for restricting the number of martyrs there to three.[16]

Episcopal zeal cannot, however, entirely explain away the special place of London and East Anglia in the story of early Protestantism. The capital, scene of sixty-seven burnings, was notorious for its sympathies. Pole complained to the Londoners 'that when any heretic shall go to execution, he shall lack no comforting of you, and encouraging to die in his perverse opinion'. Certainly London takes first place in the number of known underground Protestant congregations under Mary; and the next largest congregation recorded was in Colchester, a town notorious as 'a harbourer of heretics'. There is also the astonishing fact that four Essex parishes continued using the prescribed Edwardian services until 1555 without being disturbed.[17] The same geographical pattern was apparent when Elizabeth came to the throne. Iconoclasm in 1559, for instance, was most promptly and zealously pursued in London, 'with such shouting, and applause of the vulgar sort, as if it had been the sacking of some hostile city'. In the west country, on the other hand, the populace was devoted to the 'votive relics of the saints' and reluctant to destroy images.[18]

It is difficult to avoid writing history with hindsight. The religious opposition to Mary is often overwritten because she died before her regime was firmly established; that facing Elizabeth I is perhaps still underestimated because her settlement ultimately endured. In 1562 the bishop of Carlisle said that 'every day men look for a change', and a Yorkshire gentleman was confident 'that the crucifix with Mary and John should be set up again in all churches' before Christmas.[19] For the first decade of her reign Elizabeth moved warily and only after the rising of the northern earls in 1569, a last, forlorn Catholic revolt, did she impose a tighter religious discipline. Like all the Tudors, she had to co-operate with the J.P.s who enforced law and order in the shires and they were very divided, as a series of reports on J.P.s' loyalties sent in by the bishops in 1564 reveals.[20] Roughly 431 J.P.s throughout England were described as favourable to the Elizabethan settlement; 264 as indifferent or neutral; and 157 as hostile. 'It was a sufficient majority among those who mattered', comments A. L. Rowse – but not in all counties. In Sussex there were only 10 'favourers' to 15 'mislikers'; in Staffordshire 10 'no favourers' out of 17; and in Lancashire 6 'favourable' to 18 'not favourable'; 4 of the Lancashire non-favourers were still active justices as late as 1583. The benches in corporate towns were nearly all more conservative than the justices in the shires; the entire Hereford council was unfavourable or 'neuter', and all but two of the York aldermen. Widespread Catholic survivalism was revealed in diocesan visitations like those of York in 1567 and Chichester in 1569. In many places in Sussex chalices were kept 'looking for to have mass again'. Against these, there were radicals in other areas moving well to the left of the 1559 settlement. Independency was being tolerated in East Anglia as early as 1561, and what Patrick Collinson calls 'London's Protestant underworld' gave rise to a separatist church by 1567.[21]

By the 1570s the 'Established Church' was indeed firmly established, though assailed from both left and right. Even if Catholic recusancy of the Counter-Reformation type is beyond our brief, it is worth looking briefly at the tenacious maintenance of the older religious ways by a dwindling number of 'survivalists' who are not to be confused with the new Catholic recusants. These remained longest in what puritans were coming to call 'the dark corners of the land'. Chester, Boston, Wakefield and York, for example, kept up their medieval miracle plays until the 1570s, although so did Chelmsford in Essex. Many Catholic traditions were reported from the northern dioceses, and Archbishop Grindal found the northern province so conservative in 1570 as to seem 'another church, rather than a member of the rest'.[22] Gradually he and his ally the earl of Huntingdon, Lord President of the Council in the North, enforced conformity, though Lancashire's exemption from the Council's jurisdiction made it something of a sanctuary for Catholics. The very last open cases of survivalism can be traced in wills – Catholic phraseology by the middle of Elizabeth's reign, by a dwindling number of testators mainly in the north, can indicate only their stubborn devotion to the old ways, coupled of course with a tolerance in the northern church courts towards registering such wills. Among the last testators known to have left their souls to God, the Blessed Virgin and the saints, in full medieval form, were an alderman of Newcastle (1582), Lady Wharton of Healaugh near York (1583), and a York alderman's widow (1585). The offending phrase has been deleted in the registered copy of the Newcastle will, but the two wills in the York register have been left uncensored. In 1575 a Duchy of Lancaster official asked for prayers for his soul; in 1581 another Lancastrian left his parish priest 10s to pray for him; and in one Lancashire parish prayers for the dead were still recited at funerals in the 1590s.[23]

II

The evidence presented so far has partly confirmed the traditional textbook picture of a south and east more receptive to Protestantism during the period of uncertainty, and a north and west less so. As a crude generalisation, with many exceptions allowed, it may be acceptable. The inhabitants of London and the east-coast ports, after all, were in regular contact with the continental reformed churches, like Humphrey Monmouth and other London merchants who imported forbidden Lutheran books, or the Hull sailors who visited Bremen and Friesland in 1528 and witnessed Lutheran services. The west-coast ports traded more with the Catholic lands of Spain, Portugal and Ireland, though Bristol developed nevertheless into an early Protestant centre, as did landlocked Coventry. Something should be allowed too to T. M. Parker's claim that the greater prosperity of lowland England 'gave men more time for thought and bound them less to tradition, which always flourishes most where life is hard and experiment dangerous to existence'.[24] At any rate, some recent regional studies would appear to support the correlation: J. E. Oxley, M. Spufford and F. Heal have depicted Essex and Cambridgeshire as much more receptive than A. L. Rowse's Cornwall or Christopher Haigh's Lancashire. Many more such studies are needed for other areas, however, and it is clear that such a geographical correlation is a loose one at best. Christopher Haigh suspects that conservative Lancashire (apart from its south-east corner) was not so very different from other parts of England,[25] and Roger Manning's study of Sussex, with its strong conservatism until the 1570s, is certainly a warning against assuming that Protestantism could be easily enforced even in the south-east. Conversely, A. G. Dickens's studies showed some time ago that the north was far from being the uniformly reactionary region of popular tradition, and that Beverley, Halifax, Hull, Leeds, Rotherham and Wakefield all housed significant Protestant communities before 1558. As a further blow to geographical determinism, the radical Halifax was a clearly upland parish, whereas the city of York, in an outlier of lowland England, proved obstinately conservative. Furthermore, where highland areas did prove more difficult to control, administrative rather than physical barriers were often to blame. Much of the west midlands and the north formed before 1541 two huge dioceses, York and Lichfield, and though the creation of the see of Chester was a step in the right direction, Chester proved to be a most unsuitable centre, especially for controlling Lancashire, and was inadequately financed. Moreover, much of the north and west was divided into large parishes where detections of heresy and recusancy were inevitably difficult.

Perhaps the promising lines of future research are those concentrating on religious belief at the most local level, for regional studies have too coarse a mesh. Broad generalisations can be made about the distribution of conservatives and radicals but any determinist view based on geography or economic and social structure would ignore the vital role of committed individuals. The influence of Latimer in

Bristol and Gloucester in the 1530s, or of Bernard Gilpin in County Durham in Elizabeth's reign, are but two examples of the enormous influence of dedicated clergy in changing the local religious climate. Indeed, it was similar zeal by committed laymen, in Claire Cross's view, which made impossible any return to religious uniformity at the end of the period of uncertainty. A small number of influential nobles and gentry used their patronage to present zealous Protestants to church livings in Suffolk, Leicestershire and other counties; and both Protestant and Catholic gentry retained as chaplains men unacceptable to the established ministry. 'In the last resort the state failed to compel the laity into uniformity because the zealots, both Catholic and Protestant, disregarding the parochial system, made their own households into centres of evangelism.' The negative influence of a local magnate could be equally crucial. The third earl of Derby, who dominated Lancashire, played a waiting game in both 1536 and 1569, and though he did not in the event throw his considerable weight behind either rising, he did not actively work for the Crown either.[26]

Coupled with a realisation of the importance of the individual is a recognition that almost no area was entirely homogeneous in its religious beliefs between the 1530s and the 1570s: many villages were bitterly divided, while in the larger towns total uniformity was almost impossible to attain. G. R. Elton's survey of opinion in the 1530s identifies serious divisions between conservatives and radicals in Bristol, Rye and Gloucester as well as three Oxford colleges. Bristol remained deeply divided for another generation despite, or perhaps because of, the presence of zealous Protestants on the city council from an early date. The Catholic Roger Edgeworth, preaching at Bristol early in Mary's reign, said that, 'Here among you in this city some will hear mass, some will hear none ... some will be shriven, some will not, but for fear or else for shame ... some will pray for the dead, some will not, I hear of much dissension among you.' Similarly, when the married vicar of Orwell, Cambridgeshire, mocked the mass that he had to reintroduce he drew strong support from some parishioners but deeply offended others.[27]

London was large enough to hide a multitude of opinions and recorded dissent there may have been only the tip of the iceberg. True, most of it was radical dissent, from the bricklayer who annoyed his neighbours in the late 1530s by preaching from his window and his garden fence, to the exercises 'after Geneva fashion' being held in a church by 1559. Yet London, like Bristol, had its splits between right and left: when feasts were being abrogated by the government in 1549 and 1550 'some kept holy day and some none', and the same divisions were manifested when the festivals were restored in 1554. The Venetian ambassador clearly oversimplified when he said that the Londoners were the most disposed to obey the inconstant laws on religion, 'because they are nearer the Court'.[28] London's teeming population – it was at least ten times the size of any other English town – probably more than counteracted the pressure for conformity from the government at Westminster or the archbishop at Lambeth. After all, the capital of the northern province, York, showed no disposition to change its religion with its successive archbishops, despite the presence of their church courts in its midst, and remained as consistently conservative as London was radical.

The most vivid picture of urban division, if not the most objective, comes from the autobiography of Thomas Hancock, a Hampshire-born Protestant clergyman. In 1548 he preached against the mass in Salisbury, stirring up so much dissension that Protector Somerset forbade him to preach at Southampton. 'My lord said unto me that Hampton was a haven town, and that if I should teach such doctrine as I taught at Sarum the town would be divided, and so should it be a way or a gap for the enemy to come in.' Soon afterwards Hancock became curate of Poole in Dorset, where he found strong support, though his blunt attacks on the real presence again provoked violent controversy. A group led by a former mayor, 'a great rich merchant, and a ringleader of the Papists', attacked him in his church and the then mayor had to protect him physically. Such, at least, is what Hancock recorded long after the event, though his picture of zeal on both sides may have been magnified with distance. He proudly records a Salisbury draper's boast that 'a hundred of them would be bound in £100' as sureties for him, but his own artless testimony shows that their zeal was only moderate. When the chief justice reasonably preferred ten sureties of £10 each, the draper replied that 'it would grieve them to forfeit £10 apiece but in that quarrel to forfeit 20s apiece it would never grieve them'. Nevertheless, the picture of violent opposition to Protestant preachers in the region is corroborated from other sources: Bale, for instance, said in 1552 that attacks were being made on 'Christ's ministers' in many areas, 'chiefly within Hampshire'.[29]

Even further west, notorious to contemporaries as a region 'where popery greatly prevailed', Protestants were numerous enough to demolish any idea of uniform Catholicism. At Bodmin in 1548, schoolboys fought mock battles in gangs representing the old and new religions, and the western rising of 1549 received general but by no means unanimous support. Raleigh's father, who was alleged to have browbeaten an old woman near Exeter for telling her beads, was threatened with death by the rebels but rescued by 'certain mariners of Exmouth'. Exeter itself provides perhaps the best example of conflicting loyalties within a city. During the rising, according to Hooker's eyewitness account, the majority of citizens were Catholic, yet the city was firmly defended against the rebels because the magistrates, 'albeit some and the chiefest . . . were well affected to the Romish religion', put first 'their obedience to the King . . . and safety of themselves'. When, however, the city was tempted to join a Protestant rebellion five years later, the sheriff of Devon took no chances. Two aldermen known to be Catholics were given emergency powers to defend it, 'for as much as the mayor of Exeter and his brethren were of several religions'.[30] The precautions may have been unnecessary, for faced with a rebellion most town corporations thought of 'obedience' and 'safety of themselves' whatever their religious persuasion. Solidarity of the governing body was put before ideology and, no doubt, one fear at the back of the aldermen's minds was the disorder and looting that might be unleashed by any surrender to a rebel army. Hence the London corporation held the city firmly against Wyatt, despite the widespread support he apparently enjoyed among lesser citizens, just as York held out strongly against the Catholic earls in 1569, although some of its leading aldermen had Catholic sympathies.

It should occasion no surprise that the reception of Protestantism, like that of any new belief or ideology, had an uneven impact; making its way in a complex society divided by rivalries between individuals, families, social groups and entire communities, it was almost certain to become entangled with existing dissensions. If one man or group adopted Protestantism, that might ensure that his or their enemies remained Catholic; or – which was not always the same thing – if one rebelled, another might be the more zealous in loyalty. Such considerations applied especially in districts where lords and their tenants did not trust one another. Some gentlemen might remain aloof from a rebellion out of prudence or out of contempt for the social status of the rebel leaders; both reactions can be seen

among the Lincolnshire and Yorkshire gentry in 1536. Rebel commoners might use the cloak of revolt to work off grudges against
their lords; or arrogant lords might use the opportunities of religious
uncertainty to bully tenants. The purchaser of a monastic manor in
Sussex was accused of harassing his tenants and boasting, 'Do ye not
know that the King's Grace hath put down all the houses of monks,
friars and nuns? therefore now is the time come that we gentlemen
will pull down the houses of such poor knaves as ye be', though it is
fair to add that he denied the charge.[31]

The alignment of religious and social groups would depend on the
local situation. At St Neots (Huntingdonshire) in 1547 conservative
gentry confronted radical commoners: the parishioners removed images illegally, and the local gentlemen vainly ordered their restoration. In the west country the situation was often reversed: the 1549
rising had strong overtones of social protest by the Catholic rebels
against the gentry. Likewise in Mary's reign it was the Cornish gentry
who led opposition to her policies, while the 'stupid and backward-
looking peasantry', to use A. L. Rowse's uncharitable phrase,
remained loyal. An analysis of the abortive risings of 1554 suggests
that the distinction between gentry and commons was more explicit
in Devon than in any other area. One might conclude from studies
like A. L. Rowse's that the gentry, with their superior education, were
more open to new ideas than a stubbornly conservative peasantry,
but this would be an unjustified inference. Commons as well as
gentry could follow sophisticated arguments. Sir Francis Bigod, stirring an assembly of Yorkshire commons to renewed revolt in 1537,
used technical arguments against the validity of the King's pardon
which were obviously well understood. A Cambridgeshire
husbandman travelled to Colchester about 1555 to discuss Pauline
theology with fellow Protestants and, on failing to satisfy his conscience, seriously considered travelling to Oxford to consult Ridley
and Latimer.[32]

Social and economic grievances have also been emphasised as underlying the Pilgrimage of Grace. A. G. Dickens has drawn attention
to several riots and quarrels in York just before the rising 'over issues
unrelated to the ecclesiastical polity of the Crown', though at least
one was apparently an accusation by one merchant against another
for disloyalty to the royal supremacy. Aldermen and lesser freemen
were certainly at odds over enclosures in May 1536, yet were apparently almost united in admitting the Pilgrims without resistance in

October. However, York may not have been typical of northern communities and more research is needed on the Pilgrimage as a whole. In Lancashire it was indeed largely a religious protest but the risings in Cumbria, and probably those in Craven and Richmondshire, had the characteristics of peasant rebellions.

Religious disputes could undoubtedly become an element in quarrels between rich and poor in town as well as countryside. At Rye, between 1533 and 1538, the vicar behaved in a provocative way – attacking 'heretics'; refusing to obey the new liturgical regulations; splitting the town into two factions; and, if his enemies can be believed, openly defending papal supremacy. Cromwell had for years to deal with the complaints of the rival factions yet, when he finally stepped in, the vicar was only removed to another parish and no charges of treason were brought. The reason, apparently, was that he was strongly supported by the mayor and jurats and seventy-five 'worthy men' of Rye, whereas his enemies were 'very simple and of small substance'. 'It is clear enough', comments G. R. Elton, 'that the divisions here ran not only between adherents of the old and the new way in religion, but more especially also between the rulers of Rye and the poorer sort.' There are hints of a similar pattern at York forty years later, when Mayor Criplyng (1579–80) was in trouble with the authorities of church and state for attacking the clergy and not presenting recusants. Criplyng, apparently a survivalist rather than a recusant, was hastily disowned by his fellow aldermen when his supporters put up 'filthy and lewd' posters in the streets, and there are indications that a group of committed Protestant merchants were taking over the city council, while Criplyng was supported by some of the poorer citizens.[33]

Criplyng's case is a reminder that Tudor rulers could enforce their policies only with the co-operation of unpaid officials in the localities. All statistics of religious offenders, therefore, reflect the zeal or success of those who presented them – clergy, churchwardens, J.P.s, gentry, private citizens – as much as the actual distribution of dissent. The justices were vital to the process of enforcing uniformity, certainly after 1559, and apparently there never was a thorough purge of Catholic J.P.s in Elizabeth's reign. In Yorkshire the J.P.s did not administer the oath of supremacy even to one another until 1562 and the bishop of Winchester had great difficulty persuading his fellow justices to certify recusants. Much depended on the relationship of the bishop with the 'county community' of nobles and gentry. In Norfolk, Bishop Parkhurst (1560–75) deferred to the conservative duke of Norfolk (d. 1572) as long as he lived, but in the last three years of his life was able to follow his own inclinations and to pack the bench with radical Protestants. His successor Bishop Freake (1575–85), however, appointed J.P.s 'backward in religion' to control the puritans. Richard Curteys of Chichester (1570–82), the first bishop to make real inroads into the ingrained conservatism of Sussex, attempted to do for that county what Parkhurst had done for East Anglia, but his 'fanaticism and inquisitorial methods clashed with the attitude of practical tolerance that the Sussex gentry felt was dictated by the special conditions of local politics'. He attacked a group of crypto-Catholic justices, only to find that the bench united against him despite their religious divisions. When he pressed some of them to swear that they 'kept no company with any that were backward in religion' they replied that 'we cannot take knowledge of every man's religion and conscience that cometh into our company'.[34]

Diversity of opinion was true of the nobles and gentry throughout the period of uncertainty, though the approximate statistics in recent studies relate only to the end of the period. It has been estimated that of 66 peers in 1580, 22 were committed Protestants, 20 recusants and 24 relatively indifferent; that among office-holding gentry in Sussex in the 1560s known Catholics outnumbered Protestants two to one; and that of 567 families of Yorkshire gentry in 1570, 368 (65 per cent) were still Catholic.[35] Given such divisions, and the common preference for social solidarity among the gentry over religious opinions, the lukewarm prosecution of successive settlements in many counties is scarcely surprising. The gentry not only dominated the commissions of the peace but were also prominent on the mixed lay–clerical ecclesiastical commissions favoured by Elizabeth as instruments of religious uniformity. Christopher Haigh has shown that in Lancashire, at least, the ecclesiastical commission and the bench of justices were both unreliable instruments, including crypto-Catholic gentry and even open recusants. Nor should one neglect the lesser lay officials, the churchwardens, whose office it was to enforce church attendance. Over half the recusants returned in Cheshire in 1578 lived in nine parishes where the wardens had not been imposing the statutory fines for non-attendance.[36] In fact several recent studies suggest that the visitation procedures could cope only with minority problems: if a group of offenders were generally supported by the other parishioners, they would be unlikely to be presented. That suggests the depressing possibility that the records indicate only the distribution of small minorities of dissenters and that areas of widespread dissent might often pass unrecorded. There must have been strong social pressure on churchwardens not to betray their neighbours; and it is remarkable how often heretics presented were immigrants from other parts of England or from overseas. Given the parochial loyalties of the age, a 'foreigner' must always have stood more danger of arrest than a native.

The role of the senior clergy was, of course, equally vital in enforcing the successive settlements. Mary and Pole are often criticised for dying with five sees vacant, so making Elizabeth's settlement easier; it is less often remarked that Elizabeth unwisely left many more sees vacant after the Marian bishops were deprived, both to save money and to bargain for advantageous land exchanges with the bishops elect. Of the 22 English sees, 16 were unfilled at the end of 1559 and 9 were still vacant a year later; Oxford, the last, was not filled until 1567. Some of the longer vacancies were in the north and west and they gave Catholic survival or revival precious extra time to become more firmly established. Lichfield was not filled until March 1560, when Bishop Bentham found Catholic furnishings still retained in many Shropshire churches. At York 'the hard core of the central ecclesiastical administration' was shattered in 1559 and not repaired for two years, a crucial delay in the view of Hugh Aveling. Chester (which included Lancashire) was administered by a Catholic commissary until February 1561. Even when bishops were at last appointed – Young to York and Downham to Chester – both proved very weak instruments of uniformity. Archbishop Parker saw the danger of vacant sees clearly and complained that 'whatsoever is now too husbandly saved will be an occasion of further expense of keeping them down if (as God forfend) they should be too much Irish and savage'.[37] The position would have been worse if the Queen had accepted a scheme to keep Chester permanently vacant and pocket its revenues; she contented herself with an eighteen-year vacancy at Ely, a safely Protestant see. Nor should one neglect the vital importance of the right cathedral appointments to assist the bishops in enforcing conformity. Indeed, in Dr James's view, it was the Durham cathedral chapter who successfully established Protestantism in a very conservative diocese. These zealous graduates were theological élitists, chiefly concerned to win over the educated. Bernard Gilpin, for instance, remained unmoved when he offended 'the plebeians' by his opinions, commenting that he 'never desired the love of the vulgar'. Contempt for the religious opinions of humble folk, for which Foxe castigated the Marian bishops, was no monopoly of Catholic clerics.

Still more important than the senior clergy as moulders of opinion must have been the mass of parish clergy and unbeneficed chaplains. Despite widespread anti-clericalism and a growing tendency of parishioners to form their own theological opinions, the parish priest was the most literate and knowledgeable man in many rural communities, with the possible exception of the lord of the manor, and the character and example of both must have been crucial in many villages. It is clear that every settlement was hampered by the incumbency of clergy appointed under a previous regime. The 9000 parish priests suffered no major purges except for perhaps 2000 in 1554 (many of whom were simply transferred to other parishes after abandoning their wives) and a few hundred in 1559. Admittedly, the continuity of personnel was maintained because most clergy, like Aleyn of Bray, conformed outwardly to every settlement. A revealing anecdote from Exeter tells how in Edward's reign the rector of St Petrock's vowed never to say mass again; yet in 1554 his friend Mayor Midwinter – a Protestant – found him robed for mass. Midwinter 'pointed unto him with his finger remembering as it were his old protestations . . . but Parson Herne openly in the church spake aloud unto him, "It is no remedy, man, it is no remedy"'.[38] Or there was the ex-friar who as late as 1583 was a parish priest in Berkshire, when he was reported for saying that 'if ever we had mass again he would say it, for he must live'.[39]

Yet if most priests did not openly defy successive settlements, the presence of many traditionalist priests under Edward, of crypto-Protestants under Mary and of crytpo-Catholics under Elizabeth must have been a strong influence in hampering uniformity. Such was Thomas Dobson, the Cambridgeshire priest already mentioned. He conformed to Mary's restoration of the mass but 'before he came to the altar, he used himself unreverently, saying "We must go to this gear" with laughter'; despite this and other offences he was merely transferred to a neighbouring parish after being disciplined. A survivor of the opposite type was Robert Parkyn, the south Yorkshire vicar. He conformed with great inner reluctance under Edward (continuing to say prayers for the dead in secret); welcomed the Marian reaction joyfully; but conformed again to the 1559 settlement and retained the living till his death in 1570. There were many like-minded priests in conservative areas.[40]

The presence and character of the manorial lord must, in the countryside, have been almost as crucial as that of the priest. Alan Everitt has suggested that later nonconformity can often be correlated with a weak manorial structure or with settlements without a resident lord. Margaret Spufford agrees though she points out that the difference between large and small settlements was perhaps the crucial factor, small settlements usually having a stronger manorial structure and being easier to control; and she warns against determinism in this as in other areas.[41] No similar study has yet been made for the sixteenth century, but it would be surprising if the pattern of lordship did not prove to be of major importance.

One larger question concerns the extent of continuity in popular religious beliefs. Was there, for instance, continuity in certain areas from Lollardy to Protestantism and later to separatism, or in other areas from late medieval orthodoxy to Catholic recusancy? A. G. Dickens has drawn attention to a correlation between Lollard and puritan areas in Yorkshire, especially in the ports and textile towns, though R. Knecht has suggested that an entrenched native heresy might actually be a repellent to Protestantism.[42] There are similar difficulties in making connections between pre- and post-Reformation Catholicism, though Lancashire seems to furnish a textbook example. Both Jordan and Haigh point as an explanation to the backward state of the county, so that Catholicism was still a vital, almost missionary, influence there when it had already become stereotyped and mechanistic in other areas. Hence Protestantism was able to make little headway 'especially as the political and social structure of the county was as underdeveloped as its religion'.[43] Outside Lancashire, however, continuity on a large scale has yet to be proved and to expect it in many districts would be to lack faith in the possibility of conversions in large numbers. A. G. Dickens is sceptical of continuity between late medieval orthodoxy and Elizabethan recusancy, or between Marian heresy and Elizabethan puritanism: 'New leaders and new ideas bulk larger than old survivals'.[44]

The need for many more local studies has, it is hoped, been amply demonstrated. Not only is too little known of popular opinion, but also of its variety, which can only with difficulty be forced into the strait-jacket of 'Catholic' and 'Protestant' labels. How does one classify the testators who bequeathed their souls in full Catholic form but then added their hope of salvation solely through the merits of Christ's passion?[45] How far can one allocate the Yorkshire cases of 'tavern unbelief' to Protestant heresy and how far to age-old scepticism? Keith Thomas emphasises the oft-forgotten facts that not all Englishmen went to church, 'that many of those who did went with considerable reluctance, and that a certain proportion remained . . . utterly ignorant of the elementary tenets of Christian dogma'. The story of the popular Reformation, when it can eventually be properly retold, will probably be much more complex than can yet be imagined.

3. The Reformation and Popular Culture

IMOGEN LUXTON

ALTHOUGH the study of the world of popular culture in the sixteenth and seventeenth centuries is still in its early stages, it derives from long-standing traditions in both local history and literary studies. English local history has long included social as well as economic aspects while literary studies of the period have extended beyond national literary history to the works of provincial writers and the interests of middle-class men and women, which were the subject of Louis B. Wright's book *Middle-class Culture in Elizabethan England* as early as 1935. These two traditions are embodied in A. G. Dickens's pioneering studies of Tudor Yorkshire, in which he examined within a social context the minds of its readers and writers and formulated a range of new questions about the nature of cultural and social development in provincial England.[1] The application of this concept of social history was taken further by a group of French historians known as the *Annales* school (after the journal which they founded) whose regional studies have embraced popular mentalities as part of the *histoire totale* of local societies. Their approach has contributed to the development of the study of the beliefs, feelings and values inherent in the whole way of life not only of the literate minority but also of the majority, who were far less articulate or literate and, indeed, were often confused about their beliefs.

The most comprehensive study of popular beliefs and superstitions in the sixteenth and seventeenth centuries is that of Keith Thomas, whose book *Religion and the Decline of Magic* examines, against the intellectual and social background, the relationship between popular religion and magic, magical healing, prophecy and astrology. His extensive use of sources such as ecclesiastical court books, astrologers' case books and legal proceedings of witchcraft trials illustrates the wide range of source material, in many cases still unprinted, on

For Notes to Chapter 3, see pp. 191–3; for Biographical Notes, see p. 182.

which the historian of popular culture needs to draw. The fragmented nature of much of this evidence raises the problem for the historian of gauging how far any particular belief as revealed, for example, in a deposition in an ecclesiastical court book may be regarded as *popular*. Keith Thomas, while regretting 'not having been able to offer more of those exact statistical data upon which the precise analysis of historical change must so often depend', attempted to surmount this problem by presenting his evidence in the form of examples and counter-examples. He was taken to task, however, in a review of his book by Margaret Bowker, who argued that the use of example and counter-example was not justified unless some indication was given of the normality or abnormality of the particular cases cited, and who cast doubt, therefore, on the validity of his generalisations. In another review article, however, E. P. Thompson maintained that attempts to measure, for example, group behaviour, religious activity or literacy would always be insensitive and stressed the value of supplementing lists of examples and counter-examples with detailed case studies.[2]

The studies of popular culture which have been carried out so far have raised questions not only about the assessment of the representativeness of particular cases but also about the contribution which the social sciences can make to historical methodology. Keith Thomas, in *Religion and the Decline of Magic,* made reference to different social cultures and drew on anthropological studies in examining areas of popular culture such as the role of magic. Other social historians, notably Alan Macfarlane, have gone much further by attempting to apply sociological and anthropological concepts to their historical material. In his review article, E. P. Thompson considered the questions of historical method raised by *Religion and the Decline of Magic* and by Dr Macfarlane's book, *The Family Life of Ralph Josselin, A Seventeenth Century Clergyman,* in the light of Keith Thomas's earlier call (1966) for 'a more systematic indoctrination' of historians in the social sciences. E. P. Thompson drew attention in his article to the essentially unhistorical nature of disciplines such as anthropology, sociology and criminology, and the conflicting and often disputed nature of many sociological concepts. He went on to warn of the danger of following the method of cross-cultural comparison employed by the social sciences and using concepts drawn from wholly different social cultures without taking into account their specific historical context. He concluded that Alan Macfarlane's book, while pointing to new ways of looking at familiar evidence, did not of itself signal a new history. Nor did he consider that Keith Thomas's book offered a new methodology but rather that it represented the extension of a traditional historical discipline into new areas of research.

If the value of sociological concepts for the study of the mental history of the period has still to be determined, there can be little doubt about the value of literary evidence, as A. G. Dickens has demonstrated in his studies of provincial writers and readers. It is true that much of the cultural activity which he has examined was not itself popular. Nevertheless, he has shown that there were various levels of provincial culture and has raised questions, for example, about the existence of a proletarian or a bourgeois culture distinct from that of the provincial gentry and clergy. Moreover, the commonplace books and tracts which he has discovered have shed light on the basis of beliefs and attitudes which, in many cases, were common to all orders of provincial society.

This chapter will consider, with reference to a wide range of source material including the books which people owned, read and, in some cases, wrote, the impact which the Reformation made on provincial culture particularly at a popular level. It will make special reference to the area of the west midlands and west borders from Bristol north to Chester and will start by examining the main features of the pre-Reformation culture.*

The main characteristic of provincial culture at all levels before the Reformation was its predominantly religious content. Few secular works occur in lists of books in wills or inventories. The secular literature written in provincial England before the Reformation emanated from three main sources: monastic antiquaries interested in the history of the founders of their religious houses; town clerks turned antiquaries such as Robert Ricart who wrote *The Maire of Bristowe is Kalendar*; and noble families such as the Stanleys, earls of Derby, who continued to inspire in the north-west midlands the neo-feudal loyalties on which the ballad tradition flourished. In the west midlands there was one notable exception to this pattern of secular literature in the writings of a member of the Cheshire gentry, Humphrey Newton of Pownall Hall, whose poems comprise one of

* In the context of this chapter the term 'west midlands and borders' should be taken to mean west midlands and west borders.

the few collections of formal secular lyrics that survive in manuscript for thé early sixteenth century.[3] The majority of his compositions are in the Chaucer–Lydgate tradition of courtly love poetry from which they borrowed subject matter, motifs, images and vocabulary. They also reflect the continuing influence of a regional alliterative tradition which dated back to the 1350s when the alliterative revival of the fourteenth century developed and flourished in the west midlands and borders.

The continuing influence of later medieval religious traditions can be seen in the mystery plays which appear to have enjoyed support up to and beyond the Reformation, although becoming increasingly archaic in their literary form. In the west midlands and borders whole cycles were performed at Chester and Coventry while individual Corpus Christi plays were performed at Worcester and, according to a bequest in a local will, at Tamworth in Staffordshire too.[4] Corpus Christi pageants were also performed at Hereford. Traditionally it has been thought that the plays were presented in a processional manner before a large audience. This view has been challenged as far as the Chester cycle is concerned and the theory of a stationary performance advanced.[5] More recently, it has been suggested that the Chester plays were performed indoors before a limited audience rather than mass gatherings.[6] The popular character of the Coventry plays has not, however, been disputed. The plays seem to have been presented at several stations in the town and they attracted 'very great confluence of people thither from far and near'.[7]

Although the surviving texts of the Chester cycle and the two extant Coventry plays represent late versions of the plays, they exemplify the main features of late medieval religious culture. The essence of the play cycles was the presentation in simple, colourful and dramatic form of the scriptural narrative, ranging from the Old Testament stories to the nativity, the missionary life of Christ, his passion, resurrection and ascension. Legendary material which had grown up around the scriptural texts was uncritically presented alongside the biblical stories, while the human characterisation in many of the plays contributed a humorous element. The latter did not detract, however, from the high religious tone of the plays, whose major themes were the redemption of mankind and, reflecting late medieval eschatological preoccupations, the day of doom. The plays thus epitomised a predominantly image-orientated culture in which the basis of the Christian faith was presented visually and, in some cases,

through a cloud of legends and myths. The impact of the plays is illustrated by the example of an old man whom the Yorkshire divine
John Shaw came across in 1644 in Lancashire. Although the old man
claimed to be a regular church-goer, he maintained that he could not
recall ever hearing of salvation by Jesus Christ except in a Corpus
Christi play which he had seen at Kendal 'where there was a man on a
tree and blood ran down'.[8] His comments indicate that the impact of
the plays was predominantly visual but that the message of the Scriptures left some imprint on uneducated minds.

Other forms of popular religious drama were the performances of
the Christmas mummers; the unveiling of the Rood in churches on
Palm Sunday; and the resurrection from the Easter sepulchre on
Easter Day, through which the themes of birth, death and rebirth
respectively were dramatised. The presentation of Christian doctrines
in visual form was also the purpose of a number of half-secular
ceremonies which flourished on the fringes of the Christian year.
Among these was the custom of the boy bishop which had grown out
of both the cult of St Nicholas and the pagan feast of the Saturnalia
and which involved the dressing up of children, one of whom was
chosen to bear the title of bishop, and their participation in some of
the services of the church for the space of one or more days between
St Nicholas's day and the feast of the Holy Innocents. Bequests in a
number of local wills of scarlet gowns for the use of the boy bishop in
St Michael's Coventry and Ludlow testify to the continuing popularity of the ceremony in parts of the west midlands in the early sixteenth century. The ceremony retained considerable secular content
and, indeed, in Bristol was the occasion of some festivity, but it was
countenanced by the church because of its instructive value in showing that God himself had been made incarnate and lived on earth as
child and man. Through these religious or semi-religious observances, which were concentrated in the six months of the year
between 24/25 December and 24 June inclusive, the whole life of the
community was pervaded by the pre-Reformation church, as Charles
Phythian-Adams has shown in his study of the role of civic ceremony
and ritual in Coventry.[9]

Religious drama was inspired, too, by lives of the saints which were
the subject of plays at Coventry in 1490 and 1504 and at Shrewsbury
in 1516. The saints-cults themselves continued to appeal to all orders
of society. That vast compendium of saints' lives, Jacob de Voragine's
Legenda Aurea, compiled in the thirteenth century and first printed in
1483, was mentioned in the wills of two laymen and three of the

secular clergy in the west midlands and borders. Other bequests in
lay wills included a copy of the life of St Thomas of Canterbury and
money for a genealogy of St Anne. In Chester the local cult of St Werburgh, whose girdle was used to ease the labours of women in child-
birth, inspired Henry Bradshaw, a monk of Chester abbey, to com-
pile a life of the saint shortly before his death in 1513. The book was
composed, as Bradshaw wrote in his conclusion,

> . . . for no clerk indeed
> But for merchant men/having little learning
> And that rude people thereby may have knowing
> Of this holy virgin/and redolent rose
> Which hath been kept full long time in close.[10]

It was Bradshaw's intention that his book should not only afford
religious inspiration but should also prove 'pleasant to the
audience/contenting the mind', and the colourful fashion in which he
described some of the miracles worked by the saint must have entertained his readers.

The emphasis on saints and relics and on devout observance as a
means of attaining salvation served to obscure the teaching of Christ.
The crowds who flocked to the holy blood at Hailes Abbey did so, according to Hugh Latimer, bishop of Worcester, in the belief that the
very sight of it would put them in a state of salvation. This belief in
the protective power of relics and images was shared by the learned as
well as the unlearned. Humphrey Newton, for example, made notes,
in the same commonplace book in which he wrote his poems of
courtly love, on the pardons which could be obtained through prayer
to the shrine of St Chad at Lichfield, the Virgin at Coventry, the
Charterhouse of St Anne near Coventry and the Rood at St John's
Chester. Moreover, the accounts of the duke of Buckingham during
his residence at Thornbury in Gloucestershire contain entries in
respect of offerings in 1508 to the holy relics at Glastonbury Abbey
and in 1520 to the Rood at Gloucester, the holy blood at Hailes
Abbey and St Kenelm at Winchcombe.[11] Pilgrimages, too, were
regarded as a means of attaining salvation by the rich and poor,
educated and uneducated, and bequests of money for pilgrimages to
St Anne of Buxton and to Rome occur among the wills of men and
women who lived in the west midlands in the late fifteenth and early
sixteenth centuries.

The healing powers attributed to relics such as St Werburgh's
girdle contributed to the blurring of the distinction between religion

and magic which Keith Thomas has described. The confusion between the two is reflected in the popular account of the miracle worked by the image of the Virgin at Hughley near Shrewsbury, which was believed to have restored sight to a blind woman who made an offering to it. It was also claimed that, at the same time as the blind woman was healed, a bell hanging in a nearby house started to ring without the aid of either a clapper or human hands.[12] Holy relics, holy water and, above all, the mass itself were all credited with magical powers which could help men and women with their daily problems and they generated a mass of popular superstitions. Moreover, prayers or pieces of Scripture were sometimes uttered as though they were magical charms. John Newton, a draper and shepherd of Congleton, Cheshire, for example, who fell sick of the plague in 1492 and lay in a trance for three days, had a vision in which three black spirits taunted him and were only driven away by his invocation, 'Jesu, Jesu, Jesu, that art in heaven, have mercy on me and take me from that company'.[13]

These popular beliefs and superstitions flourished within a religious culture in which the emphasis, as has been seen, was on visual representation rather than on the written word. The role of books in the religious instruction of the laity appears to have been very limited. Mass books, primers, psalters and collections of prayers were mentioned in only twenty-five of the wills or inventories made by laymen in the west midlands and borders which were proved between 1490 and 1558 in the Prerogative Court of Canterbury or which survive in printed collections and, apart from the lives of saints already referred to, few other religious works were mentioned. The main source of religious knowledge for the majority of the laity was therefore the local clergy whose literary activity can be crudely measured by the evidence of book-ownership in their wills or inventories. For the period 1490–1558 the wills or inventories of 430 non-cathedral clergy in the west midlands and borders survive and they show that 133 (31 per cent) of the clergy were book-owners. This represents a slightly higher proportion of the sample than in the diocese of Norwich, where Peter Heath has estimated that about a quarter of the resident, active local clergy were book-owners, and in Yorkshire where A. G. Dickens has estimated that about 28 per cent of the clergy were book-owners in this period. These estimates are cautious ones and take no account, for example, of evidence in other wills of bequests of books to parish clergy whose own wills make no mention of them. Moreover, references in wills show that books were sometimes circulated among clergy in neighbouring parishes. In addition, some of the clergy had access to collections of books in their own churches. In the west midlands and borders such collections of books are known to have existed in half a dozen churches, most of them bequeathed by previous incumbents or by clergy living outside the area who wished to remember their place of birth in their wills.

While the extent of literary activity among the clergy appears to have been greater than was formerly conceded, the range of their literary interests was very limited and revolved primarily around their professional duties. An examination of the books owned by the clergy in the west midlands and borders confirms the conclusions drawn by A. G. Dickens for Yorkshire and Peter Heath for the diocese of Norwich about the narrow and conservative mentality of the parish clergy. Liturgical books were the books most frequently mentioned in clerical wills and inventories and 26 of the 133 clerical book-owners in the sample seem to have possessed no other books. Late medieval sermon books such as the *Sermones Discipuli*, the *Sermones Quadragesimales* and the *Sermones Parati* were the next most commonly mentioned category. These were all books of *sermones de tempore,* prepared for the preaching year and containing themes drawn from the gospel or epistle for the day which a priest could follow or expand on as he chose. Medieval preaching traditions were also perpetuated through preaching-manuals such as the *Destructorium Viciorum,* a comprehensive sermon encyclopaedia compiled by Alexander Carpenter in 1429, and the early fourteenth-century *Oculus Sacerdotis* of William de Pagula. Pastoral guides such as the *Manipulus Curatorum*, a popular clerical dictionary, and John de Burgo's *Pupilla Oculi* of the late fourteenth century were also traditional clerical reading.

It is true that some of the parish clergy were acquainted with the commentaries of Nicholas de Lyra, the fourteenth-century scholar of Paris who anticipated the approach of the Christian humanists in his insistence on the literal interpretation of the Scriptures. In the west midlands and borders, copies of his commentaries were left by eleven of the clergy in the first half of the sixteenth century. Nevertheless, as late as the 1550s, the great majority of the clergy appear to have relied on medieval guides to preaching or commentaries on the Bible rather than on the Bible itself. Between 1490 and 1536 only three of the clergy in the area studied left Bibles. Another three left Bibles between 1536 and 1540 and the figure rose to twelve between 1540 and 1558. This lack of familiarity with the Bible was uncovered by Bishop Hooper during his examination of the parish clergy of Gloucester diocese in 1551. His findings showed that, for example, of the 311 clergy in the diocese, 10 could not repeat the Lord's prayer; 39 could not find its text in the Bible; and 34 could not name its author.[14] The results of Bishop Hooper's visitation have often been cited as evidence of the poor educational standards of the parish clergy but Hooper's questions were testing biblical knowledge rather than general educational standards – even the book-owners among the Gloucestershire clergy could not completely satisfy Hooper's inquiries. Hooper's visitation, therefore, provides evidence not so much of general ignorance among the parish clergy as of poor knowledge of the Bible. Lacking familiarity with the text of the Scriptures, the parochial clergy were in no position to refute the popular superstitions of their parishioners or to distinguish between the legendary and scriptural stories which had become confused in the religious drama of the period.

In religion, therefore, popular culture within the framework of the pre-Reformation church reflected limited mental horizons which rarely extended beyond the customary pattern of religious or semi-religious rituals and observances or beyond local cults and traditions. Moreover, that religion had much in common with folk beliefs relating to the magical techniques of the village wizards or cunning men, who often used Christian prayers to heal, charm or to divine the future. Keith Thomas has underlined the difficulty of determining how common a figure the cunning man was. In particular, liability to punishment in the ecclesiastical courts and to secular penalties under parliamentary statutes deterred the cunning men from advertising their activities. Contemporary statements such as that of William Wycherley, an apprehended sorcerer, in 1549 that 'there be within England above five hundred conjurers as he thinketh ... and specially in Norfolk, Hertfordshire, and Worcestershire and Gloucestershire' are an indication, however, that the cunning men continued to attract clients in parts of the country including the west border counties in the first half of the century.[15]

Although the pre-Reformation church pervaded most aspects of the life of the community, its hold on the English people was never complete. Keith Thomas maintains that there is a good deal of evidence to suggest that many of the poorest classes never attended church regularly throughout the sixteenth century and beyond, whether through indifference, hostility, deliberate exclusion or some other reason. The evidence for the first half of the sixteenth century is too fragmentary to allow any assessment of the degree of absenteeism from church. F. G. Emmison's study of the surviving series of court books of the archdeaconries of Essex and Colchester for the Elizabethan period reveals, however, that throughout Elizabeth's reign several thousands of individuals from that area were presented for absenteeism from their parish church. F. G. Emmison has also documented the considerable number and variety of church and churchyard disputes which took place during or immediately after divine service and which bear further witness to the extent of popular religious indifference.[16] Moreover, even among regular church-goers, ignorance of religious dogma was widespread, particularly among the rural population. Thus in 1556 a petition on behalf of the inhabitants of Norfolk, which called for the restoration of church services in English, alleged that before the Reformation none of the laity unlearned in Latin could say the Lord's prayer in English, or knew any article of the creed, or could recite any of the ten commandments.[17]

The pre-Reformation and, indeed, the post-Reformation church was also confronted with the problem of popular scepticism. The visitation book of John Bell, bishop of Worcester 1539–1543,[18] for example, contains a series of depositions which bear witness to the continued survival of popular scepticism in Gloucestershire and Worcestershire in the 1530s and 1540s. The offending utterances include statements such as that by William Clerke of Hartlebury in 1539 that he had never believed in the seven sacraments.[19] Some of the statements reflected a common-sense rationalism as, for example, the view expressed by Matthew Price of Staunton in Worcestershire in discussion with a group of friends in a mill at Upleadon in 1539 that 'the sacrament of the altar in form of bread and wine was not the body of Christ, for the bread was made of corn with man's hand, and likewise the wine made of fruit'.[20]

As Keith Thomas recognises, it is impossible to say how representative such examples of rustic scepticism were. There can be no doubt, however, of the strength of the Lollard tradition in parts of the west midlands and borders and elsewhere. In the Forest of Dean a local cult seems to have developed around two 'martyrs', Spenser and

Griffith, who were burnt as heretics at Lydney in Herefordshire in the late fifteenth century.[21] In Bristol and Coventry the Lollard tradition stretched back to the mid-fifteenth century. The depositions of the group of Lollards in and around Coventry who were brought to trial before Bishop Blythe in 1511–12 revealed the extent of communication which took place between the Bristol and Coventry groups through the movement of apprentices and journeymen, and showed how Lollard beliefs were kept alive and disseminated throughout the country.

By the late fifteenth and early sixteenth centuries Lollard teachings had become increasingly diluted and their criticisms had come to focus on transubstantiation, the worship of images, pilgrimages and confession to priests. But the Lollard group in the Coventry area preserved the concern of the early Lollards for direct and personal study of the Scriptures in English. This had been prohibited by the Synod of Oxford in 1408, which directed that no one was to read any translation of the Scriptures which had been made in John Wycliffe's time or which might be made in the future until that translation had received official sanction, thus denying the vast majority of laymen access to the written basis of the Christian faith. The Coventry group, of whom at least forty-five members admitted to heresy during Blythe's trials of 1511–12, had an impressive collection of books of the Bible in English, some of which had been kept hidden for eighteen years. Instruction in these books was considered essential for every member of the group, whether or not he could read. In 1486, for example, John Smith of Coventry, who abjured of his heresy but afterwards relapsed and taught his beliefs to two of those who admitted their heresy in 1511–12, claimed that it was necessary for a man to frequent the 'schools' for a good while before he could attain knowledge of the true faith. Smith's concern with religious instruction was shared by the leaders of the group brought to light in 1511–12, who had held readings in their houses to promote knowledge of the Bible.

In common with most Lollard communities, the Coventry group was predominantly artisan in character and included among its members some forty skilled craftsmen. In addition, however, the group appears to have been joined by a number of the ruling oligarchy of Coventry including Richard Cook, twice mayor of Coventry in 1486 and 1503, and members of the prominent mercantile families of Coventry and Leicester, the Pysfords and Wigstons. All these families enjoyed close connections with James Preston, vicar of St Michael's Coventry from 1488 until his death in 1507 and a man of learning, who also seems to have sympathised with the group and may have offered intellectual support.[22] Thus in Coventry the Lollard group cut across social class and, through its emphasis on the Scriptures, fostered a devotion to biblical learning which contrasts with the religious ignorance of many of the laity and the scriptural deficiencies of many of the parish clergy in the pre-Reformation period.

The development of popular Protestantism in provincial England and particularly in the north and west of the country was slow and localised. In the west midlands and borders it made most headway in Bristol and Coventry where there was an old tradition of religious dissent which, in the case of Bristol, had been fuelled on the eve of the Reformation by the activities of a local bookseller, Richard Webbe, who sold and distributed religious works proscribed by the government.[23] In Bristol the pulpit became the scene of open controversy between the supporters of the new faith, led by Hugh Latimer, and defenders of the old, led by the eccentric preacher Hubberdyne. In the course of three sermons delivered at Bristol during Lent 1553 Latimer preached against pilgrimages, the worship of images, and the abuse of masses and pardons and it was reported to Cromwell that 'many in this town are infected by him, from the highest to the lowest'.[24] Again in 1559 there was a disturbance in Bristol caused by the visit of the Scots reformer, George Wishart, who was alleged to have gained many converts by his preaching,[25] and in that year depositions about heresy in Bristol were taken by a royal commission set up to investigate sacramentarianism.[26] In Coventry, too, Protestantism succeeded an earlier Lollard tradition. According to Thomas Lever, writing to Bullinger in 1560, in Coventry 'there have always been, since the revival of the gospel, great numbers zealous for evangelical truth'.[27]

Elsewhere in the west midlands and borders and, as Christopher Haigh has shown, in Lancashire also, Protestantism before the accession of Elizabeth developed as a predominantly academic movement. It was implanted by local men, converted at one of the universities, who returned to their native counties to convert their families and friends and, in the case of men such as the Lancastrians John Bradford and George Marsh, to attempt to spread the new religion through their preaching. Small, closely-knit circles of Protestants were formed such as that which Thomas Becon encountered in Warwickshire in the early 1540s and which consisted of Hugh Latimer, John Olde and 'divers other, whereof some were men very godly learned in the laws of the most highest and professors of the same' who were engaged in godly studies.[28] With the exception of a brief period during Hugh Latimer's episcopate at Worcester, however, there was little attempt by any of the local clergy to follow up the proselytising activities of the visiting preachers. In 1551, in his *Homilies on the Romans* printed in Worcester and addressed to the clergy of his diocese, Bishop Hooper lamented that the majority of the people were still ignorant of God's word. Throughout the sixteenth century Protestantism had to contend with the persistence of long-standing traditions of superstition on the one hand and popular scepticism and indifference on the other. Thus in 1579 in his dedication of his translation of a discourse by Bullinger on the authority of Scripture, John Tomkys of Bilston, Staffordshire, who was appointed perpetual preacher of St Mary's Shrewsbury and a town preacher in 1582, complained that there was no shire, city or town and almost no household which was not poisoned either by superstition or by atheism (by which he meant irreligion).[29]

The Reformation, however, did have an immediate impact on many aspects of customary life. The shrines and relics which had been the focal points of local cults were systematically destroyed and the old ceremonies and rituals abrogated. The vicar of Much Wenlock in Shropshire, for instance, recorded in his register the burning on 7 November 1547 of the bones of St Milburgh (on whose burial site had stood the priory of Much Wenlock which was surrendered in 1539) together with the images of St John the Baptist from nearby Hope Bowdler; St Blaise from Long Stanton; Mary the Virgin from Acton Round and another image of the Virgin Mary.[30] While the tone of the vicar's entries reflects his sympathies for the old order, like the great majority of the clergy and laity he conformed outwardly to the religious changes. Indeed, throughout the west midlands and borders iconoclasm and the introduction of Protestant forms met with little outright resistance. Even the protest of a townsman of Worcester against the removal of the shrine of the Virgin in Worcester Cathedral was inspired not by religious motives but by concern that the city would be deprived of a source of income from the flow of pilgrims to the shrine.[31]

Devotional attitudes were not, of course, changed overnight and the old rituals lingered on, particularly in the more remote parts of the country. In Lancashire, where traditional practices survived on a larger scale and recusancy proved far more extensive than in Cheshire, a group of seventeen preachers drew up a report in 1590 on the religious condition of the county, in which they gave details of the popish fasts and festivals which continued to be observed, particularly at funerals, marriage ceremonies and baptisms.[32] Moreover, superstitious customs persisted in ceremonies such as that at Rogationtide which the Protestant reformers had attempted to purge of its medieval associations and restrict to a perambulation for the purpose of beating of the parish boundaries. In the archdeaconry of Stafford in 1561 it was still necessary to charge the inhabitants 'to avoid superstition and such vain gazing as they used the last year and in no case that they use either cross, taper, or beads, nor women to go about but men . . .'.[33]

In other parts of the country, however, old traditions of Lollardy and popular heresy stimulated the spontaneous development of hostility to the ritual observances of the late medieval church. The activities of Matthew Price and his group of friends in Gloucestershire in 1539, for example, reflected the continuing influence of old traditions of popular radicalism which inspired contempt for the customary rituals. Holy water was held up to particular ridicule by Price, who was alleged to have sprinkled some in Upleadon church on William Baker of Staunton who proceeded to turn his back in mockery of the ceremony. The services of matins, evensong and burial were also the objects of Price's scorn, as was the sacrament of penance which provoked his comment that 'it was as good to confess him to a tree, as to a priest'.[34] Holy oil came under attack from William Bowre and William Cloterboke of Slimbridge, Gloucestershire, in 1549 when they are alleged to have said that it was 'of no virtue but rather it is meet to grease sheep and boots'.[35]

The Reformation had a destructive impact not only on the ritual observances of the late medieval church but also on half-secular ceremonies such as that of the boy bishop, which was abrogated by royal proclamation in 1541, and on civic ceremonies. In Coventry the amalgamation of the Corpus Christi gild with the Trinity gild in 1535 and their subsequent dissolution in 1547 led to the alteration and later abolition of the St George's Day, Ascension, Whitsun and Corpus Christi processions, while in Hereford it was agreed in 1548 that the different crafts should contribute yearly a certain sum of money to be used for the benefit of the city in place of maintaining their usual pageants on Corpus Christi Day. The mystery plays survived in Chester and Coventry until the 1570s, although towards the end they were performed irregularly. By 1575, when the Chester plays were performed for the last time and in face of opposition from the archbishop of York and the Lord President of the North, it was recognised that some of the plays would have to be omitted 'which were thought might not be justified, for the superstition in them'.[36]

The destruction of religious shrines and images and the abolition of the confessional left a vacuum in many people's lives. By undermining the healing power of saints' relics and images as well as the protective power attributed to holy words and consecrated objects, the Reformation deprived men and women of the prospect of supernatural aid which could help them with the problems they encountered in their daily lives. Nor was the established church of the Protestant reformers able to provide adequate substitutes to take their place in the lives of the majority of the uneducated. It is impossible to know whether, as a result, the demand for popular magic increased. Certainly, the cunning men appear to have retained their popular appeal in post-Reformation England. Moreover, the number of cases involving popular magic recorded by the church courts reached its peak under Elizabeth, but this may have been due to increased vigilance and efficiency on the part of the courts rather than to an upsurge in demand.

The Reformation did, however, give a fillip to the doctrine of divine providence as an explanation of and consolation for earthly misfortune. This teaching can be traced in popular broadsides in which national disasters were interpreted as manifestations of God's displeasure and in tracts such as Bishop Hooper's *An Homelye to be read in the tyme of pestylence*, printed in Worcester in 1553, in which he explained that the plague was the product not of chance or the influence of the stars but rather of divine displeasure at man's transgression. He urged that the remedy was for the clergy to bring the people to the knowledge of God's word. Unusual happenings in the natural world were seen as portents of things to come. A tract entitled *True News out of Worcestershire*, 1598, for example, listed recent prodigies which had been sent by God as admonishments to men to reform their lives. These included 'sliding of grounds, removing of highways, mighty floods by great abundance of rain, fearful lightnings and thunders, great fire from heaven, sudden earthquakes, strange and deformed children born, great dearth of corn, mighty plagues and pestilence'. As the schoolmaster of Olveston, Gloucestershire, explained in a tract following the terrible storm over Olveston in 1605, the faithful had no need to be dismayed by such events since they knew that the storm came from God: it was only those who did not know and acknowledge God who had cause to be terrified.[37] The pious Christian could take comfort in the knowledge that no harm could befall him unless God permitted it, and could look forward to the prospect of eternal happiness as compensation for the trials of this life.

In place of the ritual and magic of the medieval church the Protestant reformers emphasised the sovereignty of God and the importance of the word as the source of faith. The parish clergy were urged to become better educated so that they could fulfil their preaching role and proclaim the Gospel for, as Bishop Hooper recognised in two tracts and in his visitation articles and injunctions of 1551, the growth of scriptural knowledge among the parochial clergy was a prerequisite for the development of the new faith among the laity. Like Archbishop Holgate of York in his injunctions for York minster of 1552, Bishop Hooper sought to impose on the clergy a programme of self-education based on the vernacular Scriptures. This objective was pursued throughout the Elizabethan period through visitation injunctions and through systems of exercises involving regular meetings of the clergy whether organised on the initiative of the bishop, as in the diocese of Chester under Bishop Chaderton, or on that of the puritan clergy as in the diocese of Coventry and Lichfield.

The evidence of wills and inventories indicates that there was a marked increase in book-ownership among the parish clergy in the Elizabethan period. The wills or inventories of 387 non-cathedral clergy in the west midlands and borders, proved between 1558 and 1603, have been examined and of these 150 or 39 per cent mentioned books compared with 31 per cent in the period 1490–1558. The ownership of Bibles, in particular, became more widespread; of the 40 wills or inventories which mentioned specific books, 17 mentioned the Bible. A study of these books mentioned by name reveals a distinct move away from the late medieval preaching-manuals and pastoral guides which figured so prominently in the earlier period but which were mentioned in only three of the clerical wills or inventories in this area during the Elizabethan period. Their place was taken by the theological works of the church Fathers and the leaders of the Reformation. Scriptural commentaries by continental reformers such as Wolfgang Musculus, Augustine Marlorat, Rudolph Walter, Calvin and Bullinger were owned by ten of the parish clergy in the area and books of sermons by Hugh Latimer and the puritan preacher Henry Smith were also mentioned. Most of the libraries were small although there are a handful of cases of clerical libraries numbering 50 books or more and an exceptional case in 1610 of a library of some 370 books left by the vicar of St John's in Bedwardyne, Worcester.[38]

By the end of the Elizabethan period, therefore, many of the parish clergy appear to have been better equipped to preach the word of God than their predecessors. The Protestant reformers' ideal of the minister actively engaged in studying the Scriptures and carefully preparing his sermons can be seen in the notebook of Robert Dobbs, vicar of Runcorn, Cheshire, 1580–1621. This contains notes under such headings as the eight benefits of the passion of Christ; the nine rocks which hinder perfection; the five ways in which God manifests his will, all of which are supported by biblical examples and references. In addition, Dobbs's extensive notes on predestination reveal his interest in the controversy within the church over that doctrine. Dobbs started by presenting and justifying by scriptural references the strict Calvinist doctrine of the total sovereignty of God and of each man's predestination to eternal salvation or damnation by the will of God. Like a good scholar, he then set out the counter-arguments, only to refute these by reference to the Scriptures.[39]

While the clergy continued to be the main source of religious knowledge for the majority of the laity, the availability of the English Bible made it possible for literate laymen to obtain first-hand knowledge of the word of God through personal study of the Scriptures. The gradual growth of Bible-ownership at all levels of society can be traced in wills and inventories. Those proved in the west midlands and borders during Elizabeth's reign reveal that Bibles were owned by some 20 of the gentry as well as by a Bristol merchant, 3 yeomen, 1 husbandman and 7 men who were tradesmen or artisans.

As early as the 1540s there is evidence, albeit fragmentary, of the tremendous impact which the availability of the Bible in English was to make on the laity. According to Roger Edgeworth, prebendary of Bristol from 1542, the English Bible found enthusiastic readers among the Bristol merchant community. In one of the series of sermons which he preached on the gifts of the Holy Ghost towards the end of Henry VIII's reign, he observed:

> I have known many in this town, that studying divinity, hath killed a merchant, and some of other occupations by their busy labours in the Scriptures, hath shut up the shop windows, fain to take sanctuary, or else for mercery and grocery, hath be fain to sell godderds, steanes, and pitchers, and such other trumpery.[40]

Elsewhere in the west midlands and borders there are a handful of cases of men of humble circumstances reading the vernacular Bible in the 1540s. In the case of Humphrey Grynshill, a weaver of Stonehouse in Gloucestershire, his action in reading aloud from the English Bible in Christ Church, Gloucester, in April 1541 and declaring that masses for the dead were worthless, because there was no scriptural authority for purgatory, provoked a public disturbance of the kind which led to the passing of the 1543 Act prohibiting the reading of the Bible among the lower orders.[41]

The impact of biblical study on the religious knowledge of the laity can be seen too in the arguments advanced by a number of the Marian martyrs. While the offending statements of the Bristol martyrs, for example, reflected old traditions of popular radicalism, others of the martyrs demonstrated an ability to handle theological issues. Thus, knowledge of the biblical texts made it possible for John Careless, a Coventry weaver imprisoned for his faith during the reign of Mary, to hold his own in the course of his interrogation on such difficult questions as predestination and the concept of the elect church.[42]

Biblical study was further stimulated by puritanism which developed in the west midlands and borders in towns such as Bristol and Coventry which had been most receptive to Protestantism and in the eastern pastoral area of Chester with its growing trade and industry. The Bible was at the heart of puritan preaching and, in puritan households such as that of John Bruen of Bruen Stapleford in Cheshire, texts were memorised by those who could not actually read them. One of Bruen's servants, Robert Pasfield, while unable to read or write, had not only memorised the Scriptures but had developed such an understanding of them that he was 'a godly instructor and teacher of young professors'.[43]

Although direct evidence is lacking, it seems reasonable to conjecture that the availability of the Scriptures in English and Protestant emphasis on direct study of the texts may have stimulated the diffusion of literacy in sixteenth-century England. Literacy itself in the sixteenth and seventeenth centuries can only be measured statistically in terms of the ability of men and women to sign their names. The Cambridge Group for the History of Population and Social Structures are currently investigating the extent of literacy defined in this basic way. The role which writing and, more particularly, reading played in the ordinary life of local communities is not susceptible to measurement in statistical terms. It can only be assessed on the basis of contemporary statements such as that of the Chester herald and poet, Thomas Chaloner, who commented in a poem written in the 1570s that those verses addressed to the farmers were written in vain since 'the farmer meddles not with looking out of books'.[44]

If books played little part in the life of the farming community, evidence from wills and inventories suggests that there was a considerable increase among not only the gentry but also the yeomen and the urban middle classes towards the end of the sixteenth century. The proportion of Worcester lay inventories mentioning books seems to have increased from about 4 per cent in the period 1550–89 to 16 per cent in the 1590s and first decades of the seventeenth century.[45] Moreover, the stock of books maintained in Shrewsbury by the Shropshire-born printer Roger Ward indicates that there was a considerable market for books on the Welsh border. When his goods were valued in 1585 his bookshop was found to contain nearly 2500 volumes.[46] The contents were predominantly religious and included hundreds of prayer books, catechisms and psalters together with some 13 Bibles or parts of the Bible as well as commentaries on the Scriptures by Calvin and Theodore Beza. There was a large stock, too, of popular devotional works and over 200 books of sermons. Of the secular works in stock, the grammars and works by classical writers were no doubt aimed primarily at the pupils of Shrewsbury school. The range of the other secular works, however, which included almanacs, historical romances, books on the law, medicine, history, music and cookery, reflects the broadening and diversification of mental interests which took place in the Elizabethan period for reasons mainly independent of the Reformation and which added a new dimension to provincial culture.

As far as educational facilities were concerned, the impact of the Reformation made itself felt in several ways. The destructive effects of the dissolution of the religious houses in 1539 and the chantries in 1548 were offset to a considerable extent by the improvements and new foundations effected by the government. Indeed, it seems likely that the dissolutions have been overestimated as a force for good or bad in the history of education which, before and after the Reformation, continued to be largely provided in free schools endowed by private benefactors or by professional masters for a fee.

The determination on the part of the reformers and later the puritans to improve the level of religious knowledge among both clergy and laity contributed to the growth of interest in education which took place in the course of the sixteenth century. Education was one of the chief beneficiaries of the many hundreds of bequests and deeds of gift in the second half of the century which were directed to charitable purposes rather than to the church as in the pre-Reformation period. The wills of London merchants who established schools in the provinces and set up scholarship funds showed a determination to help able and aspiring children, however poor, to gain instruction not only in reading, writing and grammar but also in the holy gospel. Nor was this philanthropy confined to rich merchants. A yeoman of Wednesbury in Staffordshire made provision in his will in 1603 for a schoolmaster to give free tuition to ten poor children from families in Wednesbury.[47] By the Elizabethan period evidence from diocesan records suggests that educational facilities were readily accessible in many parts of the country. Margaret Spufford has shown that Cambridgeshire was well provided with schools,[48] while in the area of the west midlands and borders diocesan records indicate that there were, at a *minimum*, schoolmasters in some 44 towns or villages in Cheshire and some 60 towns or villages in the diocese of Hereford in the Elizabethan period. Few petty schoolmasters were licensed and recorded in the diocesan papers and the numbers of schoolmasters were also swollen by individuals such as Jacob Naishe, a yeoman of Henbury, Gloucestershire, who recorded in his will in 1574 the debts that were owing to him from their parents for teaching three boys to read and write,[49] and Mrs Reade of Campden in Gloucestershire to whom Thomas Congreve, a Staffordshire gentleman, sent his youngest daughter Margaret, aged eleven, to read and sew in 1605.[50]

The growth of interest in education is further illustrated by the large number of bequests in wills of the second half of the sixteenth century for the education of the testators' children. These bear witness to the increasing concern on the part of yeomen and the urban 'bourgeoisie' that their children should receive an adequate education. How far down the social scale this concern extended is difficult to assess. It seems improbable, as Margaret Spufford has argued in her study of schooling in Cambridgeshire, that labourers and small farmers would have been able to release their sons from work in the fields for educational purposes. Nevertheless, the provision made by educational benefactors of the Elizabethan period for the poor must have spread educational opportunities more widely, particularly in the towns.

While provincial culture at all levels at the end of the sixteenth century remained predominantly religious, its emphasis had shifted from the ritualised, visual effects of the pre-Reformation period to the printed word. The development of the printing press played an important part in this transition but, underlying it, there was the emphasis of the Reformation on the need for direct study of the Bible. This transition involved a change in the whole way of life of many local communities for it entailed the abolition not only of religious rituals but also of many civic ceremonies. Its positive contribution to provincial culture lay in the stimulus it gave to the development of an informed approach to religion which made possible the emergence by the 1640s of a whole range of different religious viewpoints. The impact of the change can be traced among educated laymen not only from the gentry but also from the yeomen and middle classes in the towns whose wills bear witness to the spread of book-ownership, particularly of the Bible, and the growth of interest in education. The consequences of this change for popular culture were perhaps even more significant – by giving humble men and women access to the text of the Scriptures, the Reformation laid the ground for the development at a popular level too of a more articulate approach to religion and the concept of religion as a pattern of beliefs rather than a series of ritual observances.

4. The Protestant Episcopate 1547–1603: The Pastoral Contribution

RALPH HOULBROOKE

EFFECTIVE reformation depended upon the efficient discharge by the episcopate of pastoral duties whose basic framework was little changed by the advent of Protestantism. The author of the *Discourse of the Common Weal* had this fact in mind when, soon after the passage of the first Edwardian act of uniformity, he asked

> what better trial or examination is there now in the admitting of the priests and other ministers of the church? What more exact search is made by our bishops for worthy men to be admitted to the cure of souls? For better execution of our canons in their visitations now than they did before? Yea, what better hospitality, residence, or ministrations, either of the Word or of other duties, do our prelates and bishops now than they did before?[1]

The author was almost certainly right in suggesting that the bishops' pastoral duties were not better discharged at this point than they had been previously. There had probably been some deterioration in the standards of episcopal oversight in the recent past. In the first half of Henry VIII's reign some outstanding bishops, competent and conscientious administrators, had been in charge of English dioceses. After about 1532, most of the bishops had been more concerned to avoid overstepping the bounds of their authority and to secure outward conformity to royal demands than to reform the abuses of a church whose future shape appeared so uncertain, and the vigour and efficiency of diocesan government suffered as a result.

Henrician conservatives from whom no more than formal compliance with the religious policy of the new government could be ex-

For Notes to Chapter 4, see pp. 193–4: for Bibliographic Notes, see pp. 182–3.

pected remained in a majority of the episcopal bench for some time after the beginning of Edward VI's reign. Many important sees came under the rule of reformers before July 1553, but most of these men held office too short a time to be able to make much of a mark before Edward's death. The most vigorous of them, John Hooper, established in his short time at Gloucester (from 1551) a pattern of the godly bishop unmatched by his sixteenth-century successors. Soon after his arrival, Hooper carried out an unusually careful and thorough visitation, and launched a programme of supervised scriptural study by the clergy, who were to attend regular meetings in each deanery to determine doubtful doctrinal points. Bypassing the conservative chancellor (chief judge) of the diocese, Hooper brought the work of his consistory court under his personal supervision, reconciling litigants and punishing evil-doers without fear or favour. Bypassing his grossly inadequate rural deans, he travelled through his diocese in order to maintain direct contact with his flock.[2] Hooper's dedication was unique; but in certain other dioceses bishops such as Miles Coverdale and Nicholas Ridley set the example of a vigorous personal ministry whose outstanding feature was regular preaching. In the limited time available to them, the Edwardian Protestant bishops could not hope to effect a reformation which was more than skin deep. The massive inadequacy of the lower clergy and the shortage of auxiliaries in the shape of able preachers or co-operative diocesan officials could not be remedied before the King's death.

Catholics as well as Protestants realised that an effective episcopate had a vital part to play in the struggle against apathy, ignorance and error. The Marian appointees to the bench were chosen for their theological learning and their loyalty to their faith. The decrees enacted in the legatine synod which met in November 1555 laid down that bishops must reside in their dioceses and adopt a more austere style of life than had hitherto been customary. They were to preach themselves and see that examinations before ordination were carefully carried out. But the records of the Marian church nevertheless lack a missionary flavour, possibly because Reginald Pole preferred peace and obedience to evangelising fervour.[3]

The first generation of Elizabethan bishops was faced with colossal problems. The rapid changes of the previous decades had engendered widespread confusion, apathy and cynicism amongst the people. The ranks of the clergy had been thinned by epidemics, deprivations, and a substantial exodus of men unhappy about the uncertain future of the church. Many benefices remained vacant long after Elizabeth's accession. The majority of the remaining clergy received the Elizabethan settlement without enthusiasm. A number of dioceses remained without Protestant bishops a long time after the settlement, their administration in the hands of diocesan officials, the majority of whom were conservative time-servers.

The Elizabethan government naturally expected that the bishops would play a leading part in converting the people to the new religion. It counted on their diligence in 'preaching, teaching and visiting of their dioceses'. But administrative convenience and the instinctive conservatism of the Queen prevented the sort of thorough overhaul of the framework of episcopal government which would have transformed the bishops into the 'pastors, labourers, and watchmen ... relieved from that royal pomp and courtly bustle' which John Jewel and other fervent Protestants wanted to see.[4] The Elizabethan bishops moved some way towards this ideal, but they remained, like their medieval predecessors, royal servants and great landowners, and their secular preoccupations interfered with their pastoral work to a considerable extent.

No longer were bishops called upon to fill the great offices of state, sit at the Privy Council board, or undertake foreign embassies. But with so few paid servants at its disposal, the Crown expected to be able to draw on their services in a whole range of secular and quasi-secular tasks. They were expected to act as members of the regional councils and as justices of the peace. Bishops were responsible for the collection of taxes paid by the clergy and for assessing their contributions towards the supply of arms and armour. They sat on the commissions set up to enforce obedience to the Queen's ecclesiastical laws in London, York and later in a number of dioceses. Above all they were called upon to supply the government with information in a series of reports and surveys.

The Elizabethan government abandoned its plans to take away a considerable portion of the bishops' lands, and instead kept them as a reservoir which might be drawn upon during vacancies and by means of grants of long leases to deserving suitors.[5] None of the early Elizabethan bishops showed any but a superficial enthusiasm for disendowment. No doubt many of them hoped to use their wealth in the service of charity, learning and the propagation of the word. Inseparable from the episcopal estates, however, were the expectations of local society: that a bishop would support a large household, maintain lavish hospitality, and entertain suits for advancement. The estates themselves had to be administered, and episcopal stewards and auditors could not safely be left to their own devices, as more than one bishop was to find to his cost.

The Elizabethan bishops had not been very well prepared by their previous careers for their onerous double responsibilities as pastors and administrators, and such success as they achieved was due to their innate gifts and ability to profit from experience during their tenure of their sees. They were indeed as a group far better qualified in theology than their late medieval predecessors. Most of them had doctorates in divinity, or received them shortly after their accession to the bench. The Elizabethan government recognised, as had both the Edwardian and Marian governments, that in a time of religious conflict it was important that the episcopate be well grounded in this respect. But their theological training did not prepare them for the conversion of the mass of the English population. Residence in a rural parish would have been the best apprenticeship for the future organisers of the conversion of England, but it seems likely that the majority had had very little, if any, experience of service in a parish, in the front line of the fight against superstition and ignorance. The proportion of men with such experience was probably highest among the first batch of bishops, dropping gradually thereafter. Few bishops are known to have gone on tour in order to preach to the people before their elevations. Well over half the first generation of Elizabethan appointees preached before or soon after their elevations to a large popular audience at Paul's Cross during the early years of the settlement, but the proportion of bishops who had had this experience grew smaller in the later years of the reign. A number of bishops owed their promotions in large part to their preaching ability, but in most cases this ability had been demonstrated in university or court. Matthew Parker probably judged his Queen correctly when he looked for *pronunciationem aulicam* and *ingenium aulicum* in those he recommended to preach before her, and these courtly qualities were not the ones most needed in an effective campaign of evangelisation.[6]

Most of the Elizabethan bishops lacked previous administrative experience. A number of late medieval bishops had been qualified in canon law, and had served apprenticeships in diocesan administration before proceeding to higher office in church and state. Very few of the Elizabethan bishops had studied law or had experience of diocesan administration before their elevations to the bench. Many had indeed been heads of houses or vice-chancellors in universities, or leading members of cathedral chapters. Such offices might well demand skill in handling men and money. But the problems encountered in the diocese were far greater, more complex and more varied than those with which the master of a college or the dean of a cathedral had to deal.

The earl and countess of Bedford summarised admirably the qualities generally accepted as desirable in the Elizabethan bishop when they recommended John Woolton for the see of Exeter in 1578 on account of his 'learning, painfulness in preaching and government, his honest life and other good parts'.[7] But the composition of the Elizabethan episcopal bench was determined by politics and patronage as well as merit, and to these we must now turn. Over three-quarters of the Elizabethan elevations and translations fell within one of five periods: 1559–62, 1570–2, 1575–8, 1583–5 and 1594–8. The two biggest rounds of promotions were the first and last of these. Those nominated at the beginning of Elizabeth's reign, when nearly all the sees had to be filled, remained in a substantial majority on the bench until the round of 1575–8, and the round of 1594–8 determined the character of the bench until some time after James I's accession. A brief survey of changing official policy in the making of appointments will show that strong Protestant commitment and learning, the qualities regarded as most desirable in a bishop at the beginning of the reign, gave way, especially after the mid-1570s, to administrative capacity and readiness to toe the official line.

Over half the first Elizabethan bishops had been in exile in Mary's reign, and many of them returned to England filled with a fervent desire for the reformation of the English church more thoroughgoing than any envisaged by Elizabeth. The exile group included Thomas Bentham (Lichfield, 1560–79), Richard Cox (Ely, 1559–81), Edmund Grindal (London, 1559–70, and later archbishop of both York and Canterbury), Robert Horne (Winchester, 1561–79). John Jewel (Salisbury, 1560–71), John Parkhurst (Norwich, 1560–75), James Pilkington (Durham, 1561–76), Edwin Sandys (Worcester, 1559–70, and later bishop of London and archbishop of York) and John Scory (Hereford, 1559–85). These men were chosen for their godly zeal and learning. A few of them were without administrative ability, a lack which was to have some serious consequences. Some of the most effective administrators amongst them, notably Cox, Horne and Jewel, grew more conservative with the passage of time as their tempers were soured by the additional complexities which puritan dissent brought to already formidable administrative problems.

From the start the Elizabethan episcopate contained a number of men considerably less radical than these. Canterbury, the most important see of all, went to the conservative reformer Matthew Parker, a man whose pride in the long history of the English church and its episcopal succession was remote from the aspirations of the exiles. Richard Cheyney (Gloucester, 1562–79) Lutheran on the eucharist, Erasmian on free will, was to arouse the fury of the puritans of Bristol by his preaching. William Downham (Chester, 1561–77) had conformed when he served as Elizabeth's chaplain under Mary.

Despite the experience of the vestiarian controversy, and Matthew Parker's strong desire to see the promotion of men ready to enforce uniformity, the elevations of 1570–2 strengthened the position of those bishops committed to Protestant reform. Emund Grindal went to York (1570–6); Edwin Sandys, dangerously lenient towards puritans in Parker's eyes, to London (1570–7). Amongst new appointees, Thomas Cooper (Lincoln, 1571–84, later bishop of Winchester) was outstanding for godliness and learning; Richard Curteys (Chichester, 1570–82), although a supporter of the official line during the vestiarian controversy, was to do more than any other sixteenth-century bishop of Chichester to further Protestant reformation.

Hopes of godly reformation of the Church of England, which reached a new height with the nomination of Edmund Grindal to Canterbury at the end of 1575, were dashed in the next two years by the rupture between Queen and archbishop which followed the latter's refusal to suppress the exercises and prophesyings. The appointments of the third round reflected Elizabeth's determination that the key sees should in future go to men who were in Parker's words 'disciplinable . . . and apt to govern',[8] men in sympathy with the Queen's own concern to achieve 'mediocrity', that is to say avoidance of extremes. The most significant appointment was that of the anti-puritan John Whitgift to Worcester (1577–83); his elevation to Canterbury (1583–1604) set the seal on the policy of reaction. Supposed readiness to impose uniformity played a part in a number of other appointments made in the period after 1575, such as those of John Young, a man 'fit to bridle innovators' (Rochester, 1578–1605), John Piers (Rochester, 1576–7; Salisbury, 1577–89; York, 1589–94) and Richard Howland (Peterborough, 1585–1600). The most important of all was that of Richard Bancroft (London, 1597–1604), the man who armed Sir Christopher Hatton with the telling arguments which he used in a vigorous attack on the presbyterian programme in the Parliament of 1586–7. He it was who ultimately succeeded Whitgift at Canterbury.

William Cecil, Lord Burghley, was the patron who bore the prime responsibility for the making of Elizabethan bishops. In the first round of elevations, his influence was rivalled by that of a strongly Protestant group which included Robert Dudley, his brother Ambrose, and the earls of Bedford and Huntingdon.[9] This group was never again to have so much influence over appointments, though Leicester was responsible for a number of later elevations, especially in the 1570s. In making his recommendations to the Queen, Burghley took advantage of the advice given him by the archbishops. It is highly probable that Grindal was, of the three archbishops, the one most congenial to Burghley, who was out of sympathy with both the gloomy pessimism of Parker's later years and Whitgift's aggressive determination to impose uniformity. It is clear that a number of Parker's suggestions were turned down in the round of 1570–2, though most of the newcomers to the bench in 1576–8, when Elizabeth was determined to impose her will on the church, were men whom Parker had marked out for advancement. During the years of his primacy, Whitgift certainly had considerable influence over appointments to the bench; but the continued advancement of a number of men of Grindalian sympathies in these years, and the comparatively slow rise of a number of Whitgift's men, were no doubt due in large part to Burghley's feelings. Robert Cecil was already playing an important part in the making of bishops before his father's death, though the earl of Essex took some part in choosing the men promoted in the round of 1594–8.

Elizabeth herself, directly responsible for the change in policy which blighted the 'promise of Grindal's church' and brought Whitgift to Lambeth, took a closer personal interest in appointments in the second half of her reign, sometimes with unfortunate results. Two of the keys to her favour seem to have been comeliness of appearance and a learned but courtly preaching style. The secret of Richard Fletcher's success, Sir John Harington tells us, was that he 'could preach well and would speak boldly, and yet keep *decorum*. He knew what would please the Queen, and would adventure on that though it offended others.' Thomas Dove owed his long and obscure tenure of the see of Peterborough (1601–30) in part to his elaborate preaching, laced with classical references, beloved by the Queen; allegedly decisive in Robert Bennet's elevation to Hereford (1603) was a sermon he preached before the Queen which was described at the time as 'all needle-work'.[10]

Patrons expected their protégés to show them gratitude and do them service. This was true even of the relatively disinterested appointments made early in the reign. Grindal, Horne, Sandys, Pilkington and Scambler all granted Leicester sinecure diocesan offices. Both Cecil and Leicester resented attempts by their protégés to enlist the help of their rivals in their efforts to gain promotion. It was perhaps chagrin at William Overton's recourse to Leicester in order to secure his nomination to Lichfield (1580–1609) that stung Burghley into his contemptuous, barely credible description of him as a bishop 'who made seventy ministers in one day for money, some tailors, some shoemakers, and others craftsmen'.[11]

In the second half of the reign, competition for all sorts of preferment grew increasingly fierce, and patrons increasingly determined that those whom they had helped should render adequate services. The tone of recent recipients of preferment became more obsequiously grateful, that of suitors for it more self-pityingly insistent. Richard Barnes wrote to Burghley acknowledging that he owed both his promotions (Carlisle, 1570–7; Durham, 1577–87) to him and undertaking to 'devow my self and service unto your honour for ever'. Richard Howland wrote to Burghley lamenting the fact that so many others had been promoted over his head since his elevation to Peterborough. He urged him to 'remember me now, for your Lordship in wisdom knoweth what a great discomfort it will be unto me to be remembered of others and to be rejected by my honourable good Lord and only Patron . . .'. This apparent threat to transfer his allegiance to another patron was, not surprisingly, fruitless. The evidence of services and rewards exacted by patrons from the men they promoted bulks increasingly large in the last decade of the reign. At the same time the government's financial difficulties forced it to resort to a greater number of episcopal leases as a means of rewarding courtiers. These conditions brought to the fore more men whose prime concern was their own advancement. They could not share the genuine interest in the reform of diocesan government and the improvement of the standards of the clergy which the exiles and Whitgift's closest associates, for all their differences of approach, had in common. There was a decline in the quality of the bench in the second half of the reign. Amongst the later Elizabethan bishops there were, however, some who were neither time-servers nor particularly anti-puritan, men accounted good bishops by members of opposing factions. The most outstanding of these were perhaps Matthew Hutton (Durham, 1589–95; York, 1595–1606) and Herbert Westfaling (Hereford, 1586–1602). Toby Matthew, too, though an ambitious prelate who allegedly owed his advancement (Durham, 1595–1606) in part to corrupt gifts, was an outstandingly diligent diocesan.[12]

The author of the *Discourse of the Common Weal* asked whether the bishops of his day had become more diligent and careful in ordination, institution to benefices, visitation, hospitality, residence and preaching. His questions provide a useful framework for an enquiry into the Elizabethan bishops' discharge of their pastoral duties, though they do not cover them all directly. The improvement of the quality of the clergy was undertaken through what we may broadly call 'in-service training' as well as the procedures governing admission to orders and benefices; the ecclesiastical laws were enforced through the bishops' courts as well as by means of diocesan visitations.

The Elizabethan bishops' first major task was to remedy as quickly as possible the appalling shortage of clergy which they found on arrival in their dioceses. In the early years of the reign they could not afford to be too discriminating if they wished to fill the large numbers of vacant parishes. Gradually it became possible to impose stricter standards. In August 1560 Matthew Parker issued an order forbidding the ordination of unlearned men who had previously followed menial occupations. The canons of 1571 insisted that candidates for the ministry be trained in good letters and well-versed in the scriptures; those of 1576 that ordinands must in future be able to render an account of their faith in Latin. The increasing supply of graduates and competition for places in the church made it possible to enforce the standards laid down. In most dioceses the proportion of graduates amongst the clergy increased during Elizabeth's reign, gradually till about 1580, and then dramatically up to and beyond the end of the reign. Was this improvement in the formal qualifications of the clergy then largely a matter of supply and demand? How far did the bishops by their personal interest make possible the enforcement of the standards laid down at provincial level?

Few records of examinations of candidates for ordination survive. Some of the best surviving were kept in the diocese of Ely. Here (as was the case elsewhere, for example in Lichfield diocese) the examination of ordination candidates was in the hands of the archdeacon, but in Richard Cox's time the archdeacons worked closely with the bishop and doubtful cases were referred to him. As early as 1561, the archdeacon of Ely rejected nearly one in six ordination candidates as insufficient; from the late 1560s onwards the proportion frequently rose to a quarter. Some degreed men with excellent knowledge of Latin were turned down because of their lack of acquaintance with the scriptures. Examiners in this diocese could afford to set high standards because it contained the university of Cambridge. In the neighbouring diocese of Lincoln, where, in Lincolnshire 14.3 per cent of benefices were vacant as late as 1576, Thomas Cooper could not afford to be so fastidious. However, in the case of some candidates Cooper withheld letters of orders for a year, setting the men scriptural study programmes. In the remoter areas of the country, the position was worse still. The conscientious John Woolton confessed that he had admitted five or six insufficient men to the ministry during the first six years of his episcopate, although his very preciseness does suggest that he had supervised the examinations fairly closely. In the diocese of Chester, William Chaderton imposed far higher standards than his predecessor William Downham, but even so little more than a third of his ordinands held degrees. In the diocese of Carlisle, so the bishop was to claim in 1598, the 'greatest number' of the clergy were utterly unlearned, unable to read English truly and distinctly. The quality of ordinands did not depend upon proximity to the universities alone. Some bishops applied higher standards than others equally well placed. This is clear from the very different fates of those who, ordained deacons in other dioceses, came to Ely to be ordained priest in Cox's time. All but one of the Norwich candidates were admitted; only one of the Peterborough deacons was considered worthy to proceed to the priesthood.[13]

The puritans and their sympathisers wanted established ordination procedures to be reformed so that no man would be admitted to the ministry unless examined by godly preachers and 'called' to a parish by its representatives. Edwin Sandys called for the implementation of a reform on these lines in a paper he drew up for the convocation of 1563. William Overton actually introduced examination by godly ministers, though his motives for doing so, and the vigour with which he enforced it, have been called in question. Whitgift, fearful lest the scheme undermine episcopal authority, soon vetoed it. In the next reign, the canons of 1604 provided that the bishop should examine candidates in the presence of at least three other clergy, but these were, if possible, to be cathedral dignitaries.

The institution of clergy to livings to which they had been presented by the patrons was the bishop's responsibility, and should have given him another opportunity to sift candidates for the ministry. Grindal as archbishop of York apparently rejected about 5 per cent of those presented to him, and from the surviving records of examinations (in some of which Grindal took part) it is clear that the expected standards of scriptural and grammatical knowledge were quite high, though one or two of the rejected candidates fell far below them. In 1576 Thomas Cooper, finding by personal examination that a presentee to a benefice was 'not capable thereof as yet', arranged that the man should present himself again after six months' study. If he were rejected again, Cooper promised to give the patron an additional five months to present a suitable candidate. Cooper was right to take such care not to infringe patronal rights. In 1571, John Parkhurst was sued in both secular and ecclesiastical courts for rejecting two grossly unsuitable candidates. It was not surprising that the accusation that they admitted insufficient ministers was one which stung Elizabeth bishops into a particularly angry response. A preacher at Paul's Cross in 1594 attacked gentlemen who

> cry out for a learned ministry, whereas in deed they do but pick quarrels with us, intending nothing less than a learned ministry, for they will willingly present none but such as are base, ignorant and beggarly, because such persons will easily accept of benefices upon unlawful conditions.

Thomas Cooper made the same point, and added that he knew some bishops who had lost more in a year through their efforts at the law to keep such men out than they had gained in institution fees in the whole time they had been bishops.[14]

The bishops themselves were patrons. They were able to place men in livings by collating them to benefices in their own gift or to those which the true patrons had failed to fill and by making requests to the Lord Keeper. The amount of patronage available varied greatly from diocese to diocese. The men placed by the bishops were not, as a group, of outstandingly high calibre. There were several reasons for this. Many of the benefices to which true patrons had failed to present were poor ones; this was often why they had proved difficult to fill. Nor were bishops completely free to choose those they considered the best men. They received requests for help from their own lay patrons and others whom they were reluctant to refuse. Some bishops used their patronage to advance members of their families. A number of bishops nevertheless promoted fit men when they could. John Parkhurst placed a number of men of puritan sympathies during the second half of his episcopate. Richard Curteys in his first six years at Chichester allegedly brought about the preferment of twenty highly competent preaching ministers. The bishops of London probably had a better choice of presentees than did most other bishops, and they used their own best livings to place a number of able domestic chaplains. Grindal helped some former exiles, while Aylmer and Bancroft chose rather to promote promising conservatives. Herbert Westfaling

> neither respected letters nor commendations of lords or knights, nor wife, nor friends, in preferment of any man, but only their sufficiency and their good conversation; so as to sue for a benefice unto him was rather a means to miss it than to attain it.

It is true that the tone of Harington's remarks suggests that he considered Westfaling exceptional in this respect amongst the bishops of the second generation, though with what justice it is hard to say.[15]

The Elizabethan bishops realised from the start that the less learned clergy would have to be trained 'in service'. The 1559 Royal Injunctions laid down that all clergy under the degree of M.A. were to possess and study the New Testament in both Latin and English. Supervision of the work was at first entrusted to diocesan officials; in 1586, by an order introduced into convocation by Whitgift, to licensed preachers who were to receive written work from those in their charge and send progress reports to the diocesan authorities. Detailed orders in the spirit of Whitgift's directive were later made in a number of dioceses.

Complementing these supervised studies there developed in a number of dioceses meetings for oral examination of the unlearned clergy ('exercises') and discussions of particular points of doctrine amongst the learned ('prophesyings'). The two types of meeting often merged into one, and might even be attended by laymen. It is in many cases difficult to tell how much the establishment of such meetings owed to episcopal initiative, how much to that of a group of godly preachers and their lay supporters. But it is at least clear both from diocesan records and from the answers sent in reply to enquiries made by Grindal in 1576 that a number of bishops approved of them and give them their warm support. Thomas Cooper, Robert Horne and John Parkhurst all enforced clerical attendance at certain exercises in their dioceses in the early 1570s. Richard Curteys played the leading part in their establishment in the diocese of Chichester, and he and the first two Elizabethan bishops of Exeter, William Alley and William Bradbridge, themselves attended them. Exercises seem also to have been encouraged in the diocese of Peterborough. In the dioceses of Lichfield, Bath and Wells and Hereford the exercises had been established without episcopal encouragement, and had indeed been suppressed by the bishops in the last two dioceses. Yet nearly all the bishops who answered Grindal's enquiry expressed approval of the *principle* of the exercises. Only if they got out of hand could they do more harm than good. Most of the group believed that the exercises were the best or only way of training the unlearned clergy. Richard Curteys was especially emphatic on this point. Even Richard Cox, who returned a negative answer, later wrote to Burghley expressing his hope that Elizabeth would consider the matter further in view of the ignorance and idleness of the large numbers of 'poor and blind priests'.[16]

The exercises survived the crisis of 1576–7. Archbishop Sandys re-established them in the diocese of York soon after his translation thither in 1577, and attendance was still being enforced by the diocesan courts in the 1590s. William Chaderton followed Sandys's lead in an initially more modest fashion; prodded by the Privy Council, he produced in 1584 a scheme for monthly exercises between February and October in five Lancashire towns. The leading puritan clergy of the county were closely involved in it. Exercises, though less strongly encouraged than in the north, were also to be found in a number of dioceses south of the Trent in the later years of Elizabeth's reign.[17]

The provision of a learned clergy was a means to a greater end: the instruction of the mass of the English laity in the fundamentals of the official religion by means of catechising and sermons. The inferior courts of the dioceses were in the main responsible for dealing with parishioners' complaints of inadequate performance of these duties. But the vigour of enforcement depended to a great extent upon the personal interest of the bishop. Edmund Grindal, for instance, by-passed the York courts in 1575, sending his domestic chaplains round the rural deaneries to make their own enquiries into the aptitudes and achievements of the parochial clergy. In a number of dioceses, bishops encouraged or ordered their clergy to join together to pay for the services of learned quarterly preachers. Some bishops clearly took more interest in the good work than did others. Cox of Ely took a wholehearted interest in the provision of effective catechising. Complaints that it was lacking were especially common during his episcopate, doubtless because of encouragement from above; before his death they declined markedly, presumably because of the progress made. In the neighbouring diocese of Norwich, efforts to make regular catechising a reality seem hardly to have begun before John Parkhurst's death in 1575.[18]

It was left largely to inferior officers, commissaries and officials, to enforce obedience to royal and episcopal injunctions amongst clergy and people. Every three years, however (in most dioceses), the bishop was able to carry out a 'visitation', to gain for himself some impression of the progress made in remoter parts of his jurisdiction, and to make contact with his flock. Since the clergy had to help to meet episcopal expenses each time visitation took place, the bishop who attempted to undertake more than his due number was likely to acquire a reputation for inconsiderate greed rather than for zeal. But Edwin Sandys, while at Worcester, and William Redman (Norwich, 1595–1602) complained that their visitations cost them more than they gained through them. For either reason or both, bishops tended to keep their tours short. The business of the visitation was dealt with in a few major centres of the diocese, usually in the parish church. After an opening sermon, the bishop or his deputy would formally charge the churchwardens and other parish representatives to make true presentments in answer to the previously circulated episcopal articles of enquiry. Clergy, schoolmasters and others would exhibit their letters of orders, licences and dispensations. The reported faults of the churchwardens and clergy might possibly be dealt with on the spot because they were present; other offenders would have to be summoned for punishment or exhortation after the visitation had finished.[19]

Some men of the first generation, such as Horne, Grindal and Jewel, threw themselves into the work of visitation with an ardour seldom equalled by their successors. Jewel's fragile health collapsed under the strain of carrying out his last visitation. Later, no doubt, less depended upon the bishop's own zeal and involvement. The crypto-papist episcopal officers who served in many dioceses at the beginning of the reign were gradually replaced by others more reliable and efficient, and the gradual improvement in the state of most dioceses after the first few years allowed an increasing proportion of routine business to be handled without direct reference to the bishop. In the diocese of London at least, episcopal visitations steadily increased in efficiency during the reign, though the bishop's personal participation in them declined. Nevertheless, the bishop was still expected to go on tour with his officials. John Whitgift made this quite clear in a directive which he issued in 1591. Six years earlier, he had demonstrated the importance he attached to personal episcopal visitation by making John Woolton answer a Cornish puritan's charge that he had never visited his diocese in person. Woolton replied that he had been two or three times in most of the market towns of Devon and Cornwall. He admitted that his two visitations had been interrupted by illness, but said he had taken some part in both. After the visitation was over, the most serious cases might be referred to the bishop's consideration. In 1597, for instance, a number of offences on the part of clergy or gentry were reported to William Redman after he had completed his visitation of the diocese of Norwich.[20]

During the visitation, in the later years of the reign, time was set aside for the performance of confirmation, the rite which brought the bishop into closest contact with his people. John Ponet spoke with a distaste felt by a number of reformers when he referred disparagingly to the popular conception of the bishop as 'a great lord . . . that carried an oil-box with him, wherewith he used once in seven years, riding about, to *confirm* children', and few traces of the rite are to be found in early Elizabethan visitation books, though several bishops prohibited the admission of children to the Holy Communion until they could say their catechism. There is, however, evidence that confirmation was still performed in some dioceses if not in all.

Thomas Bentham expected children to offer themselves for it, while Edmund Scambler sanctioned the practice of changing unsuitable personal names at the ceremony. In 1591 Whitgift deplored its recent neglect and ordered better performance in future, both in visitations and at other times when the bishop travelled through his diocese. By the end of the reign, confirmation was certainly a well-established part of visitation procedure in the diocese of Norwich. Toby Matthew while bishop of Durham 'confirmed sometimes five hundred, sometimes a thousand at a time; yea, so many that he hath been forced to betake himself to his bed for refreshment'.[21] At Hartlepool, the multitude of candidates was so great that the bishop had to conduct a great open-air ceremony in the churchyard. However brief the contact between bishop and each child on such an occasion, this description of the ceremony leaves us in no doubt of its popularity and dramatic quality. Whitgift, seeking to revitalise the relationship between the bishop and his flock, no doubt bore these in mind when he made his order.

The enforcement of ecclesiastical discipline was by no means restricted to visitations; it went on all the time. Most of the work was done by the diocesan and archdeaconry courts, but the bishops sometimes summoned to their residences those involved in weighty cases, especially if they were clergy or gentry. Occasionally, they even took charge of their consistory courts, though no Elizabethan bishop is known to have equalled John Hooper's diligence in this respect. John Jewel and Robert Horne, both of them men of administrative ability, did preside fairly frequently. Bishops could not, however, maintain constant supervision of the work of their courts, and the key to their successful running lay in the choice of able subordinates. Some bishops, such as Richard Cox at Ely and Edmund Grindal at London, managed to assemble teams of diocesan officials in full sympathy with their aims, but John Parkhurst appointed a series of chief judges who were either incompetent or else indifferent to his hopes of effective reformation. The practice of granting patents of office for life and in reversion, unfortunately extended by such Elizabethan bishops as Edmund Freake at Norwich (1575–84), made it much more difficult to remove or control officials. Edmund Freake, William Overton and John Bullingham brought down hornets' nests about their ears in the course of their attempts to remove their chief judges. Declining respect for the chief ecclesiastical sanction, excommunication, and the desire of the church court lawyers to make business for themselves had led to serious abuses; seen at their worst in the diocese of Gloucester under the lax rule of Richard Cheyney. A number of bishops were aware that the state of their courts left much to be desired, but their efforts to tackle abuses were hampered by their lack of legal training. Towards the end of his episcopate, John Parkhurst drew up a list of abuses on the part of his registrars. At Durham, a grandiloquent set of reforming statutes for the consistory court was prepared in 1573, apparently under episcopal auspices. Shortly afterwards, Edmund Grindal tried to tackle the shortcomings of the Canterbury provincial courts. Convocation, too, addressed itself to the problem, and from 1571 onwards passed a series of reforming measures which culminated in the canons of 1604. But reform in the dioceses proceeded by fits and starts, and improvement was slow.[22]

Effective ecclesiastical discipline, and in particular conformity to the religious settlement, could not be enforced without the support of the gentry. Yet, as was revealed by a survey carried out by the bishops at the request of the Privy Council in 1564, a high proportion of the foremost men in the counties, especially in the midlands and the north, were apathetic or hostile towards the settlement. A number of bishops found themselves in conflict with local magnates. Edwin Sandys's period at Worcester was marred by his struggle with Sir John Bourne, formerly Mary's secretary of state. In this case, after careful investigation, the Council supported Sandys. Richard Curteys was not to be so fortunate. He was opposed by a powerful group of conservative Sussex gentlemen. When he instituted proceedings against members of the group in his consistory court in 1577, he failed to distinguish between recusants and occasional conformers. Those of the latter category who had been summoned complained to the Privy Council of Curteys's behaviour towards them as an intolerable affront to the leaders of local society; Curteys was ordered to explain his conduct and given a stiff reprimand. The bulk of the gentry, whether conservative or puritan, no longer found prelatical government acceptable. The Council respected their prejudices; bishops were expected to act as its eyes and ears, to keep it fully informed, but to avoid any action which might provoke controversy or stir local passions. Tact and discretion – which Richard Curteys so notably lacked – came high on the list of qualities needful in an Elizabethan bishop.[23]

In order to further reformation, some of the bishops sought to bring about a closer formal association between leading clergy and gentry. In the early years of the reign many bishops suggested that commissions of clergy and laity (modelled on the ecclesiastical commission in London) with powers to fine or imprison not normally available to the church courts be established in the dioceses. A number were set up. But they could not transform diocesan government overnight, as some bishops seem to have hoped. In the diocese of Chester the commission (one of the first to be established) was rendered ineffective by disputes amongst its members. A more united body of commissioners might make the bishop the prisoner of a faction such as the militant Protestants of Devon whose desire for a commission was opposed by Bishop Bradbridge in 1577. A little later, the leading puritan gentry of East Anglia, well disposed towards the ministers whom Edmund Freake was trying to discipline, criticised him for failing to use the Norwich commission to curb recusancy in his diocese. Whitgift's associates naturally did not want to be tied too closely to the puritan gentry of their dioceses; to them, conservative opposition no longer seemed as threatening as it had to their predecessors of the first generation. From 1581 onwards, proceedings against recusants were increasingly entrusted to laymen, and the diocesan commissions became 'just another species of church court dominated by clerics and civilians'.[24] As an experiment in diocesan government they had achieved only limited success.

Much of the esteem which Elizabethan bishops enjoyed amongst their flocks depended upon their maintenance of the hospitality and residence expected by the author of the *Discourse of the Common Weal*. The Elizabethan bishops as a group certainly spent much more time in their dioceses than their late medieval predecessors had done. A number of them were reputedly good hosts; some used a portion of their revenue to support charitable activities and learning. Most bishops retained large numbers of servants. Puritans might criticise them for this, but local society expected them to provide employment. One of the most telling reproaches levelled by John Parkhurst against an episcopal collector believed guilty of embezzlement was that he had forced the bishop to reduce drastically the number of his household servants.[25]

Episcopal residences were the bases from which dioceses were governed. When John Aylmer (London, 1577–94) sought permission to use for part of the year a former episcopal residence in Essex which had passed into the hands of the Crown, he put forward as his main reason his conviction that he would

> within short space . . . bring all the whole country into so good an order, as any other part of his diocese whatsoever, both in respect of disordered persons, as such as were of lewd conversation. As his being at his house at Hadham some small time in the year had made by this time all the country of Hertfordshire (before out of order) now to be most quiet and orderly.

John Parkhurst carried out on a small scale the sort of work here envisaged by Aylmer in the little Norfolk town of Acle which lay near his residence at Ludham. Here, in the closing years of his episcopate, he met regularly with the gentlemen and yeomen of the district to punish petty offences and settle disputes. But he and other bishops could only influence a small part of their dioceses in this way. Considerations of household supply tied the bishop to his estates, often drastically pruned by the Reformation. This did not matter so much in the case of small, compact dioceses, but a number of the larger sees were left with few residences, or resources insufficient to maintain all those which they had been allowed to keep. The bishops of Chester, Lichfield, Lincoln and Norwich could not hope to rule their enormous dioceses from their one or two remaining residences, especially when these lay in one corner of their jurisdiction. These bishops' knowledge of, and control over, the outlying parts of their dioceses was bound to be slender, a fact well illustrated by the episcopal reports of 1564, particularly that furnished by Thomas Bentham of Lichfield. The solutions were to break up the larger dioceses into manageable smaller units or to increase their endowments so as to facilitate control from a number of houses as envisaged by Aylmer. But the Elizabethan government could afford neither of these.[26]

Of all the duties of a bishop listed by the author of the *Discourse*, ministration of the word was perhaps the most important. The Elizabethan bishops were well aware of this fact, and even their most outspoken critics did not tax more than a handful of them with neglecting preaching. We may be fairly sure that the Elizabethan bishops did preach fairly frequently, but there is depressingly little evidence to show how often or where they did so, or what effect they had upon their audiences. William Harrison, writing in 1577, believed that few bishops would not be found preaching somewhere within their dioceses every Sunday or oftener. A number of individual bishops, including William Alley (Exeter, 1560–70), Richard Curteys, Edwin Sandys, John Whitgift and John Woolton, were specifically stated to have matched this ideal: many others were more vaguely alleged to have been diligent preachers. John Whitgift regularly preached two Sunday sermons while at Worcester, one in a neighbouring church in the morning and another in the cathedral in the afternoon. John Woolton preached on his country benefice. Did Elizabethan bishops also travel round their dioceses to preach? Most of them probably preached sermons during their visitations. Whitgift showed in a directive of 1591 that he expected his brethren to 'travel abroad in the diocese to preach' at other times as well. John Jewel was supposedly exceptionally diligent in this respect. In the autumn of 1578, Richard Barnes launched a scheme for the preaching of additional sermons by learned clergy in the diocese of Durham. He himself undertook to provide twenty-four, twice as many as any of the other participants. Unfortunately we know little about the contemporary reaction to episcopal sermons. John Woolton's were 'practical rather than controversial, and yet were full of learning'. Those of William Day (Winchester, 1596) were said to be delivered in 'a good plain fashion, apt to edify, and easy to remember'. No Elizabethan bishop, however, is known to have had an effect on a popular audience comparable with that of Latimer or Hooper, though Toby Matthew may have come somewhere near to achieving it. It was his 'beloved work' (we are told) to preach to the poor, going each Sunday to some parish church in his diocese of Durham. On one such occasion he found that only three people had gathered to hear him. He nevertheless preached to them, and on the following Sunday, when he returned, he found the church packed with people who had heard reports of his earlier sermon. Anxious care went into the composition of his sermons, yet of the nearly two thousand he delivered, none has survived in print.[27]

The Elizabethan bishops were butts both for the courtiers who coveted their lands and for the puritans who resented their enforcement of conformity. A rich fund of anecdotes about their ambition, arrogance, servility, uxoriousness, nepotism and parsimony has presented a standing temptation to historians. This essay has attempted to portray some of the positive achievements of the episcopate. For the first time in many centuries there was established in England a body of bishops who were nearly all normally resident in their dioceses, regular in visitation and assiduous in preaching. Faced with enormous problems, the first generation of Elizabethan bishops set to work with a will on the tasks of improvement and conversion. That the results were not always commensurate with their hopes was due in large part to their inexperience, the opposition of the gentry, the timid conservatism of the Queen, and the inherent defects of the system they had to run, in particular the excessive size of dioceses. Yet much was achieved.

The triumphs of the Elizabethan settlement were overshadowed by the tragedy of internecine strife. Energy and talents which should have gone into the struggle against ignorance and superstition were diverted into a fratricidal conflict which obscured the fact that the bishops and their critics held many objectives in common; objectives which many members of the later Elizabethan bench continued to pursue.

It would, however, be idle to suggest that the hierarchy did not undergo profound changes before 1603. Whitgift and his associates responded to puritan attacks with an increased emphasis on hierarchy and order; in 1589 Bancroft publicly countered presbyterian dogma in a sermon which seemed to suggest that episcopacy was divinely ordained. It was no coincidence that Whitgift called only two years later for the more assiduous performance of confirmation, that quasi-sacramental rite which only bishops could perform. The later years of Elizabeth's reign saw too the reappearance of the courtier prelate, and Whitgift's appointment to the Privy Council marked the beginning of churchmen's return to government. Under James I, the episcopate was to become even more closely identified with the court. Assured of support such as Elizabeth had never given, Bancroft and Neile began a determined effort to defend and where possible extend the church's rights. The Jacobean episcopate was far from united in outlook and aims. Takeover by Laud, Neile and their associates, when it came, was to seem abrupt. But some of the characteristic features of their rule were nevertheless the fruits of developments which can be traced to roots in the late 1570s.

5. Economic Problems of the Clergy

FELICITY HEAL

THE late medieval church was a vast but amorphous corporation: the institutional manifestation of the body of Christ, constructed by centuries of papal organisation, and locally evolving custom. Its social and economic functions, while subordinated to its key religious purposes, were of vital importance to a society that was permeated by ecclesiastical structures and values. Those functions can be divided into two general categories. First, there were the rights and duties that derived from the clerical office itself: these were broadly similar in all the countries of western Christendom, and were carefully safeguarded by the canons of the church. It was the right of a beneficed cleric to receive the tithes and the offerings of the congregation, and to hold as inalienable all those lands and other properties that had been given throughout the centuries for the maintenance of the church. His duties included the maintenance of an assigned portion of the church fabric, and the provision of hospitality and alms for the needy. Other functions and duties sprang from the particular position of the clergy in society. Even in the sixteenth century the higher clergy remained enmeshed in the feudal system. Their lands were held of the King and had been granted to them not as a charitable endowment but as a means of furnishing men and revenue for the monarchy in time of need. The parochial clergy also had obligations as subjects of a temporal prince: in England in particular they were required to meet fairly regular demands for taxation. All clerics worked within a network of more local relationships, which strongly influenced their capacity to discharge their prime function of the cure of souls. The parish clergy might be forced to act at the dictate of their patrons: they could be vicars, holding only a limited portion of the revenue from tithes, the rest being appropriated to a monastic foundation. The higher clergy played an important role in secular affairs, both as advisers and officers of the realm, and as leaders of local politics.

It is perhaps inevitable that we can discover a great deal more about clerical performance of duties towards realm and locality than about their discharge of such general functions as hospitality. In the pre-Reformation period little more can be said about the latter than that charity was constantly enjoined upon the clergy. English synodal decrees regularly insisted upon charitable and hospitable behaviour from the clergy: the idea was that about a third of net income should be used by incumbents for this purpose.[1]

Sermons and literature of the fifteenth and early sixteenth centuries contain complaints that charity and hospitality were neglected; but such neglect, if it did occur, was not considered sufficiently serious to warrant investigation in episcopal visitations such as those of Lincoln for the early sixteenth century. The failure to provide charity or to fulfil one's duties to the community in no sense entitled the laity to withhold from the priest his rightful tithes but there probably was some popular feeling that the two were closely related. This is best expressed by the reformer Thomas Becon, who in his catechism argued for the maintenance of the traditional system:

> The bishop's house, the parson's house, the vicar's house, the priest's house, the archdeacon's house, the dean's house, the prebendary's house etc., are all God's house; and tithes and offerings be brought into these houses, not for the incumbent's sake only, but also for the maintenance of the poor, that the needy may have whereof to be relieved at their hands.[2]

When one turns to the clergy's relationship with the Crown, a very different set of social and economic expectations are encountered. The church as an institution was one of the most valuable and co-operative assets of the Crown. It had long been established that the monarchy had the right to tax all the clergy, not merely its own tenants-in-chief, and income from the church was peculiarly valuable, since the clergy were rarely as politically demanding and assertive as the laity. Thus the early Tudor monarchs were able to raise large sums from the church: the best estimate is an average of about £12,000 per annum. This excludes the benevolences and loans which the higher clergy, in particular, had to produce in time of war. The bishops and prebendaries and other officials of the ecclesiastical hierarchy were most exposed to the Crown's fiscal demands in the pre-Reformation period: in addition to the direct taxation burden, they could also be forced to participate in a game of 'musical chairs'. Whenever a cleric who held lands directly of the Crown had his temporalities restored to him on his appointment, a substantial fine had to be paid to the royal coffers. Henry VII was particularly adept at raising revenue by these means, moving some of his unfortunate bishops from see to see four or five times. Even the lowliest clergy could not evade royal taxation: although the unbeneficed and those with an income of less than £8 did not have to pay tenths and subsidies, after 1496 all clergy earning more than 4 marks were subject to the archbishop of Canterbury's charitable subsidies.[3] The church was also for the monarchy an invaluable source of patronage, and the place where administrators could most easily be found. At every level the monarchy invaded the structure of the church and made its demands upon it: only the capital endowment of the clergy seemed safe. In this respect, at least, the Yorkists and Tudors, until the 1530s, were loyal sons of the church: they showed no inclination to follow the promptings of the Lollards and take back the land and wealth which their forefathers had bestowed upon the clergy.

In addition to the general demands of the Crown and the obligation to charity, most of the clergy had other specific duties imposed upon them by law and custom. The bishops and others who held appropriated livings, together with all rectors, were responsible for the maintenance of the chancels of their churches, and of the dwelling-houses of the clergy. Failure to make these repairs was a more obvious source of friction between parishioners and clergy than the more general failure to provide charity. The parish clergy had to pay costs such as procurations and synodals – the monies paid to the ordinary at time of visitation. There were also the charges arising from the proper fulfilment of their spiritual office: payments for wine, bread and other liturgical necessities, and often the relatively high cost of employing a chaplain or assistant. Of the unbeneficed there were few expectations, beyond the fact that they must pay their taxes, which was as much as their poverty allowed.

Two questions must be asked of the income of the pre-Reformation clergy: was it, in theory, adequate to allow the clergy to discharge these duties and live in reasonable comfort; and did the clergy in practice use their income to fulfil the expectations of the laity? Any discussion of clerical income immediately encounters the problem that the secular church was incredibly diverse in its resources and wealth. It used to be assumed that there were essentially two tiers in the late medieval church: the higher clergy (bishops, ecclesiastical officers, candidates for high preferment), and the mass of the clergy, beneficed and unbeneficed, who performed the actual cure of souls and who, if they were pluralists, were so only by the accident of their local connections or poverty. Recent research upon the clergy of Kent, Lancashire and Coventry and Lichfield suggests that this model needs to be refined. A third tier of clergy can be separated from the second. The division between the beneficed and the unbeneficed is shown to have been very sharp: the church rarely provided a path of upward mobility for those who entered her ranks as unbeneficed assistant curates.

While this three-tier division is useful principally in analysing the personnel of the church, it also has some relevance to questions of income and wealth. The lowest group in the church, the unbeneficed curates, have been accorded less attention by historians than the rest, partly because they appear far less often in the regular records of the church than the beneficed clergy. However, the evidence that has been assembled from dioceses such as Lincoln, Coventry and Lichfield and the counties of Kent and Lancashire indicates that they were poorly paid as well as insecure. Throughout much of the area studied the maximum of 8 marks or £5 6s 8d, laid down in a statute of 1414, was the norm for assistants' wages. In Rochester and Canterbury dioceses the average in the 1530s was about £5, although in 1526 the Lincoln assistants were blessed with the slightly higher average figure of £5 3s 2d. In north Lancashire in 1524 the average income of £2 6s 9d did not even approach the norm.[4] It is difficult to offer a useful estimate of what an assistant needed to live and perform his minimal duties to society, but Peter Heath's guess of between £4 and £6, depending upon whether he lived with the incumbent, would seem reasonable.[5] Since many chaplains were obviously earning less than this, and since both inflation and taxation must have begun to affect these low salary earners during the early Tudor period, it must be assumed that many of them existed in a state of poverty. The problem at this level was not so much that the clergy were neglectful of their social duties, as that their financial rewards gave them little incentive to devote themselves wholly to the cure of souls.

Higher expectations were entertained of the beneficed clergy by parishioners and church authorities, since they had security of tenure and usually cure of souls. A great diversity of income characterised these occupants of the middle ranks of the church: a diversity created both by the benefice itself, which might be rich or poor, appropriated or not, and by plurality and non-residence among the clergy. The incidence of pluralism and non-residence greatly complicates any discussion of the wealth of individual clerics. Margaret Bowker's research upon Lincoln diocese suggests that almost a quarter of the parishes were held by non-residents between 1514 and 1520; in Kent, Warham found about 15 per cent of his clergy absent in 1517; in Lancashire pluralism alone created a 30 per cent absentee rate by 1520.[6] The absentee might hold a second living in plurality or have a second source of income from church, state or private patron. The wills of the clergy, especially those proved in the Prerogative Court of Canterbury, are more often a guide to the success of the individual in multiplying his offices, than to the profit to be made from a particular ecclesiastical living. In the pre-Reformation period it seems generally true that the richer the benefice, the more likely it was to be held by an absentee. The rich Lancashire rectories, valued at an average of £34 in 1535, were rarely occupied by their incumbents. Poor benefices, on the other hand, at least in the diocese of Lincoln, rarely had absentee priests, in marked contrast to the post-Reformation situation. This can be attributed in part to the vigilance of the bishops in enforcing residence, but is also evidence of an abundant supply of clergy willing to take such poor cures. Indeed, an important element in the analysis of the economic difficulties of the clergy at this point is that there is no evidence of men failing to enter orders because of the poverty of many of the church's livings.

Most estimates of the wealth of the parish clergy must continue to depend upon the valuation of individual benefices. The key source is the great survey of 1535 known as the *Valor Ecclesiasticus*. There are difficulties involved in using the *Valor* as the data is not uniformly detailed. However, its general accuracy has been proved for the monasteries and some of the higher clergy, and there seems little warrant for the assumption made by Christopher Hill that the vicarage figures are distorted by the inclusion of great tithes paid to the appropriator.[7] The *Valor* may have underestimated the potential income to be derived from glebe and tithes, but it remains the best available survey of income actually obtainable in the 1530s. It shows that the average net receipts for those dioceses which have been studied in detail varied between about £10 and £13 per annum per parish. Vicarages consistently fared worse than rectories: to take an extreme example, in Lancashire the averages were £12 for vicarages and £34 for rectories. Elsewhere an average differential of £5 was not uncommon. It has been estimated that a beneficed cleric needed a gross income of £10 to fulfil all his obligations, or nearer to £15 if an assistant was employed.[8] If this was so, only a quarter to a third of the benefices in the country would have been able to support a priest effectively.

It is probable, however, that the sources of an incumbent's income were more important than their precise valuation, even in the early sixteenth century. Benefices with a large glebe that was not on long lease – and long leases seem to have been extremely rare before the Reformation – should usually have been able to support a reasonable standard of living. Glebe has been given far too little attention by early sixteenth-century historians, largely because the evidence for it derives from later glebe terriers. Stephen Lander has shown that vicarage glebes in Chichester diocese altered little between the original ordination of the vicarages and the preparation of the terriers in the seventeenth century. We may, therefore, with caution use later evidence for this period, except in areas seriously affected by enclosure. In Chichester most of the rectories and 40 per cent of the vicarages for which evidence survives had more than five acres of glebe; in Warwickshire 87 per cent of the rectories and 40 per cent of the vicarages had substantial glebe.[9] Stephen Lander suggests that where a benefice had more than five acres of glebe and some tithes in kind, the £8 set as the lowest level of income for the payment of parliamentary taxation was sufficient for the needs and duties of a beneficed clerk. This seems a more reasonable figure as most benefices clearly did remain viable not only in the 1530s but in the inflationary years that followed. The really vulnerable clerics were those who, like the unbeneficed, lived on a salary from their appropriators, or who occupied parishes that were too small or depopulated to yield much tithe. Both these types of living were frequently found in urban areas where the high concentration of churches created small parishes, and the absence of agriculture made it difficult to collect tithes. York, to take a rather extreme example, had parishes with an average value of only £4 in 1535.[10]

The bishops, cathedral clergy and richest pluralists who formed the upper ranks of the church had few of the immediate problems of subsistence that confronted many of the parish clergy. Yet they had social and economic responsibilities that often made heavy demands upon their resources. The richest English sees – Winchester, Canterbury, Durham and Ely – all commanded an income of over £2000 a year, and they were usually held by men with state office, their resources partly used to pay the high costs of diplomacy and hospitality. Almost all bishoprics, and some other positions such as that of dean, normally involved their incumbents deeply in local affairs, if only in paying part of the costs of administration and providing hospitality when they were resident. The scale of hospitality was of particular importance: Bishop West of Ely was considered generous, but by no means unique among his fellows, and he is traditionally supposed to have had a household of 100 men, and to have maintained 200 poor men at his gates, feeding them warm meats. Hospitality was also a considerable charge on a prebendary who wished to enter into residence. At Wells in the later fifteenth century the chapter decided that such a man needed an income of £40 a year apart from his prebend to sustain his initial obligations to the cathedral community.[11] There is little doubt that the resources of the higher clergy were more than adequate to face these duties, and to pay the heavy taxation demanded by the Crown. For those below the rank of bishop, there was usually the opportunity to hold livings and prebends in plurality; for the bishops themselves, their lands and revenues usually sufficed. The generosity with which the early Tudor episcopate endowed colleges and schools is clear evidence of the surplus wealth that many were able to accumulate. Bishop Oldham of Exeter, whose income and expenditure accounts survive, had an average income of £1600, and a total household expenditure of £850, which indicates a comfortable surplus even after the payment of taxes.[12] Nevertheless, the bishops could already encounter financial problems: the Welsh sees, Rochester and Carlisle were always poor, and so much was expected of the archbishops of Canterbury that their household charges consumed almost all their available revenue.

The image of the pre-Reformation church is, therefore, one of immense financial diversity. A substantial section of those in major orders had benefices or incomes that were scarcely viable even before a period of inflation and heavy taxation, and were suffering strain from both of these by the early 1530s. On the other hand, those with the influence to obtain good livings, or with access to the higher ranks of the church, can rarely have had difficulties in meeting their expenses by acquiring other benefices if necessary. Among the higher clergy it was perhaps only the poorer bishops that had difficulty, as a group, in meeting their obligations, as they were normally prevented from holding any second living. The system, constructed as it was to provide support for a large non-resident élite from the resources of the parishes, was not the ideal means of providing for parochial care. Yet, as both Margaret Bowker and Christopher Haigh have argued, it is doubtful whether many of the graduate pluralists would have resided on their livings even if they had been strictly limited to one benefice. Although more and more university-trained clergy were being promoted to parochial cures in the early sixteenth century, it is not clear that the parishioners appreciated or needed a priest whose costly education supposedly entitled him to high financial rewards. The key role of the priest remained mediatory rather than expository: the sacrifice of the mass was the corner-stone of the priestly function and, while sermons and other forms of instruction were undoubtedly more widely used than the traditional view of the pre-Reformation priest suggests, the priest was judged above all else upon his adequate performance of this central duty. Good conversation, attention to the needs of the congregation and a sober style of life were important secondary requisites, stressed both in the moralising literature of the period and in the complaints of parishioners at visitation. In the early sixteenth century these expectations, which in some measure justified the uneven distribution of resources within the church, were beginning to be challenged both by the higher clergy and by a small but vociferous section of the laity. Those humanists, both within the church and outside, who stressed the importance of education and instruction in the faith, and who strove to increase the number of graduate clergy, helped to foster a more critical attitude towards clerical standards which was to be of increasing significance in the later sixteenth century. The uneven distribution of the church's resources became a focal point of this critique, for if educated clergy were to reside and teach in their parishes, they had to be rewarded with an adequate living.

One of the more remarkable features of the English Reformation is that the system of financing the English clergy was scarcely altered between the reign of Henry VIII and the Civil War. Until the emergence of the radical sects in the English Revolution no serious alternative to financing the parish clergy through tithe and glebe was contemplated. The only marked change in the nature of a cleric's rights was that the common law became more and more involved in tithe litigation. Rectories and vicarages continued, only the rectories formerly appropriated to religious houses were now normally impropriated to laymen, who regarded them as pieces of secular property and showed little concern for the vicar. It is symptomatic of the institutional continuity of the English Reformation that this vital change from monastic to lay impropriator was accepted with scarcely a comment during the great dispersal of monastic lands under Henry VIII. The parochial assistants remained as they had been, with only the loss of the chantry chaplains under Edward VI, and were often paid precisely the same sums on the outbreak of the Civil War as they had been a century and a half earlier. Among the higher clergy there were more institutional changes: notably the creation of six new bishoprics and twelve secular cathedrals from the ruins of the monasteries. The bishops also lost much of their land to the laity before the end of the sixteenth century. Yet even in this upheaval the semblance of continuity was maintained – most of the land taken was recompensed by rectories and other spiritual sources of income which helped, in theory, to give the bishops the same revenue as before the Reformation. This sense of continuity, of a church still endowed with a substantial portion of the wealth of society, is very important in explaining the hostile attitudes of many contemporary laymen. Both those who were envious of that wealth and those who were opposed to the religious policy of the establishment were able to compare critically the economic stability of the church with the failure of the clergy to play a generous role in society. The archbishops of Canterbury from Cranmer to Laud were almost all forced to answer serious criticisms that a rich church was failing to discharge its obligations.

In reality the church was ground between the upper millstone of inflation and the nether millstone of lay power. This process was not such a complete crisis for the church as is sometimes suggested, but it was fundamental in changing the way in which church and society interacted. Since the worst of the demands of Crown and laity and the most intense inflationary pressures occurred within the same period, it is often difficult to attribute the problems of the church precisely to one or to the other. Traditional accounts tended to ascribe all difficulties to rapacious laymen: some recent historians, on the other hand, have too casually invoked the notion of inflation, whose effect upon the various sections of the church is still imperfectly understood.

Inflation was certainly vital, for there were large groups in the church whose incomes were fixed and inflexible, some of whom had already been near the edge of poverty even before the Reformation. The most obvious were the unfortunate parish assistants who in the 1560s, and even in the 1620s, often had to exist on payments of £5 per annum or less. At the end of the sixteenth century the notoriously poor chapel curates of Lancashire were being paid an average wage of £4 whereas in London and some of the more affluent parts of the country assistants were sometimes paid as much as £20.[13] Inflation at this level resulted in a rapid decline in the number of assistants. Incumbents could no longer afford to employ them at a tolerable wage and, moreover, the disturbed state of the Tudor church gave men no incentive to seek ordination merely to occupy these poverty-stricken positions. The number of assistants increased during Elizabeth's reign once more but Lancashire had difficulties in filling its curacies under James I. Vicars who were dependent upon a money payment in lieu of tithes were almost as vulnerable as the assistants. On occasion impropriators augmented the vicarages from their own tithe profits: some bishops made conscientious attempts to persuade impropriators to augment benefices. Yet the evidence so far available suggests that only a tiny fraction of benefices had been augmented by the time that the Laudians made a systematic campaign for improvements. The vicars with no glebe and few or no tithes must have had very inadequate resources after the great period of inflation. It was these benefices which succumbed first to the difficulties of the Tudor church, and were left unfilled in the middle of the century. In 1563 thirteen of the livings left vacant in Ely diocese could not be filled 'for the exility of the living' and approximately the same number were held in plurality because of their poverty.[14] Urban clergy suffered particularly from fixity of income. Also, after the Tithe Act of 1549, it became virtually impossible for them to collect the personal tithes which were normally their only other source of income.

Clergy with land in lease were also potential victims of inflation. Long leases of glebe and/or tithes effectively fixed a cleric's income. That this was a serious problem is suggested by the efforts of the Elizabethan bishops to prevent leases of more than three years duration.[15] Even short leases did not guarantee rental adjustments which reflected the economic value of the land. Bishops and cathedral clergy consistently used the beneficial lease – a grant for a fixed rent, often with an entry fine attached. Indeed, the higher clergy probably suffered rather more from the problems of leases than did the parish clergy. Their land was almost all in lease even before the Reformation and the grants were often for thirty- to forty-year periods. When the demands of Crown and laity also had to be met, grants of sixty to ninety-nine years became common, and no fine could possibly retrieve the full value of the lands for the clergy. Throughout the Elizabethan period the bishops and chapters had to live with the consequences of grants made under Henry VIII and Edward VI and to try to counter the effects of inflation by exploiting the few resources that they kept in hand: woodlands, a home farm or two, and ancillary rights such as mining or fishing. By the end of the period the situation of the higher clergy was on the upturn: they had greater security in their lands under James I, and the lucrative leases of the previous century began to fall in. They were renewed for very large fines – at the beginning of Charles I's reign Buckeridge made £4000 in a few years at Ely – but usually still at fixed rents for shorter periods.[16] It was not until after the Civil War that the bishops became as efficient as landlords as many of the aristocracy had been since the reign of Elizabeth.

One final way in which the clergy might condemn themselves to a fixed income was by agreeing to a *modus decimandi*. This involved the commutation of some or all tithes for a money payment. Traditional *modi* on tithes that were highly perishable or not readily divisible into ten parts obtained in many parishes. More damaging, however, were agreements to commute on a particular tract of land or to commute the tithes of a whole group of parishioners. Urban clergy were often the worst sufferers as the difficulty of collecting personal tithes made it tempting to agree to a fixed payment instead. London clergy suffered when, by statute, tithes and offerings on lands in lease were commuted to 2s 9d in the pound on the rental value of the houses thereupon. The extent to which tithes were commuted can, however, be exaggerated: D. M. Barratt's work on Gloucester and Worcester has shown Usher's assumption that most tithes were commuted by the end of the sixteenth century to be erroneous. Stephen Lander's study of Chichester suggests that few parishes had their tithe wholly commuted even in the 1630s.[17] Outside the larger towns, the main problem was probably that any commutation *lessened* the incumbent's chances of combating inflation rather than that the battle was lost by wholesale commutation.

This catalogue of woes suggests that most clergy could not escape the consequences of inflation. Yet there were those whose livings kept pace with rising prices and who may even have profited from the rapid increase in food costs. Rectors and vicars who farmed their own glebe or collected and sold their own tithe were well placed to benefit. Dr Hill's figures for sample rectories show an increase in value by 549 per cent between 1535 and 1650. Even vicarages improved by 404 per cent. These figures are supported by Rosemary O'Day's sample of Derbyshire livings over the same period. The Phelps Brown index, designed with building workers rather than incumbents in mind, shows an increase of 331 per cent between the 1530s and 1650s. This suggests that a substantial section of the parish clergy were able to survive inflation quite comfortably.[18] It is likely, however, that if detailed figures were available for the sixteenth century, they would show a less sharp increase in the value of livings. Until well into Elizabeth's reign, indeed perhaps until after the bad harvest decade of the 1590s, the parochial clergy suffered from problems which must have made the improvement of their revenue very difficult. In the 1580s Whitgift alleged that almost all the clergy were overtaxed by the 1535 valuation, except for a few rectories and 'here are not many undervalued, all things considered: and the best in every place are in lease to temporal men for many years'.[19] The increase in leasing seems to have been one of the major problems of Elizabeth's reign. The length of leases became extended as the reign progressed. This was but a part of that process of lay involvement in the church which is a central theme of Christopher Hill's *Economic Problems of the Church*. As impropriators and particularly as farmers the laity were making it more difficult for the clergy to counter inflation and it was frequently they, rather than the clergy, who were involved in litigation with parishioners to extract the full economic value of the tithe.

The more fortunate higher clergy were able to maintain their income with difficulty. Most individuals did this by accumulating pluralities, possible even after the statute of 1529. The bishops were debarred from holding benefices in plurality but even they could rely upon being given livings *in commendam* by the Crown if their financial plight became too serious. A few corporations and individuals tried to improve their position by a more vigorous policy as landlords. Richard Cox of Ely and Edwin Sandys of York both tried to extend their home farms and sell surplus produce on the market, but fell into conflict with the local laity because of their aggressive policies. The archbishops of Canterbury under Elizabeth more slowly and cautiously began to take rents in kind again – grain and meat proved to be useful hedges against inflation.[20] Of the groups so far studied, however, only the dean and chapter of Durham were apparently outstandingly successful in countering rising food prices. The prebendaries managed to find technical deficiencies in several of the long leases of central demesne or 'corpes' lands. By this device the dean and a number of the prebendaries were able to resume possession of considerable tracts of land and farm them, or lease them for very short periods only.[21] This foreshadows the policy attempted more widely under Laud, but few of the Elizabethan higher clergy had the courage, energy, or luck to follow Durham's example.

Most of the bishops suffered in some degree from the fixity of rents and the difficulty of improving their income. Their letters of complaint are scattered through the Elizabethan state papers, although they were probably by Elizabeth's reign more secure and better able to increase their revenue than they had been during the mid-Tudor years. The new sees founded by Henry V I I I were often the worst sufferers: Chester, for example, had been given an endowment of little more than £300 in the 1540s, and its bishops gave such lands and rectories as it held in long lease to gain local influence.[22] Such a see had very little chance of remaining unencumbered by debt in an inflationary century.

Inflation was probably responsible for the most fundamental economic problems of the sixteenth-century clergy but it was the appearance of an assertive and aggressive laity that often prevented them from countering the effects of the rise in prices. The Crown had had such a substantial role in the affairs of the church before the Reformation that the clergy could be forgiven for believing the rhetoric of liberty in the Reformation statutes, which suggested that the church would be more independent for the loss of the Pope. In reality the 1530s saw a great increase in royal demands upon the church, for now its property was at the full disposal of the supreme head of the church. Taxation was no longer granted by favour of Convocation but was taken as the right of the Crown. The first fruit and tenths legislation brought within the sphere of direct royal taxation almost all parish clergy, and was a totally new tax for all except the wealthy clergy who had previously had to pay common services and annates to Rome. From the 1540s onwards further sums were raised from the church, as the Crown regularly asked for subsidy as well as the fixed tenth. As William Harrison complained in Elizabeth's reign, the payments of the clergy were 'certain, continual and seldom abated . . .'.[23] For the parish clergy the new powers of the Crown in economic affairs meant primarily this claim to increase taxes: in the 1530s many of the seditious comments for which the clergy were reported to Cromwell focused upon the Crown's fiscal demands and, as late as the reign of James I, resentment at the inequality between lay and clerical taxation was often voiced by ecclesiastical writers.

For the higher clergy, the Crown posed a threat to their whole estate and position within society. The practice of the Tudor monarchs and their advisers varied considerably from the authoritarian paternalism of Henry VIII, through the frank exploitation of the duke of Somerset, to the circumspect but still assertive attitude of Elizabeth. The monarchs all agreed that the Crown had the right to dispose of the lands of the clergy as it wished, however. The basic position had been enunciated in the 1530s: 'The clergy have submitted to the King, from whom they have immediately jurisdiction and goods . . . and have acknowledged that without his assent and confirmation they could pretend none other'.[24] Only Mary and, later, James I demurred: Mary for religious reasons; James because the continual demands upon the church brought the whole hierarchy into disrepute. The monarchy was, in its turn, constantly subjected to the demands of aristocracy and others for land and patronage and only in the golden age of monastic appropriation had the Crown the land and resources to satisfy these lay demands. Both Henry VIII and Elizabeth tried to have the best of all worlds by using church lands as a source of patronage while appearing to do justice to the bishops and cathedral clergy by maintaining their nominal income with exchanges. In 1559 Elizabeth formalised the idea in a statute which allowed the Crown to take manors from the bishops, giving in exchange the equivalent value in spiritual revenues. Since many of the lands given to the Crown under this statute were on long lease, and would have brought the Elizabethan bishops a fixed income anyway, the transactions were often not seriously inequitable in the short term. Nevertheless, the Jacobean bishops had every reason to bemoan the loss of these potentially valuable lands.

Yet the major damage inflicted by the Crown upon the clergy was psychological rather than purely financial. Constant changes of religious policy and the Crown's failure to support the clergy against the laity created a climate of insecurity which lasted for most of the sixteenth century. This insecurity, combined with the inflationary pressures of the mid-century, led to a sharp decline in the number of men receiving orders. It was this failure of recruitment which made the problems of poor cures and inadequately paid assistants so urgent by the early Elizabethan period.

The ambivalence of legislative policy added to the insecurity of the parish clergy. While most legislation sanctioned by the Crown professed to clarify the rights of the clergy, there was a tendency for customary rights to be defined away by statute. This is nowhere more marked than in the Tithe Act of 1549, which redefined the method of levying predial and personal tithe and abolished the oath as a means of examining tithe defaulters. This is an unusually marked instance of discrimination against the clergy and legislation was sometimes used to uphold the shaky power of the church, especially under Elizabeth. On the other hand, any proposals for major adjustment of the *status quo* in favour of the clergy met with little favour from Crown or laity before the reign of Charles I. Schemes for the augmentation of poor livings, such as those put forward in 1540 and 1563, had no chance of success: only Mary took some genuine initiative towards improving the economic situation of the clergy when she returned Crown impropriations to the bishops at the very end of her reign.[25]

The bishops and cathedral clergy were particularly vulnerable in this climate of insecurity, since the Crown gave no official discouragement to a host of plans to put their lands to better use. Social reformers, advocates of a stronger monarchy, and those with a purely mercenary motive, all expected the Crown to complete in the secular church the work it had begun in the monasteries. This expectation rose to fever pitch in the 1530s, towards the end of Henry VIII's reign, and again towards the end of that of Edward VI. Even in the relative calm of Elizabeth's reign speculation continued and schemes for appropriation were revived during the financially difficult years of the Spanish war. Doubts about the Crown's intentions left the bishops unwilling to invest seriously in their lands or plan policies

with the future profits of their sees in mind. Those bishops who took
no principled stand against alienation and who acceded to lay
demands were merely responding to this atmosphere and taking what
profit they could. Even those who resisted royal demands found it
difficult to formulate an acceptable theory of opposition, because
almost all of them upheld the idea of the royal supremacy. The most
effective argument was that an identity of interests between Crown
and clergy meant that the latter should remain economically strong
in order to support the former. It is an argument normally associated
with the Arminian wing of the church and, certainly, Charles I was
the first monarch wholly to support it. Yet it occurs in the writing of
the bishops throughout the post-Reformation period and it found
strong proponents among Elizabeth's first generation of bishops.
Richard Cox, for example, in opposing the legislation for the exchange of bishops' lands argued 'when the bishops' lands are gone,
the Kings and Queens of this realm shall never have such present
relief anywhere else, as they may have of the bishops, if need should
require'.[26] Church lands were too valuable a source of patronage for
the Crown to grant the bishops formal security in their lands in the
sixteenth century. Elizabeth, indeed, developed the insecurity of her
bishops to a fine pitch. Only after James I placed a positive prohibi-
tion on the alienation of episcopal lands in 1604 could the bishops
begin to plan seriously to improve the economic situation of their
sees.

While the Crown certainly had positive views upon the uses to
which church wealth could be put, it was often cast merely in the role
of adjudicator between the rival interests of church and laity. When
the Crown was weak, especially under Edward VI, laymen found it
relatively easy to invade the wealth and privileges of the church. At
every level the laity increased their economic influence: as purchasers
of monastic appropriations; as farmers of benefices; and as lessees of
episcopal land. Of course there had been farmers of benefices, and
lay tenants of the bishops, long before the Reformation but,
thereafter, it is the laity who often assume the dominant role in the
economic affairs of the clergy. An increasing number of lay farmers
brought tithe litigation in the mid-sixteenth century. In York
between 1540 and 1560 76 per cent of tithe causes involved a lay
farmer or impropriator, as compared with the 16 per cent involving a
farmer between 1500 and 1540.[27] Such lay involvement with church
lands required little theoretical justification and must not be con-

founded with feelings of anticlericialism. Many laymen must have felt as did Michael Sherburne's father, who justified his profit from the local abbey, whose spiritual services he had valued, by saying, 'might I not as well as others have some profit of the spoil of the abbey? For I did see all would away and therefore I did as others did'.[28] The impropriated rectory became strictly a piece of property. The simple desire for increased property rights and profits became entangled with the puritans' wish to control benefices in order to promote godly preaching. In the early seventeenth century, therefore, puritan piety and incursions upon church property and rights often went hand in hand. For the sixteenth century the equation is less obvious: perhaps a more familiar pattern until the later years of Elizabeth's reign was for the reforming clergy to be defending the wealth of the church against the theologically neutral demands of Crown and laity alike. For many of the Protestant clergy church wealth was a means to an end – the nurturing of education and the encouragement of learned preachers.

In the midst of these demands from Crown and laity, and in a period of unprecedented inflation, the church was expected both to maintain its traditional role in society and to adapt to the new standards of the Reformation. The success of its endeavours cannot easily be evaluated objectively – least of all in a society polarised by religious differences. The activities of the bishops as a group are the best documented and it was they who were often most criticised by contemporaries from diverse standpoints. The conception of the functions of a bishop underwent surprisingly little modification even in the reforming years of Edward and Elizabeth. Despite a diminished real income, the bishops were expected to play an important part in local politics, and offer generous hospitality, in addition to all their spiritual obligations. Some of the more radical prelates, such as Latimer and Hooper, did indeed try to give these duties a Protestant emphasis by offering hospitality primarily to the needy and using their manors as centres for preaching campaigns and clerical supervision. The influential laity and many of the bishops themselves, however, saw the first social function of the prelate to be the provision of a focus of hospitality and political stability in the locality. The Reformation tended to reinforce this concept because few of the bishops were detained in London upon government business for long periods and because the married Elizabethan or Jacobean prelate had a stronger interest in placing his own family among the gentry than had his unmarried predecessors. Criticism of episcopal families often arose not from resentment at such attempts to insinuate them into county society but from a feeling that some bishops neglected their political and social duties to amass profits for their children. Sandys and Cox were both charged with such neglect, while a bishop such as Martin Heaton of Ely, who did remarkably little for the church, won laurels after his death for his hospitality. The bishop of Rochester proudly boasted in the 1590s that, although he had to spend three-quarters of his net income on food and drink, he kept 'as good a table as any in England, excepting that which is prodigal'.[29]

The parish clergy were also preoccupied with the issue of hospitality. Visitation articles of the late sixteenth century often enquire what provision clergy had made for hospitality: even in a period of extreme difficulty in the early 1560s, Parker thought it worthwhile to enquire of his diocesans whether hospitality was kept in the parishes.[30] This concern may be seen as part of a wider attempt by the clergy to justify their remaining economic power. Yet as the duties of charity and hospitality were also enjoined upon the laity, some other justification had to be sought. This lay in the argument that the wealth of the church, through their actions, could be used for the support of learning, the universities and hence godly preaching. This was already a traditional duty of the bishops and the emphasis upon it had been greatly reinforced by the humanist prelates under Henry VII and Henry VIII. To the humanist idea that there should be a large group of educated and articulate clergy to serve church and state the Protestants added their urgent emphasis upon biblical exegesis. It became generally accepted that a degree was the necessary basis upon which the Protestant cleric should build. This notion had far-reaching implications: it meant not only more provision for potential clerics in the universities but also the provision of adequate financial rewards for their long training. The most that the bishops could do was finance some university students. Few, however, could do as Matthew Parker did – he gave at least £2500 to Cambridge.[31] A far more radical readjustment was needed than could be provided by the surplus wealth of the bishops.

By the Elizabethan period sections of the laity were echoing this demand for a preaching, Protestant ministry, particularly in urban centres and in counties such as Northamptonshire. Yet the economic and institutional arrangements of the church made it almost impossible to answer the demand at parish level. William Harrison estimated that at least £30 was necessary for the support of a learned minister, and the figure must have increased steadily until the end of James I's reign. Ralph Josselin expected £80 from the Earl's Colne congregation in the early seventeenth century.[32] A preaching minister had to be resident and it was, therefore, the ideal of the puritan to abolish pluralism and non-residence. This was the ultimate ideal of the bishops also, but Whitgift was not alone in seeing puritan demands for the abolition of plurality as a threat to orthodox learning in the church. Such abolition, he argued in 1584, would discourage 'the best sort of the clergy' and encourage the factious to take livings. If one accepts the figures quoted by Harrison and Josselin, there must have been only a minority of benefices, perhaps between a quarter and a third of all livings in the country, that could support a graduate of their own, and a number of these would still have been occupied by non-resident pluralists. The puritans argued passionately that the bishops could help the situation by augmenting their impropriated benefices or, preferably, by surrendering all their endowments to a fund for support of learned ministers and by receiving in return a salary for honest maintenance.

By the late sixteenth century the argument between bishops and puritans was often expressed in terms of economic issues and particularly of the inadequacy of parochial livings, but it was by then an ideological conflict first and foremost. Neither side was able or willing to effect the massive alienation of property rights necessary to place the majority of parishes in a prosperous economic position. Moreover, the failure to attract enough learned men to the parishes must be attributed largely to factors other than financial difficulties. While the stability and survival of the English church was in question, which it was at least until the 1570s, there was little incentive for graduates to enter the church at this level. In this sense Elizabeth, by her very survival and by her largely successful attempt to maintain political stability, did more for the improvement of the church than many of her vocal puritan critics. In the late sixteenth century the financial lure of some rectories and vicarages probably helped to attract more graduates into the church. A few years later, at the end of James I's reign, the pattern had shifted again and a degree had become an almost automatic qualification for ordinands. A penalty for this development was, as Christopher Hill has shown, an increase in plurality in some areas, as graduates were unwilling to make do with the poor financial rewards of their parishes. As Rosemary O'Day has suggested, however, it is by no means clear that the scale of the economic expectations of graduates was much different from that of their non-graduate forebears.[33]

Promotion at parochial level still depended far more upon patronage than upon suitable educational qualifications. All too often there was justification in the puritan complaint that good livings were filled by men who had neither the capacity nor the interest to perform the cure of souls and instruct the people. But by the early seventeenth century social expectations had shifted so markedly that such men had to lay claim to a degree. At the other extreme were men who offered the full Protestant ministry in poor parishes. The case of Richard Greenham, the learned puritan divine, who spent most of his life ministering to the poor and unrewarding parish of Dry Drayton, Cambridgeshire, is a good example of the lack of correlation between good ministry and adequate parochial endowment.

It is perhaps less easy to say what the ordinary laymen expected of the clergy in the early seventeenth century as opposed to the early sixteenth century. The interest in expository preaching was certainly widespread and, in those parts of the country most influenced by puritanism, was seen as the key part of a minister's activity. Yet the older concept of the cleric as part of the community, providing the rites of passage and regular Sunday prayer and worship for parishioners, continued alongside and intermingled with the newer ideal. It was in this context that such customary socio-economic duties as the provision of hospitality, the care of the poor, and the maintenance of church fabric remained a key part of the minister's job. Visitation returns, particularly for rural areas, remained preoccupied with these traditional duties, even when the articles of enquiry gave priority to the issue of preaching. The emphasis which Christopher Hill places upon the dynamic urban and 'bourgeois' values of late sixteenth-century and early seventeenth-century society tends to underestimate these traditional priorities, which still played a major part in the predominantly agrarian society.

The clergy were faced with one very serious economic problem: the English government had not made the fully Protestant change to an expository ministry, financed by the congregation directly, and with economic responsibilities which were commensurate with the salaries. Instead the traditional system of finance continued and with it many of the customary expectations, which inflation, lay intrusions and clerical marriage made it more difficult to fulfil.

6. The Disposal of Monastic and Chantry Lands

CHRISTOPHER KITCHING

THOMAS FULLER'S *Church History of Britain,* published in 1655, contained a section on the dissolution of the monasteries dedicated to William Compton whose ancestor, Sir William, though chief gentlemen of the bed-chamber to Henry VIII, was among the courtiers who had received no monastic lands. Fuller therefore felt that Compton's descendants were among the few persons of any standing in his day who might 'wash their hands in the same basin to have no abbey lands sticking to their fingers'.

Until late in the nineteenth century historians commonly believed that there was little to be said about the disposal of the monastic lands. It was considered a sin or a crime on the part of Henry VIII and those who had benefited at the expense of the church. 'Spoliation', 'pillage' and 'sacrilege' were the words most frequently employed in discussing the matter; it was deemed self-evident that the nobility and gentry close to the court had received handsome bargains in land through Henry's largesse and that as far as the nation at large was concerned little benefit had resulted. Few of his contemporaries would have disagreed with Abbot Gasquet that 'the greater portion passed out of royal possession without serving any useful purpose whatever'.

As long as historians and antiquarians drew their inspiration from established oral traditions about the fate of the lands, from a few easily accessible documents and, particularly, from ruined monastic sites, no different interpretation was possible. Margaret Aston has recently shown (1973) the impact of the ruins themselves on men's view of history over several centuries. But a fundamental mistake had been made in historical method: sweeping generalisations had been based on what later turned out to be only a small part of the evidence.

For Notes to Chapter 6, see pp. 195–7; for Bibliographical Notes (including details of works referred to by publication date in this chapter), see pp. 184–5.

More recent approaches to the subject reflect the growing sophistication of historical method at large: the quest for further source materials; the analysis of old sources in new ways; the attempt to apply techniques from other disciplines (such as mathematics and statistics); the regular reshaping of historical consensus on the issues raised and a developing awareness of their complexity.

Our field of study may instructively be compared with an archaeological site. For generations men were satisfied with established tradition as to its nature and content and a few pieces of evidence found near the surface were enough to confirm their beliefs. But in the past century or so successive specialists have cut cross-sections through parts of the site, from differing angles, and reported their findings. Each in turn felt that his own cross-section might hold the clue to the real nature of the site as a whole, only to discover later that the next man's findings in some respects modified or contradicted his own. This model is also valid in other respects: for instance, some of the evidence no longer survives and some of it is buried so deep that it may never be unearthed. The final report has yet to be written but we already have a formidable amount of analysis before us to warn that there is no simple answer to most of the questions we should like to ask and that we can only begin to understand the whole 'site' by noting the angle and limits of some of the cross-sections.

Accordingly, the first part of this essay examines some of the 'excavations' that have been made and draws attention to certain weaknesses inherent in them. No attempt is made to recount the chronology of the dissolutions or to analyse the political background. The facts and figures for the monastic lands should be sought in the admirable works of A. G. Dickens, David Knowles, G. O. Woodward and Joyce Youings which are mentioned in the accompanying bibliography. We shall have space here only to note some of the methods used by historians and the way in which the study has developed. The second part of the essay introduces the question of the disposal of collegiate and chantry property which, as we shall see, is rather a different field.

I

Only towards the end of the nineteenth century did historians really become aware of the wealth of surviving evidence on the disposal of the monastic lands. The way was prepared by publications of the Record Commission, especially *Valor Ecclesiasticus*;[1] by the establishment of the Public Record Office (which led to the centralisation and classification of the historic records of government departments); and by the publication of surveys such as the Deputy Keepers' Reports and calendars like the *Letters and Papers* of the reign of Henry VIII. There was too much material here for any one scholar to master, producing a definitive monograph on the monastic lands which would not be overtaken by subsequent research. But a start had to be made somewhere and, although W. A. J. Archbold was one of the first in the field with his *The Somerset Religious Houses* (Cambridge 1892), it was the work of foreign scholars that had the most formative influence on later research.

A. Savine of Moscow university produced a masterly study of *Valor Ecclesiasticus* (1909) and went on to examine the letters patent by which the Crown granted away many of the lands. His research at once demonstrated that the accepted tradition was wrong: much of the land had been *sold* by Henry VIII or exchanged for other plots then in private hands. Much less had been given away than earlier scholars had assumed. Other writers have gone on to show that good prices were paid for most of the lands sold; that sales began in earnest after the fall of Cromwell and accelerated from 1543 as warfare made increasing inroads into revenue. It is now accepted that even much that was given away was 'earned by public or personal service, or by private expenditure on government business'.[2]

The patents were also used by Savine and by the Swedish scholar S. B. Liljegren (1924) to determine who received the lands and to categorise them by class. Savine's figures passed into historical canon through H. A. L. Fisher's *History of England* but they have been challenged by subsequent commentators.[3] Even if we accept their mathematical validity, they present only a vague picture, for the status of over half the recipients – men who paid some 45 per cent of the total for purchases – was unidentifiable. A more important reservation is that later scholars have shown that the patents cannot be used on their own; they have to be supplemented from other sources if we are to obtain an accurate picture.

Joyce Youings (1954) and H. J. Habakkuk (1958) dug deeper, studying the particulars for grant which preceded the issue of a patent, containing valuation of the lands by a local Crown official. They demonstrated (as others who had previously used the particulars had failed to demonstrate) that the patentees who actually paid over the money to the Crown were often no more than London agents acting on behalf of clients in the country. This opened up a new discussion on the profits of such middlemen and whether any of them could rightly be described as speculators. Few firm conclusions are possible on this last point because the documents by which they conveyed their interest in the properties to their clients rarely state the sums paid, sometimes cloak them under a vague term such as '*pro quadam competenti pecuniae summa*', or merely repeat the price mentioned in the patent itself, which does not preclude a separate, unrecorded fee or commission. As a result of these studies it became apparent that tracing the actual purchaser was much more complex than Savine, by analysing only one documentary stratum, had supposed.

Given this new understanding of the evidence, it was clear that scholars had to work on selected regions, attempting to assimilate every layer of evidence, rather than hope to cover the whole country. Joyce Youings's pioneering studies in the disposal of monastic lands in Devon have inspired other regional projects on individual counties and townships. But A. G. Dickens and, indeed, Joyce Youings herself in her more recent work have pointed out some of the considerable regional variations in the findings, which make it dangerous to rely too heavily on figures produced for any one area.[4] A vertical specialisation (by area), then, has almost as many pitfalls as a horizontal one (by type of document). Yet without such studies we should never get any nearer to our final report on the impact of the dissolution on English society.

Historians are now agreed that most of the land disposed of by Henry VIII went to persons already well placed in the social or governmental hierarchy. Most of the nobility, including the dukes of Norfolk and Suffolk and Lords Russell and Clinton, acquired lands by gift, exchange or purchase. But the majority of sales were made to gentry, courtiers, Crown officials, lawyers and townsmen, many of whom already had strong local connections. Prominent among them were figures of national as well as local importance: Sir Richard Southwell in Norfolk; Sir Richard Grenville and Sir William Petre in Devon; Sir Thomas Heneage in Lincolnshire. But many others whose names are less frequently encountered in the pages of national history are represented too, as the local studies have shown. It is likely that men who already had the spending power would soon have deployed their assets in some similar investment even without the dissolution which, however, must have speeded up the process, perhaps giving an especial boost to younger sons who could not expect to inherit family estates. For some, receipt of the land was the clinching factor which raised their social status and responsibility by turning them into lords of the manor or enabling them to become J.P.s. But for others, similar purchases in the private land market could equally well achieve the same result, and we have no reason to suppose the monastic lands peculiarly beneficial in this respect.

In an important local study, J. E. Kew has recently shown that, at least in Devon, there were more dealings in the private land market, in terms of both the numbers of transactions and the amount of land changing hands, than in the Crown land market following the dissolution.[5] If this was so over the whole country it would further minimise the special role of the dissolution in affecting the social balance. Kew's work shows that we may not view the dissolution in isolation from other economic and social developments. Returning to our archaeological analogy, there might well be important evidence over the hedge in an adjacent site!

A similar warning against regarding the dissolution in isolation has often been sounded by those who have studied the pattern of land tenure at earlier dates.[6] The monasteries themselves had already leased a good deal of land to laymen, many of whom acted as stewards or other officials of monastic manors, thus being favourably placed to acquire control of the lands when they came on the market after the dissolution. This was another factor which minimised the resulting social change.

The Act in Restraint of Appeals (24 Henry VIII, c. 12) stated that 'the King's most noble progenitors and the antecessors of the nobles of this realm' were those who had endowed the church with honour and possessions. But after the dissolution there was, despite arguments in its favour, no planned redistribution of wealth favouring the nobility over other classes. Except in the case of the Crown itself, which took care to protect its own interests and those of its foundations, founders generally received no free gift of the property they or their ancestors had given. They had to acquire leases or buy the lands back, sometimes in competition with others.[7] A few men of humble status were even able to buy or lease plots in which they had been the sitting tenants, though this was not the norm, the freehold usually being disposed of over their heads to wealthier men.[8]

Historians discussing the rise of the gentry or the 'crisis of the aristocracy' have differed widely in their interpretation of factors affecting mobility within and between classes and even in identifying the component parts of a given class. But it is generally agreed that such processes can only be safely studied over a long time-scale, taking as many individual examples into account as possible. In so far as mobility was affected by the ownership of lands at all, developments subsequent to the dissolution of the monasteries seem to be more important than the dissolution itself: the resumption of lands by attainder; the impact of price inflation; the later sales of Crown lands; the development of estate management techniques and so on. The pioneer in this neighbouring field, R. H. Tawney, observed that 'the first fruits of confiscation do not always rest where they first light',[9] but few studies in the disposal of monastic lands have continued beyond the year 1558, nor have studies of the later sales of Crown lands singled out former monastic lands for attention.[10] The long-term effects of the dissolution have, therefore, not been systematically explored. The broadest view of land-ownership has been taken by F. M. L. Thompson, who suggests that if one thinks of 'great estates' rather than concepts such as the 'aristocracy' or 'gentry' one can detect a general trend towards consolidation of property in the hands of a few owners from the sixteenth down to the eighteenth century.[11]

The importance of local studies in correcting data drawn solely from records of the central government machine has been repeatedly demonstrated. The American scholar F. C. Dietz concentrated on the central records of the treasurer of Augmentations, notably the receipts for the sale of monastic lands, comparing them with Crown revenue from other sources.[12] His figures give a clear idea of the magnitude of the operation and prove conclusively that it was only the profits of the dissolution which enabled the Crown to pursue its expensive foreign policy without imposing crippling taxation. (Ironically, the absence of extra taxation was only an intangible benefit compared with, say, expenditure on schools, poor relief or public works which could have been seen and understood by all. The complaints of social reformers that the monastic assets had been squandered all too easily passed into popular tradition. The records tell another story.) But we should not place too much credence in the mathematical precision of Dietz's central figures. Joyce Youings has pointed out that local officers of the Court of Augmentations might, with due authority from the centre, spend money on the spot which, therefore, never saw its way into central books such as Dietz used.[13] Only an intensive study of local records like the yearly accounts of the bailiffs (ministers) and receivers would allow us to assess the real cost or, indeed, the real profit to the Crown from the disposal of the lands and movable goods. These records have been surprisingly neglected so far by historians.[14]

Even the important *History of the Court of Augmentations* (1961) by another American, W. C. Richardson, fails to come to terms with these subsidiary, local documents. It describes the administrative machinery by which the Crown accomplished the dissolution, passed grants and leases, drew revenue from the properties which it did not at once sell off, and coped with the flood of resulting litigation. Of the work of bailiffs, receivers, surveyors and auditors little is said in detail. Here again, it is the work of Joyce Youings which makes up for much of this deficiency, especially by describing the duties of the local officers.[15] But we still know only too little about the regional offices of the auditors, the venue of the audit, the cost of so many officials travelling about the counties and up to London to present their reports. A great number of receipts and vouchers survive from which some of this story might be reconstructed, together with letters and papers of regional officers like Clement Throckmorton and Thomas and Walter Mildmay. At present, however, many of these are buried deep in classes of document only partially listed or bearing descriptions such as 'miscellaneous' or 'subsidiary', and they must, therefore, be reckoned among the evidence which it is most difficult to retrieve.[16] Even a random dip into this stratum of material is enough to show that the dissolution was difficult to administer locally, that the officers frequently found it impossible to come to terms with the terrain allotted to them, or made mistakes in book-keeping, and that a variety of excuses was offered for non-payment of rents by those who should have handed over money to the Crown after the dissolution. These and similar factors go a long way towards explaining why the concealment of lands and revenues from the Crown was so widespread.[17]

A better acquaintance with the ministers' and receivers' accounts at an earlier stage in the analysis of the disposal of the lands would also have broken historians of the habit of foreshortening the time-scale of their studies. The ministers' accounts for revenue received from former monastic lands in Lincolnshire and Yorkshire were still sufficiently large even in the reign of Charles I to justify entry on account rolls separate from those for other Crown lands.[18] Rentals, surveys and views of account among the records of the Augmentation Office of the Exchequer and the auditors of the land revenue confirm that monastic lands occupied a good deal of attention well into the seventeenth century,[19] and we shall see that the same was true of chantry lands. In addition, local studies have shown that many choice sites remained in Crown hands long after the dissolution, often being leased at first and only sold much later. The Middlesex lands of Syon abbey, for instance, were leased by Henry VIII; under Edward VI they were granted to Somerset but on his fall they were resumed by the Crown which then retained the freehold until 1604 when it was finally granted to the earl of Northumberland. The humbler site of Burnham abbey remained Crown property until 1834.[20] The Crown did not dispatch its choicest properties as quickly as has sometimes been supposed. Even if estimates are correct that only between a third and a half of the monastic estates remained in Crown hands at the death of Henry VIII, this still represented a considerable increase in the Crown's landed holdings compared with those before the dissolution, which had in themselves been quite difficult to administer efficiently. The estates which Henry did not sell were not unattractive property which nobody wanted to purchase. Indeed, they formed the reserve of land from which many of the later sales by Edward and Elizabeth were made. The full impact of the dissolution on English government and administration cannot be ascertained from studies confined to the reign of Henry VIII, not can the impact on English society be fully understood without taking into account later sales and the leases by which so much of the property was held until well after the reign of Henry VIII. Only recently have scholars begun to extend their horizons in these directions and little of their work has yet been published.

A further respect in which our time-scale may need to be extended is in the study of resulting litigation. It was not to be expected that the greatest simultaneous transfer of property ownership in England since the Norman conquest would be achieved without complicated legal disputes over the claims of individuals to property, tithe, advowsons and other rights associated with the dissolved institutions. Many thousands of tenants suddenly found that they had a new landlord. Disputes arose between tenant and landlord and between new landlord and Crown. The records of litigation subsequent to the dissolution have not yet been fully appraised.

Some disputes arose over the terms of leases granted by the monasteries on the eve of the dissolution, yet it could be many years before a long lease became the cause of friction or litigation. For instance, at the very end of the sixteenth century the Exchequer was asked to determine whether a lease granted by Syon abbey was valid or not. A glance through the special commissions of the Exchequer in Elizabeth's reign shows that a fair percentage of cases were still trying to unscramble claims associated with the former monastic lands.[21] Even into the eighteenth century there were recurring disputes over tithe on such lands.

But the further away we get in date from the dissolution, the more difficult it is to see whether the cases have anything to do directly with the Crown's confiscation of the lands or whether external factors are more important, such as clashes of temperament between landlord and tenants or attempts by landlords to keep pace with inflation by raising rents or cutting down the tenants' former privileges. Three decades after the dissolution a dispute arose between tenants on Burnham abbey's former estates in Buckinghamshire and the Crown's then lessee, Peter Wentworth.[22] The tenants claimed pannage for their swine in Abbess Wood, which Wentworth denied them despite the fact that the previous lessee, William Tildesley, who had just died, seems to have given them the benefit of the doubt. It is not clear whether Wentworth was trying to cut back tenants' privileges and charge them for what had previously been a free right or whether the tenants were taking the opportunity of the granting of a new lease to claim rights which they had never freely exercised, though the balance of the evidence points in the latter direction. Vague though the outcome is, the case illustrates the tensions which might arise with a change of landlord. And since the tenants were asked to state what had been their rights under the abbesses, their depositions are also instructive in showing that the memory of the monasteries might be revived after many years and their regime compared favourably with what had followed. The tenants said that 'in the life of two of the late abbesses [they] were never interrupted of their said common'. Of such reflections legends were born about the sympathetic role of the religious as landlords, many of which have been doubted by modern scholars. Recent historians have also observed that, by being dissolved when they were, the monasteries escaped the worst of the inflation in the sixteenth century; it was the landlords who succeeded them who bore the brunt of the unpopularity resulting from increased rents and improvements such as enclosures.

Much more could be said on the methods employed by historians in studying the disposal of monastic lands, not least about the mathematics of the exercise, which raise important questions of procedure (for example, whether to assess purchases by the prices paid, the number of manors involved, the number of grants, the modern equivalent valuation, and so on). To this we shall briefly return when discussing the chantries. But the general conclusion which may be drawn from all we have seen so far is that we must not be misled into thinking that small samples of the surviving evidence are necessarily typical of the whole. More studies, local and central, are still needed. More evidence is still to be quarried and there may be valuable clues also in neighbouring fields. Above all, we must not select too short a time-scale for our studies.

II

The disposal of collegiate and chantry land has attracted nowhere near as much attention from historians as has that of the monastic lands. Yet the net value of these and similiar endowments surrendered or confiscated under Henry VIII and Edward VI has been estimated at about a quarter that of the monasteries: no negligible sum.

The buildings of many colleges survived as parish churches. Chantries frequently had no separate chapels of their own but were founded at altars within existing buildings. Even where chantry chapels had been added to parish churches, their demolition was rarely insisted upon at the dissolution. The free chapels which were pulled down at this time were for the most part humble buildings. Taking all this into account, we can see that there were few spectacular ruins left in the wake of the dissolutions, which no doubt helps to explain much of the scholarly neglect of the subject. It was for long treated as a mere footnote to the dissolution of the monasteries: another example of officially sponsored pillage. And because there had been specific promises under Edward VI that proceeds from the dissolutions would be put to educational and charitable uses, those who did interest themselves in the disposal of the lands were especially concerned with what happened to schools, poor relief and public works as a result of the removal of the endowments, rather than with what became of the lands themselves, and what effect their disposal had on English society.

No monograph has yet been published on this aspect of the dissolution of the chantries, though it has recently received much attention from W. K. Jordan (1968, 1970) in his work on the reign of Edward VI. Very few samplings have been made of the evidence for individual counties. Perhaps it has been generally assumed that the lands were disposed of to much the same persons as had received the monastic spoils and that nothing more needed saying. In a recent essay on church lands even Joyce Youings failed to mention the chantries.[23]

Scholars have also steered clear of these smaller institutions because the endowments were mainly quite different from those of the monasteries, consisting of tiny, scattered plots of land and a large number of annuities and free rents. These are more difficult to trace through the various documentary stages of sale or lease than the compact monastic estates.

We do not even know with any certainty how many institutions were dissolved, nor what was their total value: all the totals quoted in standard works on the subject are estimates which must be treated with caution (though they doubtless give a reasonable idea of the magnitude of the operation). This is primarily due to defects in the source materials. No document similar to the *Valor Ecclesiasticus* was compiled for these foundations. The *Valor* itself is both too limited in scope and too remote in date to help us significantly in assessing which ones had survived until 1546 or 1548. Many chantries never paid tenths and were, therefore, not recorded in the *Valor*. Besides, there were a host of short-term endowments for prayers in the 1530s and 40s after its compilation. Yet, unfortunately, the figures most often quoted (90 colleges, 2374 chantries, 110 hospitals) are based on the *Valor*, and this results in a considerable underestimate of the number of foundations dissolved.[24] The chantry certificates of 1546 and 1548, which recorded the known institutions parish by parish, and many of which have been published by local record societies, are all worth reading but they are sadly incomplete. It is only by supplementing the picture from other sources, such as the ministers' accounts after the dissolution, or returns to Augmentations and Exchequer commissions investigating claims and counter-claims to exemption from the terms of the dissolution statute, that we can discover the total number of institutions involved. This has not yet been done for the country as a whole; and, since the work is both long and tedious even for a single county, it is possible that it may never be attempted on a large scale. We know quite enough, however, to say that in some measure every parish throughout the country must have been affected by the removal of these endowments. Prayers for the dead, donations for the benefit of their souls, and all the related ceremonial ceased to be part of the English way of life. The impact must have been more direct than that of the dissolution of the monasteries for most parishioners.

We need not here spend long in disproving earlier suppositions that chantry lands were squandered on courtiers. W. K. Jordan has shown that, even though the amount given back to charitable uses was not as high as social reformers of the age demand it was nevertheless not negligible.[25] Some errors of judgement were made in deciding which social amenities, allegedly provided by certain chantry endowments, ought to be allowed to continue. But townsmen who made a fuss in defence of their amenities, petitioning the Crown for protection, were often successful. Those of Lynn and Coventry fought the issue in Parliament but many others did so afterwards, like the townsmen of Beverley who defended their collegiate church against threats of demolition. Others who quietly accepted the dissolution perhaps had nothing significant to defend, for the general acquiescence does not suggest that the Crown misjudged popular requirements. Most old attempts by historians to prove that education and poor relief suffered were based on a far too rosy reading of the chantry certificates, for we know practically nothing about most of the 'schools' which certain chantry priests kept, and we have no proof that these men stopped teaching at the dissolution.[26] As for poor relief, the payments made to the poor at an obit were no more than a random dole, not a system whereby the truly indigent were aided. W. K. Jordan's study of charitable endowment after the dissolutions[27] suggests that none of these social amenities suffered in the long term; any temporary deficiency was soon more than made good by private or public benefactions.

It is true that during the reign of Edward VI more land was given away to loyal servants and supporters of those at court than was restored for charitable uses. But most of these free gifts consisted wholly or partly of monastic rather than chantry lands. In fact, the great majority of chantry land that was disposed of was sold or leased at realistic rates by commissioners under increasing pressure from successive governments to obtain good money quickly, especially for the war effort.

The State Papers and records of the treasurer of Augmentations amply testify to the sincerity of the government's repeated claims that it needed the money to defend the nation. They record in detail payments made to military commanders and their men, garrisons and works on a very distended front including Alderney, Portsmouth, the Isle of Wight, Dover, Calais, Boulogne, Berwick and Ireland.[28] There was also the sad necessity to curb rebellions at home, sparked off mainly by other government policies and by the opportunities afforded by the reign of a weak king. During the sale of chantry property in 1548, the treasurer kept the chantry account separate from that of other income and expenditure, perhaps so that he could readily explain how the profits had been spent. And whatever criticisms may be made of Northumberland's largesse later in the reign, the records show that there was no decline in the vigilance of the commissioners for sales in 1552 and 1553: prices were higher than in 1548; full payment for all purchases had to be made within twenty days of the sale; and all paper-work was checked and double-checked for errors.[29]

If chantry lands were not being squandered, we must treat with caution even so recent an appraisal as W. C. Richardson's that they went to 'greedy harpies at court', whereas the monastic lands, he thought, went to 'countless individuals who were shrewd enough to make the most of an advantageous market'.[30] It is very doubtful whether we can rightly make such a simple distinction between the motives of the two generations of purchasers.

The only attempt on a national scale to analyse the purchase of chantry lands is that by W. K. Jordan. But the mathematical basis of his discussion raises many questions. Translating all the figures into 'capital' sums by applying a multiplier of twenty to the yearly value confounds any attempt to compare his figures with those for the monasteries, augments twenty-fold any errors in the original figures, and is at best a rough and ready method of establishing true values. He himself admits that different properties were sold at widely differing rates during the reign. His conclusions on the distribution of the property by class after the dissolution are vitiated by his reliance solely on the patents to establish the identity of the grantees. As with the monastic property, the land might change hands four or five times, through various agents and middlemen, before it reached the end of the chain. We must, therefore, seek other evidence to correct and supplement what Jordan has been able to tell us.

When it was known that colleges and chantries were to be dissolved, there was a flood of enquiries from prospective purchasers, reminiscent of the letters to Cromwell about the monastic lands.

These requests were directed to Somerset, to other principal courtiers, to M.P.s and to officials of the Court of Augmentations. Many astute individuals, as well as a number of civic corporations looking out for specific properties, employed servants and agents to keep them informed of the prospects. Robert Swift, a servant of the earl of Shrewsbury, complained to his master that the commissioners for sale 'hold everything so dear'.[31] but he sent back information about Yorkshire chantry properties in which, as it transpired, Shrewsbury showed only a very modest interest. Thomas Chamberlain recommended Richard Pate of Lincoln's Inn to Lord Paget in case the latter wanted to buy any chantry property. Pate had been on the chantry commission for Gloucestershire and eventually, in league with Chamberlain, bought up a lot of Gloucester property, some of it for the corporation of Gloucester itself.[32] A complete list survives among the Cecil manuscripts at Hatfield of all those who bought through the patronage of Somerset.[33]

The particulars for grant often show the name of the person for whom the property was priced or 'rated'. Bundles of separate valuations, often rated for different people, were frequently stitched together and the properties passed under a single patent. We can discover by this means who was the second link in the chain between patentee and purchaser. When Sir Michael Stanhope and John Bellow, two Yorkshire officials of the Crown, obtained letters patent for chantry lands, their grants included properties in London and Westminster, Nottinghamshire and Yorkshire rated for Stanhope, and in Yorkshire for Bellow.[34] But in addition they bought land in nine counties rated for fourteen other men, including courtiers and officials but also some obscure provincial figures. This multiple purchase is typical of many others in which some of the 'ratees' are known only by name. Such grants channelled through one patent may have been officially encouraged, to speed sales and reduce clerical effort. A glance through the *Calendar of Patent Rolls* will show that there were many larger grants than this one.

If the particulars had not survived we should doubtless have assumed that the person named in the patent was the actual purchaser. But we have learnt to question this and we must go a stage further, having found the name of the ratee. The question then arises of where we should look for further transactions relating to any particular property. For the monastic lands this was comparatively easy: the larger estates were mainly held by knight service from the Crown and before a purchaser could sell again he had to obtain a licence to alienate. For chantry property this was rarely the case, for little of the land was valuable enough to be held by knight service.[35] If we are to succeed in tracing the descent of the property, therefore, everything depends on the survival of conveyances. Some such grants were enrolled on the close rolls in Chancery, some in King's Bench and some in Common Pleas, but most enrolments were doubtless made locally and the records have mainly now perished, save for a few surviving examples in collections of private deeds. This is a major obstacle, which means that we shall never know as much about the disposal of chantry lands as we do about monastic ones. But we can find some indications of what must have happened.

There were, of course, some desirable properties; sales in the early months were particularly brisk.[36] In London especially the opportunity arose for many to purchase a town house. Hot competition tended to push up the prices asked and another of Shrewsbury's agents reported that the sale of the city would be 'a great thing'.[37] Strangely enough, no study has yet been undertaken to see who bought up the London property and in what quantity, though the city livery companies bought back the tenements which had been confiscated from them because the rents had been put to 'superstitious uses'.[38] They continued to dispute the Crown's right to this property for half a century after the dissolution.

Despite reports of brisk trading, we should not assume that the Crown was quickly able to dispose of all the revenue, even of the London chantries, to eager buyers. A good deal of the total was derived not from real estate but from free rents or annuities payable as lump sums each year to the priest but giving him no right to any property. In such cases, the Crown only acquired at the dissolution the right to receive these yearly sums of money. Thus, when the best of the chantry property had been sold, the Crown was left with the plots that nobody wished to buy, a great many of which were rent charges, and had to continue administering them. So notorious did they become that the very term 'chantry rents' seems to have been used in the seventeenth century to describe all remaining income resulting from the sixteenth-century dissolutions whether monastic or chantry. As late as September 1660 a Crown official was still accounting yearly for the sum of £607 for London and Middlesex alone from these sources, noting that 'the chantry rents etc. lie dispersed throughout the whole city of London and county of

Middlesex, and consist of very small parcels, very troublesome in the collecting'.[39]

In the provinces too some of the choicest properties were quickly sold: prebendal mansions of the colleges and good town houses being among the more popular, along with some of the collegiate estates which were more akin to those of the monasteries. Most of these seem to have gone to the established local gentry and merchants, though they often acquired only small, individual sites. There was not the same desire to amass large quantities of this sort of land.

Bulk purchases were common for the movable goods of the chantries, which were then presumably sold off locally at a profit. For example, Edward Pease bought up all those for Derbyshire and Robert Waller those of Nottinghamshire.[40]

W. K. Jordan tells us that by the end of Edward's reign only the 'debris' of chantry property was left in Crown hands.[41] This assertion is apparently based on his own calculations, whose reliability is challenged above. The ministers' and receivers' accounts of the Court of Augmentations appear to tell a rather different story, and merit further investigation. In an unpublished survey covering the Yorkshire and Nottinghamshire chantry lands it is concluded that no less than three-quarters of the original chantry income of 1548 in those counties was still being accounted for in Augmentations at Michaelmas 1553.[42] Some of this arose from rent charges (such as those for London described above) which were not a readily marketable commodity. In addition, some property might justly be described as the 'debris', particularly the numerous urban tenements reported as being 'in decay' (which might mean empty, falling down or merely needing some repair). But the majority appeared to be reasonable property for which we might well have expected buyers to come forward. Ministers' accounts for the same date in other counties show that what was left at the end of the reign could be far more than the dregs.[43] Jordan's estimates therefore seem to misrepresent what actually happened.

It is easier to demonstrate that this was so than it is to explain why. The cost of implementing the dissolution and paying pensions to the dispossessed chantry priests had to be met from the yearly income of Augmentations. Yet there was apparently no attempt to hold back enough chantry lands to keep this part of the account self-financing. Several receivers' accounts show that the bill for pensions alone in 1553 exceeded the income from the remaining chantry lands, and other Augmentations revenue thus had to be deployed to meet these costs.[44]

Explanations for the large remaining quantities of land may well vary from county to county, and generalisations are out of place given the present state of our knowledge, but some of the conclusions from Yorkshire may have a wider application. Much of the otherwise attractive collegiate land there was held on leases with many years still to run. Such an encumbrance would deter prospective purchasers. The Crown continued to receive yearly rents from these properties and in many cases renewed the leases when they expired years later. Secondly, in Crown manors and particularly in the Duchy of Lancaster there was a consistent refusal to sell off the lands. The alternative solution favoured by the Crown was to let them out to farm, receiving a yearly fixed sum as for a lease. This resulted in a modest consolidation of the Crown's estates apparently by deliberate policy. Another form of encumbrance was the copyhold tenure. Certain copyhold tenants, by devious enfeoffments to use, had devoted their rents to the support of chantry priests. To protect the interests of the lords of the manor (in many cases the Crown itself) and of the tenants, these properties were sold only to the sitting tenants or to agents acting on their behalf. We can perhaps begin to understand what lingering administrative problems there were following the dissolution.

There are also signs that the local officials of the Court of Augmentations had to work hard to get potential buyers to come forward for the chantry lands. John Bellow toured the East Riding trying to stir up enthusiasm by announcing that 'if any would buy any lands, the King was disposed to sell lands and he would help him to it'.[45] In the few cases where enough conveyances survive to trace the property with any certainty to its post-dissolution owner or lessee, it appears from the Yorkshire evidence that the sitting tenant was often the person at the end of the chain. This is perhaps what we should expect, especially where the properties are tiny and scattered. When we find purchasers buying up in bulk all the lamp and obit lands of the county or other local region, as did Sir Edward Bray for those in Lindsey and Buckinghamshire, surely the most likely outlet for these is the sitting tenant: who else could possibly want them?[46] We may at least safely say that such men had a much better chance of buying them than had been the case when the monastic lands were put on the market. If this was really the situation on a large scale, the dissolution of the chantries had very little impact on patterns of land tenure or property ownership at large, though we are not yet in a position to say that this was so with any degree of confidence.

Our survey has been all too concentrated and it has not been possible to treat the two dissolutions in the same way. It is nevertheless clear that in both fields there is a need for more research at a local level. For the present we must realise that we are still far short of the final answers to our questions and that, in interpreting the material, we must identify the limitations both of the original sources and of the studies based upon them. Too much faith must not be placed in the available statistics where they themselves are based on imperfect evidence. We should not restrict our interests to lands which were sold or given away, nor should we stop at the end of Edward's or Mary's reign. We may well conclude by echoing that post-Restoration rent collector and saying that the data in both these fields have been, and seem likely to remain, 'troublesome in the collecting'.

7. Ecclesiastical Patronage: Who Controlled the Church?

ROSEMARY O'DAY

PATRONAGE made the early modern world turn round. He who possessed patronage possessed power – power to control people, politics and events; power to delegate power; power to command respect. If a historian is to understand anything of the workings of that world, and specifically of the church within that world, he must certainly lose himself among the labyrinthine paths of patronage. But what was patronage? The concept is somewhat elusive. It can be described as the *action* of one person with some sort of power or influence using that influence to aid another party. Such help might be freely given or solicited, either with money or service, by the recipient or by a third party on his behalf. The client of a patron might receive something concrete from his benefactor – a place in church or state, for example – or he might benefit only in terms of general encouragement and support.

It quickly becomes evident that patronage in the post-Reformation church was of extreme importance. After the Henrician Reformation the church in England was in continual flux. The first generation of Elizabethan bishops had one thing in common: they did not accept for one moment that the initial Elizabethan religious 'settlement' was a settlement at all. Many accepted sees in the first place because they wanted to be able to shape the church from within according to the guidelines of the continental reformed churches. Very soon it became apparent to them that they had insufficient authority to mould the church in the way they wished. Their activities were restricted by the position of the Queen as supreme governor and patron (and her lack of sympathy with their goals) and by the fact that there were others competing for patronage (and thereby control)

For Notes to Chapter 7, see p. 197; for Bibliographical Notes, see pp. 185–6.

in the church, or resisting the attempts of bishops and others to seize control of patronage. The emergent character of the Church of England was dependent upon the distribution and exercise of patronage: for this reason it is imperative that one should determine how ecclesiastical patronage was distributed and how it was exercised.

At first sight it might appear that the bench of bishops controlled the church and some contemporaries certainly believed this. In fact, the power of the bishops was very limited – Charles I seems to have been the first post-Reformation monarch to concede that it was the bishops and not the Crown who had the right to determine doctrine.[1] However, it was true that the choice of bishops could affect markedly the complexion of the church – witness the difference in character of the early and late Elizabethan churches under the respective rules of Parker/Grindal and Whitgift/Bancroft.[2] In theory all episcopal appointments rested with the Crown. Rarely in the reign of Elizabeth did the Queen make a personal selection, yet it can be said that the bishops selected at various points in the reign did reflect rather accurately the Queen's current position regarding ecclesiastical politics. The Crown seems to have followed a policy in some respects: for example, there was a tendency to appoint Welshmen to the Welsh sees and to encourage the appointment of local men to English sees. Nevertheless, a close examination of the distribution of favours during the reign suggests that others selected the bishops. Lord Burghley was paramount among the distributors of patronage at this level. Leicester was instrumental in the furtherance of several careers. Bedford, Huntingdon, Hatton and Robert Cecil all had a hand in such patronage. The Crown permitted others to exercise its patronage as regards such appointments – to assume that it did so carelessly would be wrong. During the later years of the reign Elizabeth favoured a more conservative approach to the church's affairs and accordingly gave Christopher Hatton and Archbishop Whitgift considerable say in the choice of bishops. Earlier she had respected Burghley's judgement and had excluded her archbishop, Matthew Parker, from direct favour. Elizabeth had been forced to work with the continental reformers before 1580; at that point, drawing her own conclusions from Grindal's blatant insubordination, she selected her own archbishop, against advice, and determined the direction which her church was to take. The 'settlement' of 1560–2 was indeed not permanent, but it was not the first generation of Elizabethan bishops who would shape it but the Queen's men. Elizabeth would not be deflected from this conservative course even by the importunities of her new favourite, Essex. This is stating the case in rather bald terms. It would certainly be incorrect to suggest that the court was divided into warring camps who proposed entirely different candidates for promotion to the bench. Whereas William Overton was unquestionably Leicester's man and Richard Curteys of the Cecil faction, others such as Grindal, Cooper and Chaderton had been supported by both factions, for different reasons perhaps but with the same effect.

James I's selection of bishops has been the subject of some dispute. H. R. Trevor-Roper claimed that the Jacobean bench was filled with courtiers in clerical clothes, who had been chosen for this reason and not for their outstanding abilities as theologians, ecclesiastical politicians, administrators or pastoral bishops.[3] A. P. Kautz has contested this view and pointed out that James tended to elevate or translate men who had proved useful to him in ecclesiastical policy.[4] George Abbot, cited by H. R. Trevor-Roper as the prime example of James's distribution of patronage at the whim of his favourites, was, according to Kautz, already in James's good graces as the successful converter of the Scottish church to episcopacy. Bishops Barlow and Andrewes and Dean John King were elevated or translated as a result of their services at Hampton Court. George Carleton found the key to preferment when he completed a treatise against the new Arminian doctrines. Those who sympathised with Arminianism met with no such favour. James was also a connoisseur of sermons; and good preaching, while it did not guarantee preferment to a bishopric, did secure the King's attention.

Both historians agree as to the unpredictability of the selection procedure under James. The King was always willing to listen to the latest opportunist: where preferment was concerned, a promise made long ago was worthless when the man in favour was promoting someone else's cause. The influence of certain royal favourites was noticeable. Abbot was finally translated to Canterbury because of the memory of the late duke of Dunbar. After 1619 Buckingham was able to place his own clients on the bench – even some who did not have the King's personal favour, the most prominent example being that of William Laud. A. P. Kautz also draws attention to the far-reaching influence of Richard Neile in the selection procedure. He was initially planted in the royal household by Bancroft to counterbalance the influence of Cecil in guiding royal appointments to the bench. The hand of Bancroft and Neile can be seen in the preferment of Abbot, Andrewes, Barlow, Parry and Ravis. Even after Bancroft's death, Neile exerted considerable influence.

In fact, although it may be true that James accorded his favourites more freedom in ecclesiastical patronage than did his predecessor, both monarchs kept a relatively tight hold on preferments to the episcopal bench, being generally unwilling to prefer men whom they found personally obnoxious in terms of policy or doctrine. James was more affected by theological issues than was Elizabeth. Her prime concern was for the direction of the church along conservative lines once the contemporary situation permitted it. It would be easy to see their patronage of the bench in terms of a grand design but both, in fact, adopted a pragmatic approach and both were aware of the value of ecclesiastical patronage in terms of secular politics.

The main point to retain from this argument is that whereas the Crown delegated to laymen the power to choose individual bishops and ecclesiastical courtiers, it did so while retaining an active veto on all appointments, which had to be reconcilable with the broad sweep of current ecclesiastical policy. Neither monarch allowed the situation to get out of control.

In England, until the dissolution of the monasteries, the bulk of ecclesiastical patronage pertained to parish livings. This patronage took two main forms – advowsons in the hands of religious houses (appropriate rectories), and other advowsons, for the most part appendant to manors. At the dissolution the picture was altered with the redistribution of monastic patronage. This was inevitable: in Lincoln diocese, for example, before the Reformation nearly half of the patronage was in the hands of the religious orders. Between 1495 and 1520 there were 2760 presentations to parish churches in Lincoln diocese: the religious presented 1331, the Crown presented 123, the two bishops presented 85, and the remainder of the patronage was fragmented among collegiate bodies and a large number of individual laymen.[5] The Crown was undoubtedly the greatest beneficiary at a national level at the dissolution although many advowsons were subsequently, often almost immediately, purchased by local laymen. In general, monastic lands were passed on with their appendant advowsons – an incidental acquisition by the land-hungry. Patronage itself, therefore, remained exceedingly fragmented in its distribution after the Reformation. It was, however, a redistribution heavily in favour of the laity rather than ecclesiastical bodies.

Nationally, and in many dioceses, the Crown was the single largest advowson-holder. This was not always the case: in Worcester diocese between 1585 and 1664 the dean and chapter actually held more advowsons than did the Crown, but this seems to have been the exception rather than the rule. When the Crown passed on the advowsons it had claimed at the dissolution it tended to grant them to laymen rather than to ecclesiastics. In Surrey for example the Crown retained only 19 of the 80 advowsons which had come to it, but few went to the bishop or dean and chapter: in 1616 ecclesiastical patrons of all sorts in the county held only 12 advowsons.[6] Only in London did the church benefit greatly from the redistribution of advowsons at the dissolution. Granting the strong position of lay and ecclesiastical patrons in given areas, generally speaking the Crown was dominant. Within Salop (Shropshire) archdeaconry in the later sixteenth century, the Crown controlled 29 parishes out of 72.[7] Neither the bishop nor the dean and chapter possessed *de iure* patronage rights therein. Only seven laymen owned more than one advowson apiece and there were no individual blocks of patronage of significant size. Clerical patrons are conspicuous by their absence.

We have said that patronage meant control. Theoretically the Crown was in a position to organise its patronage distribution to create a Crown party within the church or, at least, to ensure that the church possessed a preaching, subscribing ministry. Through the Lord Keeper of the Great Seal alone, the Crown presented an average of 106 clerics a year to livings throughout the country worth less than £20 a year. A further 34 clerics per annum were presented by the Crown to more valuable livings. The Crown had the right to present to many more livings than it owned in law: livings in the gift of Crown wards, livings which had been left vacant for eighteen months, livings to which a simoniacal presentation had been proved, livings of which the incumbent had been deprived – all fell to the Crown's gift.[8]

But did the Crown use this opportunity? Did circumstances allow it to do so? The Lord Keeper's patronage was certainly highly organised, with a bureaucracy. A number of examining chaplains were engaged also to ensure that candidates for Crown livings conformed to certain minimal standards. Some of the Keepers did formulate a policy and envisage themselves as adhering to certain principles in distributing favour. Thomas Egerton sincerely attempted to supply worthy ministers to Crown livings. In the 1590s he was making some presentees enter into obligations to deliver a given number of sermons per annum in their new benefices. He was trying to further the interests of a learned preaching ministry, so far as the clerical recruitment situation of the day would allow. Most Lord Keepers tried to endure that simony did not enter into Crown presentations although Lord Keeper Puckering was accused of allowing his servants to sell church livings during his term of office in the early 1590s.

The extent of the patronage in the Keeper's hands made organisation imperative and, in effect, it also meant that the Keeper could not choose the recipients of his favour from personal knowledge in the majority of cases. He had to delegate the process of selection to some person or persons and retain only the ultimate responsibility and the right of veto. This gave laymen and ecclesiastics throughout the land the opportunity to exercise patronage to which they had no legal claim. At the beginning of Elizabeth's reign there appears to have been a deliberate attempt to give the bishops considerable say in the distribution of patronage and the returned exiles as a group were certainly highly favoured. The high point of episcopal influence occurred in the mid- and late 1560s and was probably due to Nicholas Bacon's personal sympathies. Just under half of the clerics preferred in 1563 were presented upon petition or commendation of one of the bishops (36); a further 22 owed their success to some other eminent ecclesiastic. A similar picture emerges in 1567.

Notably, the Lord Keeper in the 1560s was granting patronage to the returned Marian exiles – men who were often holding episcopal or other office in the early Elizabethan church. Alexander Nowell, dean of St Paul's, Thomas Lever, archdeacon of Coventry, Edmund Grindal, bishop of London, Thomas Bentham, bishop of Lichfield, and many other bishops and archdeacons were prominent in petitioning for Crown livings on behalf of clients. Most of them sought to exercise this patronage within their own jurisdictions. Apart from the two archbishops, only the bishop of London regularly petitioned for benefices outside his area of immediate influence. His wider influence may have been attributable not only to personal dominance but also to the fact that superior national information regarding vacancies was available to London clerics via the *Si Quis* door of St Paul's. Moreover, clerics may have felt that the bishop of London had easy physical access to the Lord Keeper.

Granted that most bishops appear to have exercised influence largely within their own sees, one might expect that the value of livings to which they succeeded in presenting in this way depended upon chance rather than design. For example, the bishop of Hereford provided to several extremely impoverished livings in his diocese, yet, as he practically monopolised Crown patronage therein, one must assume that this reflected little upon his influence although it did little to help him improve the quality of clerical personnel there.

It was through the Lord Keeper that the bishops, chancellors, archdeacons and colleges were able to supplement their existing patronage resources and prefer more men of their own choosing to livings within their jurisdictions. The bishops of Lichfield, for instance, had *de iure* patronage of several benefices but most were prebendal stalls or archdeaconries and so the opportunities to present to parochial livings offered by the well of Crown patronage were most welcome.

But as Elizabeth's reign progressed, the bishops and ecclesiastical leaders lost their near monopoly of royal patronage and gave ground to individual courtiers and gentry. Prominent courtiers such as Huntingdon, Leicester, Bedford, Warwick and Pembroke were seeking to extend their own patronage by nominating to Crown livings. These leading Protestant noblemen were acutely aware of the importance of patronage in ensuring that the church had a Protestant preaching ministry. In this goal the puritan noblemen were not so far removed from the ideals of the returned exiles – they had a rather different conception of lay participation in the newly reformed church, perhaps, and they remained radical longer than did their ecclesiastical contemporaries – but they were certainly of a different breed from the new generation of Elizabethan bishops who were being elevated from the early 1570s onwards. In granting them patronage, the Lord Keepers were assisting the advanced Protestant cause. But they were doing more than this – they were granting the laity a leading role in selecting the personnel of the church at local level and robbing the ecclesiastical hierarchy of its earlier predominance. The Reformation had removed *de iure* patronage rights from the church by the sale of monastic lands and advowsons but, for some years afterwards, the hierarchy had retained some control because the Crown had allocated it influence over royal patronage – now this favour had been removed.

Does one want to imply that this was a piece of conscious engineering on the part of the Crown? In effect one is faced with a curious situation: the Queen's 'little black husband', her personal and un-popular choice as archbishop of Canterbury, John Whitgift, was in the ascendant, a man who had little sympathy with the goals of the radical noblemen – and yet the Crown was granting increased exer-cise of patronage within the church to a group of leading Protestant noblemen who belonged to the more radical wing of the church. It is true that, until the discovery of the Marprelate presses in the 1580s, there were attempts by the Privy Council to compromise with the puritans; criticisms of existing clerical personnel were accepted as genuine constructive efforts to improve rather than to undermine the Elizabethan church by men who had no real objection to conformity given the establishment of a preaching, teaching pastoral ministry. Moreover, the situation may have been an example of those politic balancing acts of which the Elizabethan government seemed so fond – balancing the puritan nobles and gentry against the conservative Whitgift and Bancroft. Certain of the Lord Keepers involved were in personal accord with the aims of the puritan nobles. Finally, the group were prominent at court: the Crown regarded ecclesiastical patronage as just another link in the chain of patronage which was much wider than the ecclesiastical world, which bound individuals to the regime, and which provided a not insignificant source of revenue. It was absolutely natural that the Crown should elect to favour the most prominent men in the kingdom in this way. Moreover, the courtiers in question were *actively* seeking patronage in the church.[9]

Of course, patronage was not entirely removed from the hier-archy even at this time – the archbishops still retained influence. In 1591 and 1621 the Great Seal was put into commission and, in 1591 at least, the commission was largely an ecclesiastical one. There is some reason to believe that the hierarchy was again favoured by the late Jacobean and Caroline Keepers such as Bishop John Williams of Lincoln (1621–5) and Thomas Coventry (1625–40). Laud himself ad-vised Coventry on the exercise of Crown patronage on occasion. Charles I and his government were more sympathetic to the claims of the hierarchy in church government than had been either Elizabeth or James, and Charles probably granted it more practical favour.

The policy which the Lord Keepers adopted of allowing a third person to nominate a cleric to a Crown living removed the patronage initiative from the Crown in all but a minority of cases. The Keeper retained the right to veto and his chaplains existed to ensure that presentees were conformable. Certainly the Crown protected its property rights in patronage in this way but an examination of the recipients of Crown patronage suggests that it did not use its patronage very effectively to secure even a conforming clergy. In 1578 the radical puritan Humphrey Fenne was presented to the Crown living in Holy Trinity, Coventry; in June 1599 Humphrey Leach, M. A., later charged with Catholic leanings and eventually a formal convert to Roman Catholicism, was presented to St Alkmund's vicarage, Shrewsbury, with the personal support of the Lord Chancellor. Thomas Hodgkinson, the rebellious vicar of Hillmorton, Warwickshire, who in 1623 rejected a summons to appear before the ecclesiastical consistory court, saying that he 'cared not for such baubles nor for his shitacions [sic], scorning in very ridiculous and upbraiding manner' the court's authority, was himself a Crown protégé.[10] On the other hand, the Crown was also favouring many of the leading diocesan clergy. Presentations of nonconforming ministers were normally the result of lack of personal knowledge of the candidate by the Keeper and his chaplains. Nevertheless, it is surely surprising that the Crown allowed such men into leading urban pulpits without more careful examination of their conformity and character.

Neither is it at all evident that the Crown succeeded in raising the educational standards of the parish clergy through the discriminating exercise of its patronage. Indirectly the Crown tried to improve the situation by devoting the revenue from prebendal stalls worth less than £20 per annum to the support of needy theology students at university early in Elizabeth's reign. James I and his son were aware of the need to lure educated men away from the more lucrative professions and into the ministry but they were able to contribute little of a practical nature to this goal. The administration of Crown patronage itself meant that the Crown had to rely upon the integrity of patrons as regards selection of suitably educated candidates. But even had these patrons all sought learned clerics it is doubtful whether this effort in itself would have improved the educational quality of the pastoral ministry in Crown livings very much. Patrons were dependent upon supply – ordinands in the 1560s and 70s had far inferior qualifications to those of ordinands in the 1620s. Once educational expansion was under way patrons had the opportunity to present more qualified candidates. By the 1620s, a degree was so commonplace among ordinands that any patron, however uncaring about such matters, was almost bound to present a university graduate to his living. Of 1380 presentations to Crown benefices between 1627 and 1640, 825 involved presentees with M.A.s, 301 men with higher degrees and 97 men with B.A.s Only 157 presentees were non-graduate. This represented a startling increase upon the 1558/9 to 1579 lists, although the situation had already improved somewhat by the 1590s. Patrons may have been instrumental in inspiring prospective ordinands to attend university before entering the church but this is rather a different problem, and is dealt with in some detail elsewhere. A cautionary note should be struck here. Candidates in the 1560s and 70s were more poorly qualified on paper than candidates in the period 1596–1640 but they were not necessarily less vocationally suitable or less acquainted with the Scriptures. Even so, it is fair to conclude that the rise in the number of graduates presented by the Lord Keeper was commensurate with general educational expansion and the rise in graduate entry to the church as a whole.

Lay patrons who had an active interest in the shaping of the church in England were very aware of the important role which patronage could be made to play. Historians interested in the operation of patronage have concentrated upon the activities of these lay patrons. It is true that there were some influential laymen who were dedicated to the puritan cause and whose exercise of patronage was primarily dictated by religious considerations. The group of nobles clustered about Leicester and Huntingdon was the major case in point. Moreover, there were individual laymen, equally devoted to the goal of providing a preaching ministry but with rather less personal command of patronage, who tried to acquire patronage and use it to that end. In the case of Sir Richard Knightley of Northamptonshire the effect was to provide the area in which he lived with a small core of committed puritan clergy and with unrelenting support for their activities when the authorities tried to suppress them. Sir John Coke, Secretary of State to Charles I, had very little *de iure* patronage. Yet he secured the *pro hac vice* right to present to his home living of Melbourne, Derbyshire, from its patron, the bishop of Carlisle, because he wished to ensure that the vicar was of puritan sympathies and suitable to be his personal religious mentor.[11] Sir Samuel Tryon, a London merchant, was so committed to his puritan chaplain, Immanuel Bourne, that he went to great lengths to secure him a good living in Derbyshire.[12] Numerous instances of such bonds between individual patrons and clergy could be cited. Some were as conscientious as Sir John Harington of the diocese of Bath and Wells in giving clients for preferment practical preaching trials.

The exercise of much patronage was undoubtedly religious in motivation, at least in part. But the implication is often that there was a *concerted* puritan patronage movement in operations in the period. Certainly men like Huntington, Leicester and Warwick had great and wide-ranging territorial influence and accompanying patronage: they did have opportunities to present considerable numbers of ministers to livings and they exercised these opportunities conscientiously and with reference to puritan standards. Such were the exception rather than the rule – most puritan patrons could present by right to only one or two livings in a lifetime. Statements by the historian R. G. Usher to the effect that patrons during Elizabeth's reign were buying up blocks of advowsons in given areas to ensure the success of the Reformation fuelled this impression that there was an organised patronage programme. This may have been true in Norfolk, Essex and Northamptonshire but it was certainly not true of Worcester, Oxford, Gloucester or Coventry and Lichfield dioceses. Independent studies of the sale of Crown lands and appendant advowsons during Elizabeth's reign suggest that most of the sales consisted of small purchases intended to consolidate existing holdings rather than to build new territorial empires.[13]

Even in Northamptonshire, where Usher cited Sir Richard Knightley, Sir Francis Hastings and Sir Edward Mountague as the dominant lay patrons, there was much fragmentation of patronage. William Sheils has recently refined the picture of patronage in the county.[14] Half the ecclesiastical patronage in the diocese of Peterborough was in lay hands but no one layman controlled this patronage – rather there was an intricate web of patronage connection. A landowner would own the advowson appendant to his manor. There were, nevertheless, interested puritan patrons who made the best possible use of their influence. In Rutland the Cecils and the Haringtons controlled seven livings apiece and used them to support a puritan ministry of a moderate kind. In mid-Northamptonshire the recusant influence of the Treshams and the Griffins was more or less balanced by that of the puritan Mountague and Mildmay. In the west of the county, Knightley held only four livings which he used in the interests of the puritan cause to provide a radical nucleus. Around the city of Northampton the clergy themselves built up a radical tradition. In the east of the county patronage was much fragmented. There was a recusant element which puritan families such as the Mildmays, Zouches, Lynnes and Fitzwilliams co-operated very informally to defeat. The co-operation was effected as much through social and kinship connections as through religious ones – there was no cabal sitting to ensure that puritan clergy were preferred; it was simply inconceivable that one of the group would present any other variety of cleric, and when no suitable candidate sprang to mind, help could often be secured from a friend of similar religious persuasion. All puritan laymen did not seize every possible opportunity to exercise influence. The earl of Leicester did not manipulate Crown patronage in this area where he was a landlord and where he was publicly expressing support for the leading puritan clergy. The diocese of Peterborough contained a sizable puritan element but the puritan clergy – the activists – formed no more than a significant minority among the clergy at any one point. They were significant because they had powerful lay support, were vocal, were by their nature troublesome to the authorities (particularly after 1575) and were interested in controlling the diocese's pulpits.

As has been noted, the ecclesiastical hierarchy were also aware of the importance of patronage for the shaping of the church. The amount of their patronage varied from area to area. The bishops of Peterborough controlled three livings and one disputed living. The bishops of Lichfield presented by right to four parish livings in the diocese, although they also had considerable control over personnel in the cathedral chapter. The bishops of Lincoln and London were in a stronger position. Ecclesiastics were predominant among city of London patrons: in addition to livings to which the bishop could collate directly (13); 17 were in the collation of the dean and chapter of St Paul's. Within the city but outside the bishop's jurisdiction was the archiepiscopal peculiar, the deanery of the Arches: 7 of the 13 churches there were in the collation of the archbishop of Canterbury and 6 were presentative rectories in the gift of the dean and chapter of St Paul's. Within the city of London, then, the hierarchy had an unusual degree of control over parish incumbents. So great was it that the laity were forced to endow separate lectureships in the parishes if they wanted independent control over the city's pulpits. It is true that many of the lectureships were held by city incumbents (often of the same parish) but, nevertheless, to fill such a lectureship one had to earn the approval of the patron concerned, be it layman or group of laymen.[15]

The exercise of patronage by the bishops of Lichfield provides a useful case study of a different type.[16] The bishops had few patronage opportunities at parochial level yet the first Elizabethan bishop of Coventry and Lichfield, Thomas Bentham, made an effort to encourage the substitution of learned, enthusiastic Protestants for those clergy deprived at the beginning of Elizabeth's reign. He also sought to promote clergy via the Lord Keeper's patronage. Like other bishops he was particularly concerned to provide places for his own chaplains and officials and, on occasion, this led to the abuse of pluralism. But out of 147 separate presentations during the period 1560–70 the bishop was responsible for only 5 and 3 of these had fallen to him by lapse. The position was only slightly alleviated by indirect patronage. Such a bishop had to concentrate upon making the most of such personnel as he already had – supporting vigorously the few available preachers, encouraging if not initiating the exercises which provided in-service training for the clergy, and trying to improve the financial situation of the curates and vicars whom he presented.

Later bishops of the diocese were forced back even more upon their own sources of patronage – the royal well of favour was almost dry. They tended to bestow most of their patronage upon their personal chaplains and servants. Richard Baddiley, secretary to Bishop Thomas Morton (1618–32), obtained a degree and the position of official of Gnosall peculiar with his master's help. Isaac Basire was befriended by Morton, who paid for his studies at Cambridge and ordained him. Basire became domestic chaplain to the bishop in 1631/2 and followed the bishop to Durham where he was given preferment, eventually becoming archdeacon of Northumberland. There is little doubt that the domestic chaplaincy was the accepted route to high preferment in the church during the period. The outstanding example, of course, is that of Richard Neile's household during the Jacobean period.

The bishops were able to sponsor clerics in other ways. Morton, a strict-living bachelor, used his income to support poor scholars at university. He encouraged the existing link between his old college, St John's Cambridge, and Shrewsbury school by ensuring that scholarships from the school to St John's, envisaged in the school's statutes, were established. He also sought to raise the academic standards of the school. Morton took a lasting interest in the careers of certain individuals – George Canner, for example, was a blind boy from Lancashire, whose education at both school and university was financed by Morton and whose livelihood was provided for by a curacy in Lichfield diocese. Canner's predecessor in this curacy of Clifton Campville had also benefited from Morton's patronage. Joseph Leigh, a Cambridge graduate, served as curate of Slaidburn, Yorkshire, while studying for his M.A., and was preferred to Clifton in 1619. He served there only briefly before Morton presented him to Duffield, Derbyshire, in 1620. Later in 1620 Morton preferred him to the relatively rich living of Hanbury, Staffordshire. In this way Morton offered patronage to a select group of like-minded and well-educated clergymen. His was not a wide-ranging patronage but it was effective in supplying leadership for the diocese. Archbishop Neile used similar methods to staff the major clerical administrative posts in his diocese of York. The method probably had some detrimental effects for the parishes directly concerned because turnover tended to be rapid and continuity of pastoral service was lost.

Turning away from the bishops, there were other types of ecclesiastical patronage in the realm of pastoral service than that involving control of the advowson to a living. Control of the pulpit was perhaps the most important of these. In many areas preaching was not controlled by the hierarchy even in the negative sense of licensing. In London preaching was extremely important. The royal injunctions of Henry VIII (1538) had laid down compulsory quarterly sermons in every parish and such a demand became an invariable feature of metropolitan and diocesan visitation articles. The Interpretation of 1560–1 had seen monthly sermons as the ideal. The 1604 canons ordered Sunday sermons by resident preachers and instructed non-preachers to procure monthly sermons for their congregations. Court proceedings following visitation survive in London for 1583 and 1601: on only one occasion was an incumbent presented for not fulfilling his minimum preaching duties. Several parishes supported virtually permanent lectureships to provide sermons. For example, St Botolph's Aldgate, which was served by a non-preacher from 1564 to 1594, maintained a lecturer to preach twice weekly (Sunday morning and Thursday evening), to catechise on Sunday afternoons, and to provide funeral sermons and other sermons as required and paid for. When the lecturer was eventually appointed perpetual curate there, he cut down his preaching duties considerably, suggesting perhaps that an outsider was more diligent in preaching than an incumbent, who had other competing pastoral duties.[17]

The supply of sermons in the parishes was most often controlled by the vestry or by the incumbent himself. But there was one important source of preaching under the direct control of the bishop – the Paul's Cross sermons. Sermons preached at the Cross had always been of a controversial nature and reached a wide audience. In 1560 Jewel estimated an audience of 6000 people of both sexes, young and old. Many of the listeners took notes and handed over written comments to the preacher. Sections of the congregation were known to assault unpopular preachers physically. The hierarchy actively encouraged parishioners, particularly where there was no preaching incumbent, to attend the Paul's Cross sermons: before 1579 curates were ordered to end morning service by 9 a.m. to allow their congregations to hear preachers at the Cross at 10 a.m., and Aylmer's visitation injunctions of 1583 reiterated the order.

It was, however, difficult to obtain preachers before the reign of Elizabeth. By then many of the radicals were willing to preach at the Cross, causing some concern to Bishop Aylmer. Difficulties in recruitment were caused by poor remuneration for the job, the probability of a critical response from the audience, and the confusions involved in making appointments. In Edward VI's reign the city authorities had claimed a share in the nomination of preachers at Paul's Cross. Grindal had scarcely been the man to reassert episcopal authority. In Archbishop Parker's correspondence there are indications that the Lord Mayor and Leicester in addition to Bishop Grindal had made appointments prior to 1566. The association of several of the preachers with nonconformity during the vestiarian controversy drove Parker to vet candidates and reject the nonconformable. But in 1573 Sandys was allowing prominent nonconformists to preach at the Cross. Bishop Aylmer, however, on his appointment as bishop in 1577 was quick to reassert episcopal authority. He still found it difficult to make suitable appointments: the elimination of the nonconformist element restricted the pool of potential preachers; many others, while conformist, were unwilling to be used as instruments of episcopal propaganda (it was Aylmer's practice to 'help' into print sermons denouncing schism, faction and nonconformity); the posts were still inadequately paid. Arrangements were made which proved reasonably satisfactory in the mid-1590s – at least they ensured that orthodox sermons were preached regularly.

Eventually the sermons at the Cross underwent a revival, largely because Aylmer himself bequeathed £300 for their maintenance in addition to a sum of £100 left at his disposal by Elizabeth, countess of Shrewsbury. A situation was reached where the sermons were used for propagandist purposes by both Aylmer and his successor Bishop Bancroft. Because of this potential, episcopal patronage of the preaching was most significant and the bishops tried to make it more so by encouraging large audiences and printing the more satisfactory sermons. Much attention has been given by historians to puritan control of the pulpit and press: perhaps a little more should be given to episcopal manipulation of both media – it is too easy for the layman to assume that the pulpit in England was under uncontested puritan control. Of course, it is true that the outstanding example of an organised attempt to secure a preaching ministry in England, particularly in urban areas, was puritan-inspired. The efforts of the feoffees for impropriations in the 1620s and 30s must be recognised in this context.

Three of the more obvious sources of ecclesiastical patronage have been examined: the Crown, puritan laymen, the ecclesiastical hierarchy. But the distribution of patronage was in the hands of many and the situation was further complicated by the action of *de iure* patrons in alienating (by gift or sale) the right to present to a living for one or more times. By such a grant the recipient became the *pro hac vice* patron of the living. The religious houses in the early sixteenth century had made many such grants; the device remained very popular in the later sixteenth century but was rather less so in the early seventeenth century. In some dioceses up to 25 per cent of presentations were made by *pro hac vice* patrons in the mid- to late sixteenth century (Worcester, for example) whereas in others the practice was never so common (Coventry and Lichfield diocese).[18] The willingness of certain patrons to allow a third party to present enabled a large number of lesser gentry, professional men and yeomen to present to ecclesiastical livings. The true patron might reap between £30 and £100 from the transaction. From the purchaser's point of view, this would be a worthwhile investment if dedicated to the career of a relative. In many cases, the cleric himself would put up the money and stage the transaction through a third party to avoid possible charges of simony.

There can be little doubt that the system opened up a huge reservoir of ecclesiastical patronage to people who would otherwise have had none. There is little evidence of concerted action by groups of puritan laymen to buy up grants to present their protégés. Rather one finds evidence of individuals, often from the same locality, buying up opportunities to prefer relatives, friends or importunate ordinands. Very occasionally the grants were made to servants by way of reward. Ecclesiastical patrons seem to have been as anxious as any others to benefit financially from the system but they tried to retain a greater degree of control over the use of grants.

The system of grants had several effects, some of them disturbing. It did provide a source of patronage for the gentleman, well-to-do yeoman or professional man; often the clergy obtained preferment for their own sons in this way. It may have led to an increase in the incidence of technical simony although it is difficult to determine whether this was any more of an abuse than excessive social or economic dependence upon a patron, or to say whether it was detrimental to the ministry. The device probably increased the importance of the diocesan registrars' offices for the distribution of information about vacancies and patronage. Many of the advowsons held by the religious houses had been held in gross – that is, where there was no manor. At the dissolution many of these passed to patrons with no connection with the parish. To some extent the practice of granting presentations to third parties redressed the balance, allowing local men to exercise patronage in favour of local clergy.

The existence of the practice, however, completely invalidates any estimates of lay and ecclesiastical patronage based on the ownership of advowsons. It also served to complicate the contemporary situation. Owing to grants made by monastic houses and cathedral bodies in the critical period 1530–60, there were probably fewer clergy appointed by ecclesiastics then than for centuries before or after, with the exception of the commonwealth period. All along, ecclesiastics were more prominent in selling grants than were laymen – for instance, the bishops seem to have sold grants fairly frequently in the early seventeenth century when the over-all market was declining. At a time when the bishops and other ecclesiastical officials had little enough patronage at any level, it is surely surprising that they chose to alienate what they had. Their actions may be explicable in terms of their precarious financial position, their need to reward domestic servants and chaplains, and their ability to retain control over the choice of candidates by *pro hac vice* patrons. The system also served to obscure the true ownership of advowsons on many occasions, leading to legal disputes and much confusion.

In a short essay it is not possible to treat all the implications of the patronage system within the English church. Rather it has been possible to draw out some of the major themes which emerged from the dissolution onwards. The most important trend seems to have been the loss of control of ecclesiastical patronage by the bishops themselves and by ecclesiastics in general. By the beginning of James's reign the bishops were claiming that five-sixths of ecclesiastical patronage was lay-controlled. The trend by which patronage was removed from the church at the dissolution was not reversed during the Edwardian Reformation and was only temporarily halted when the early Elizabethan Lord Keepers showed favour to the returned exiles. Moreover, one gains the impression that the bishops were often only interested in limited patronage: they wanted to control the appointment of leading clergy. Many seem to have been willing enough to alienate their patronage and few seized every available opportunity to exercise patronage.

The Crown's use of patronage is also of great interest. The Crown did not employ its extensive rights of presentation in order to create a Crown party within the country. Such a policy was not practicable even had it been felt to be desirable. The Crown saw its patronage rights as property rights, which it jealously guarded. It used them to reward petitioners. Through the Crown a wide variety of individuals and groups gained some control over the shape of the English church and the Crown used its patronage to balance the opposing factions within the church.

For a variety of reasons, it is the puritan lay patrons who have captured the attention of historians, in regard both to their use of Crown patronage and to their approach to control of the parochial ministry. It is this incursion of the laity into the control of church personnel which seems most important. Puritan patrons were significant because they were active in the pursuit of an ideal and because they appointed vocal, troublesome and able clerics to livings in their gift. It would be wrong to assume that puritan patronage was numerically predominant or that it was highly organised. Indeed, the most highly organised puritan effort was dedicated to circumventing the existing parochial system and substituting congregationally controlled lectureships.[19] Puritan patrons do not seem to have made much use of the device of buying grants of next presentation in order to increase their patronage opportunities. The practice seems rather to have brought patronage within the reach of those somewhat lower on the social ladder, to have strengthened clerical dynasticism, and to have restored the local character of the patronage system.

Enough has been said to make it clear that he who controlled ecclesiastical patronage did not in fact control the church un-hampered. The exercise of patronage was limited by a variety of factors, some of the more obvious being politics, availability of personnel, and finance. Moreover, ecclesiastical patronage was so fragmented in its ownership that no one group was able to pursue a coherent policy without impediment. Elizabeth and her ministers used this fragmentation to good effect; James preserved the balance; if William Lamont is correct, Charles I may well have destroyed the hierarchy's influence in the church by granting it too much patronage and too'much control.

8. Religion in Provincial Towns: Innovation and Tradition

W. J. SHEILS

I

THE importance of the English towns in the spread of religious ideas and their influence on the character of those ideas has long been recognised and, indeed, did not escape the notice of contemporary observers. In 1584 the puritan earl of Huntingdon stated: 'I do all that I can to get good preachers planted in the market towns of this county' and, looking back on the period, Richard Baxter saw a clear connection between the urban communities and the parliamentary cause in the Civil War. It has been in relatively recent times, however, that the connection between the towns, puritanism, and the Civil War has been a central theme in the attempt to understand late sixteenth- and early seventeenth-century English history. The influence of Max Weber's pioneering analysis of the rise of Protestantism in north German towns, *The Protestant Ethic and the Spirit of Capitalism*, was acknowledged by R. H. Tawney in his own masterly essay, *Religion and the Rise of Capitalism*, which examined the English Reformation. For Tawney puritanism was the 'true English Reformation' and its principle environment for growth was among 'the trading classes of the Towns, and of those rural districts which had been partially industrialized by the decentralization of the textile and the iron industries'.

The insights of Tawney have been refined and restructured by the extensive corpus of material produced by Christopher Hill, through whom many dark corners of the land have been illuminated. His work has done much to take the debate out of the realm of theoretical discussion about the relationship between puritan theology and the emerging capitalist economy, and has provided a framework of facts to assess the means by which a puritan tradition was established in

For Notes to Chapter 8, see pp. 197–9; for Bibliographical Notes, see p. 186.

the period up to the 1640s. The corner-stones in establishing this tradition were the market-day lectures and corporation lectureships, but these devices were supplemented by a variety of means outlined in *The Economic Problems of the Church* and subsequent essays; they included the augmentation of livings by voluntary subscription, the securing of the patronage of town livings, and the reorganisation of the parochial structure in some larger towns. In addition to these there occurred confrontations over jurisdiction between corporations and cathedral bodies in the cathedral cities. The scope of Christopher Hill's work has encouraged and informed many local studies, and a more general work by P. S. Seaver, *The Puritan Lectureships.* The sub-title to Paul Seaver's work, 'The Politics of Religious Dissent', indicates however that, within this welter of information, the basic framework, whereby these lectureships are identified with puritanism and with a puritanism largely explained in terms of opposition to and alienation from the establishment, remains intact.

More recently Patrick Collinson has suggested a reinterpretation of the role of the towns or, more accurately, of the lectureships in the history of the reformed church in England. He has shown that the relationship between the puritans and the establishment was far from clear-cut and that, in the early years of Elizabeth's reign, many of the religious initiatives of urban corporations enjoyed widespread episcopal support, and some never lost that support. Wherever market-town lectureships were put down they were, as often as not, raised up again after a time. Most important among these lectureships were the 'lectures by combination' in which the beneficed clergy of a district would provide a rota for regular preaching of sermons, usually in the market town, and which survived within the normal diocesan framework throughout the period. These lectures, perhaps embodying the highest ideal of the 'Grindalian' churchmanship of the 1570s, sometimes called reformed episcopacy, covered the whole spectrum of Jacobean preaching and, though some exercises were more radical than others, 'the institution in its total setting was more typical of the church of this epoch than of alienation from it'. If this preaching activity can be placed within the life of the church, then other initiatives such as the purchase of advowsons and the reorganisation of parishes were clearly attempts to work within the conventional framework of the established church. Opposition and alienation were not the most pronounced features of local initiative.[1]

The great expansion in the network of inland trade meant that, by the seventeenth century, wayfaring traders were a common sight in most English towns. In addition to commodities these traders brought with them news, rumours and ideas and the markets and fairs were distribution centres for more than mere goods. Interestingly it was at Stourbridge fair time, one of the greatest of the midland fairs, that the leaders of the *classis* movement chose to meet in 1589. Recent concentration on the marketing functions of English towns has highlighted the close interdependence between the town and the surrounding countryside in the distribution and production of the basic necessities of life. The majority of towns had populations of between 600 and 1500 and in communities of this size, as at Cheltenham or Ripon, there can have been no sharp distinction between urban and rural lifestyles. Indeed interdependence between town and country was paramount in both social and economic activity, and in the religious context that same interdependence was nicely expressed in the market-day exercises wherein the beneficed clergy of the surrounding rural parishes foregathered for preaching followed by discussion and dining, often at a local inn like the Bull at Northampton. In those larger towns known as shire towns, such as Leicester or Colchester, in cathedral cities like York and Exeter, or in major ports like Bristol and Hull, the contrast between town and country was more pronounced. Many of these towns were governed by prosperous craftsmen or merchants trading and squabbling with their counterparts in London and other large towns, who were to lay the foundation for that urban *rentier* class, the town gentry of Hanoverian England. This latter process was still at an early stage, however, and even in these larger towns the close connection between town and country was well established. Borough corporations often looked to the leaders of county society to protect their privileges and usually elected their members of parliament from the local gentry: the influence of the earl of Huntingdon in the debates of Leicester corporation in the reign of Elizabeth was reflected by the influence of the earl of Leicester and Sir Richard Knightley at Northampton and, no doubt, by others elsewhere. What recent urban history has underlined is that the prosperity of most English towns rested on the produce of the countryside and that, though each had its own tensions and problems, there was no sharp dichotomy between urban and rural society.[2]

The divisive effect which puritanism could have within an urban community has recently been illustrated by Paul Slack's study of the conflict in Salisbury over the administration of poor relief in the 1620s, and the puritan order of Northampton established by Percival Wiburn in 1570 was quickly suppressed by the bishop with the support of hostile elements in the town. For the most part, however, research has concentrated not on the influence of religion on the internal history of particular towns, but on the part played by towns in the wider religious history of the period. In this context Patrick Collinson has suggested that a list of lectureships would read like a gazetteer of the market towns of England. When other forms of local initiative in ecclesiastical affairs are considered the problem becomes one of too much rather than too little information. Nevertheless before discussing the attitude of the hierarchy to such initiatives and the response of the town governors to the ecclesiastical authorities, some indication of the range of activity is called for.[3]

II

In two areas urban authorities were clearly working within the conventional framework of the established church: in their attempt to acquire the patronage of town livings and also in the reorganisation of the parochial structure. Securing the advowson to a living provided the inhabitants of a town with some guarantee of control over the beneficed cleric, and Christopher Hill has provided a list of corporations, including Boston, Ipswich, Coventry, Newcastle, and Plymouth, which owned the patronage of churches in their towns. Initiative in this matter was not confined to large corporations however and, in the clothing district of Gloucestershire, the inhabitants of Painswick purchased the advowson of the vicarage in the early seventeenth century. This was done at a time of recession in the town, when the clothiers and their market were losing trade to their rivals at Stroud, a better situated town four miles south-west. Stroud, with a population of about 900 adults, was itself an ill-endowed living, having grown up as a clothing settlement within the parish of Bisley, to which it was a chapelry. The salary of the curate was woefully inadequate and he was supported largely by the contributions of the inhabitants who also, at this time, claimed the right of appointment. Similarly at Devizes in Wiltshire the corporation purchased the lordship of the borough in 1624 and four years later the advowson was also assigned to them. In addition to outright purchase of the right of appointment, which was not always possible, an enterprising corporation could exert influence on the process by which a clergyman was presented to a living. This was particularly true of the large amount of patronage in the hands of the Crown, and administered by royal officials open to pressure from local interests. At Northampton the chief living of the town, the vicarage of All Saints, was a royal appointment and for most of the period the corporation were able to secure puritan clerics sympathetic to their views.[4]

As a result of shifts in population and of the effects of the Reformation changes on the ministry, the parochial structure in some major towns, where a large number of parishes were served by poorly paid clergy, became increasingly anachronistic. The pastoral need for some reorganisation was clear and, combined with the economic advantages to be gained from removing redundant churches, to some corporations the possibility was an attractive one. A statute of 1545, whereby two parish churches less than a mile apart could be united if one had an annual income of less than £6, provided enabling legislation. The corporation at York secured a local act in 1547 and, in the reign of Edward VI, 14 churches were closed and their parishes united to others. After Mary's reign the exact legal position became obscured but in 1586 the archbishop, the recorder, mayor and six aldermen of the city ratified the unions retrospectively, adding one further church to the number dissolved. Even so York retained 23 parishes, most of which were poorly endowed, and like Gloucester, where only two parishes of twelve were said to have incomes of over £10 a year in 1603, had difficulty in attracting able men to parochial livings. Other corporations were to follow York: at Lincoln 24 parishes were reduced to 9, and at Stamford 11 were united to make 6. At Winchester the bishop, with the support of the corporation, attempted unsuccessfully to reduce the number of livings, the poverty of which he held partly responsible for religious conservatism in the early years of Elizabeth's reign. At Exeter such a harmonious relationship between bishop and corporation did not exist and the bishop thwarted two attempts by the corporation, in 1581 and 1601, to have the number of parishes reduced from 19.[5]

The religious conservatism noted at Winchester was a great problem in the north, where in many market towns the inadequacies of the parochial structure were the reverse of those discussed above. In the north of England many market towns found themselves at the centre of enormous parishes, some in excess of 30,000 acres, with a multiplicity of secondary settlements. The problems of serving such communities were great, and the institutions of the established church needed adapting if recusancy and radicalism were not going to prosper. It was the laity who usually provided the initiative for such adaptation. At Whitby in the North Riding conservatism was the problem: during the 1580s recusancy had made great strides in a moorland area with many isolated settlements. Whitby was the chief town of the district but, having an impropriate rectory whose tithes accrued to the archbishop, was a fairly poor living with seven dependent chapelries to serve. Many of these were so poorly endowed that they remained unserved. The earl of Huntingdon, who had done much to establish lectureships in Leicestershire and at York, took a lease of the rectory from the archbishop in 1593 and proposed to reorganise the parish in order to make Whitby a preaching centre which could challenge the growth of Catholicism. To do this he transferred the usual rectoral responsibility for finding curates in the chapelries to the archbishop and, instead, retained £20 a year of the profits of the rectory for the maintenance of a resident, preaching minister in the town. Faced with the growth of Catholicism, Huntingdon thought that one able preacher in the market town could do more than seven ill-paid curates in isolated moorland villages. In other areas of the north the large parishes produced different problems, particularly in the clothing districts of south Lancashire and the West Riding. Here shifts in population meant that towns had emerged which, in terms of population, were larger than many southern parishes and had little or no provision for their spiritual needs. The towns of Liverpool and Toxteth were in the parish of Walton and, on the other side of the Pennines, those of Elland and Heptonstall were in the parish of Halifax, and curates in those places were supported largely by contributions from the inhabitants. Given that wholsesale parochial reorganisation was out of the question, such local initiative was often the only answer to the pastoral problems posed by the shift in population. It was an answer which took some measure of control into the hands of the urban corporations who, not unnaturally, sought to have a voice in choosing the cleric they maintained. Many of these areas did, in fact, become identified with puritanism and, in the 1630s, were in confrontation with authority. By the end of James's reign, however, these congregations

were still very much within the established church, and many initiatives received episcopal support. A few people may have been un-
easy about this sort of local control, but it was not voiced loudly until
1634 when Archbishop Neile expressed concern over the arrangement for the patronage of the new chapel of St John in Leeds which
was vested jointly in the corporation and vicar of Leeds, although the
'best men' of the town had already purchased the advowson of the
parish church in 1588 without arousing comment from the
authorities.[6]

Voluntary financial support for the clergy brings us to an area in
which the initiatives of local congregations moved beyond the usual
institutional framework of the established church. This support took
two forms, the augmenting of inadequate incomes for beneficed
clergy with parochial responsibility and the endowment of lectureships. The former, although it often brought close contact between
congregation and minister, was in response to a situation created
largely by impropriations. At the Reformation impropriate rectories,
formerly held by monastic houses, were transferred to laymen,
colleges, and senior clerics who enjoyed the great tithes of the parish,
which came to be served by a vicar supported by the small tithes or by
a curate with a stipend. In these livings some augmentation was often
necessary and, moreover, it was a problem recognised by Laud
himself. He wrote: 'the vicars in market towns, where the people are
very many, are for the most part worst provided for', and the point
was underlined by the puritan *Certificate from Northamptonshire* of 1641.
In that county, where almost half the benefices were impropriate, the
parishes of nine market towns out of fifteen were served by vicars or
curates 'commonly left so poor and destitute'. In the diocese of
Gloucester the situation was even worse. The problem in Gloucester
itself has already been mentioned, but a survey of 1603 throws light
on the other market towns in the diocese. The survey deals with 30 of
the 33 remaining towns and, if those decayed towns with less than
200 adults are excluded, then the livings in 22 of the remaining 26
towns were impropriate. In some of these towns, as at Marshfield, the
small tithes of the vicarage provided a decent living, but in the majority of cases vicars were poorly paid and the plight of curates
parlous. At Cirencester the curate was said to have no certain stipend
but by courtesy of the inhabitants, and at Tewkesbury, where the
curate received a stipend of £10 from a rectory estate worth £200 a

year, the corporation claimed in 1650 that they had been supporting the minister for fifty years.

The attempts by the inhabitants of Cheltenham to procure an adequate income for their curate from the profits of the rectory deserve closer attention. The rectory was owned by the Crown who farmed it to lessees responsible for maintaining curates at Cheltenham and Charlton Kings. The terms of the lease required the farmer, Mrs Baghott, to provide adequate salaries for the curates but, in 1603, she was paying them only £10 a year each. The inhabitants complained to the bishop in 1609, who preached in the town urging Mrs Baghott to provide suitable incomes for preaching curates. Unsuccessful in this, the bishop and the inhabitants launched a succession of appeals to the Lord Chancellor who responded by threatening the farmer with loss of patronage. The impeachment of Chancellor Bacon meant that Mrs Baghott ignored appeals and threats with impunity. Both parties, inhabitants and lessees of the rectory, then began to petition the court and agreement was reached whereby the tenants of the rectory agreed to pay £80 a year divided equally between two curates. Ultimately the parish got two adequate curates, one a B.D. and the other a D.D. The Cheltenham example is important because, in this instance, there was no mention of puritanism and the essential demand was for 'a worthy preacher and a very good scholar'. In fact Cheltenham's curate was Dr John English, a follower of Laud, and, at the outbreak of the Civil War, the chief parties in town affairs came out on the royalist side.[7]

Coventry provides an early example of a radical lectureship held in 1560 by Thomas Lever, an exile during the reign of Mary and without preferment in the established church, who preached in the town supported by the townsmen solely because of the 'free kindness and love' they bore him. Such independence was uncommon at this early date and, in the majority of towns, sums of money originally laid aside for sermons were clearly intended as a supplementary source of income for local beneficed clergy who could preach. This was so at Barnstaple where, in 1576, the corporation paid Mr Parson of Parracombe 25 shillings for a quarter's salary for preaching, and also at Lincoln where, in 1571, the corporation granted an annuity of £5 to a preacher who was also beneficed within the city. The status of the preacher was likely to change and at Lincoln in 1583 a salary of £20 was given for a preacher who was also required to teach and to visit the sick. Such a preacher was obviously more dependent on the corporation and less dependent upon the established church, but it was not necessarily an attempt to set up a contentious lectureship and the corporation were concerned to stress other aspects of pastoral work also. At Barnstaple the corporation tried a variety of expedients: in the 1580s there appears to have been an exercise based in the town and the corporation paid 50 shillings to the Friday preachers for fifty sermons in a year, and at the end of the century there was a short-lived experiment with a salaried preacher at £30 a year. Whether because of expense or of rows with the town vicar the arrangement ceased and by 1612 the exercise appears to have been revived, for we find the corporation paying for a dinner for the preachers 'at their conference about a lecture'. It was not until the reign of Charles I, possibly in response to the Arminian policies of Laud, that the corporation again went to the expense of a full-time lecturer at a salary of £50 a year. At Rye in Sussex the same sort of experiments with a variety of devices can also be seen.[8]

Paul Seaver, using printed sources only, has identified 74 parliamentary boroughs where lectureships were known to exist before the Civil War, and the indexes to the works of Patrick Collinson and Christopher Hill testify to the universality of the practice, in the north of England as much as in the south. Indeed at Chelmsford and at Norwich the lectureship was said to contribute to the well-being of trade in those towns, bringing in a good crowd of people to the market. Lectureships thus became part of the normal facilities associated with town life. As has been indicated, however, lectureships could exist in a variety of forms, and it is important to disentangle some of these before considering their relationship with established ecclesiastical authority. Four principal forms of locally supported preaching can be identified: lectureships endowed for sermons preached by a beneficed cleric of the town or locality; those with sufficient financial provision to render the lecturer independent of preferment within the established church; combination lectures, or exercises, provided by a group of beneficed clergy from the vicinity of a market town; and public fasts held on special occasions and incorporating sermons from one or more local ministers. From time to time one type of lecturing merged into or coexisted with another and, as at Barnstaple, some towns tried a variety of devices.

In most larger towns the original lectureship foundation was assigned to a particular cleric, beneficed in the town or a neighbouring parish, although a few corporations, such as Coventry mentioned above or Colchester in 1576, established lectureships with preachers drawn from outside the ranks of the parochial clergy. The decision to retain a lectureship assigned to a beneficed clergyman or to seek a preacher from outside the ranks of the parochial clergy often resulted from local circumstances. At Boston in Lincolnshire, where the corporation owned the patronage of the living, the lecturer was always the parish priest also, though it must be said that the greatest part of his income and his chief responsibility derived from the lectureship in the early seventeenth century. In other towns which could not influence ecclesiastical appointments or where diocesan authorities were vigorous in silencing puritan incumbents, there was greater incentive to establish a full-time lectureship independent of the established church. This was done at Gloucester and at King's Lynn in 1619 following confrontation between local vicar and local preacher, and at Exeter in 1610 where the bishop and the corporation were in dispute.[9] Such lectureships could, if circumstances changed, be attached to parochial appointments again. The amount of money needed to provide a full-time preacher meant that, unless there was some private benefaction, most small towns could not support one. With their more limited resources the inhabitants of Tewkesbury and Daventry preferred to augment the salary of their curate and to provide exercises or lectures by combination. This was less expensive, usually entailing the provision of hospitality for the local ministers, who welcomed the opportunity to meet for discussion of local and professional matters in addition to engaging in theological debate and preaching to members of the congregations assembled from the town and surrounding countryside. In the early seventeenth century such exercises sometimes coexisted with stipendiary lectureships, as at Leicester, and can be found throughout the country. For example, in the diocese of Lincoln in 1614 there were exercises at Grantham supported by 14 ministers, at Market Rasen with 7, at Louth with 12, at Grimsby with 9, at Alford with 12, and at Horncastle with 21, as well as at other towns where the numbers participating are not known. The clergy conducting these lectures were not free-lance preachers and were far from the 'alienated intellectuals' of seventeenth-century England as seen by some. They were, for the most part, beneficed clergy, considerable numbers of whom were engaged in this sort of extra-parochial preaching and mutual discussion. These exercises were the descendants of the prophesyings of the 1570s which, with episcopal support until their suppression in 1577, attempted to improve the intellectual standards of the clergy and provide sermons in towns for the many congregations with non-preaching ministers. Some exercises survived undisturbed until the reign of James I when they once again became a familiar part of the ecclesiastical scene. Indeed some, like those at Oundle in 1589/90, at Beverley in 1594, and throughout the diocese of Chester, were actively supported by bishops who enforced attendance. Elsewhere an element of continuity was provided by two means: through the *classes*, essentially clerical gatherings designed at establishing a national church on Presbyterian lines, which were suppressed by the authorities in 1590, and through public fasts held on particular occasions. In Northamptonshire *classes* were established at Daventry and at Kettering where lectures by combination were later to appear, and the practice of the public fast is well illustrated by that held just over the county boundary at Stamford in 1589. This fast gained some contemporary notoriety, being held by the corporation in defiance of Lord Burghley and with the doubtful support of the bishop. The fast involved a show of strength by the local clergy, two of whom were nominated to preach sermons which were 'not yet much above five hours, which time was thought to be little enough for them'. These were preached before local congregations and members of the local gentry, some of whom took notes to which they referred when defending the preachers against the charge of subversion.[10]

Mention of attendance by local gentry underlines the interdependence of town and country noted earlier, and some town lectureships, of whatever character, owed their origin to the initiative of local gentry rather than to the town governors. Sir Richard Knightley and the earl of Leicester were instrumental in establishing a lectureship at Towcester in 1572; Lord Zouche played a prominent part in the founding of the Rye lectureship while that at Lewes in the same county was organised by a group of local gentry. On his own testimony, the earl of Huntingdon provided the early impetus to urban preaching in Leicestershire.[11]

Patrick Collinson has recently provided a description of the immediate context in which a lecture often took place, not stopping simply with the sermon but going on to general discussion among the clergy *ad clerum* with further exposition and debate between the godly and individual ministers over points raised, such as no doubt took place among the Cranbrook clothiers. The practice of the Sunday afternoon lecture at Boston in 1614, not a combination lecture but supported by the corporation, was typical and was described by a hostile witness as follows:

(1) They have prayers with psalms after the lesson;

(2) After the second lesson, a psalm being sung, the preacher of the town bestows two hours in a sermon;

(3) After his sermon, a psalm being sung, the clerk of the parish calls to certain families for their youths to be catechized, every one of which as they stand dispersed in the congregation answers aloud as they use to do at a sessions 'Here Sir';

(4) After this calling the Minister of the town makes a long prayer;

(5) His prayer being done, he turns himself to the boy who must give him his first answer, and so to the second and third etc. for he knows beforehand every boys station that answers him . . . ;

(6) This being done he spends two hours more in the explanation of these his own questions and answers, so that they keep the same tenor all the year which they did when we were with them, their afternoon worship, as they used to term it, will be five hours, where, to my observation, there was as many sleepers as wakers, scarce any man but sometime was forced to wink or nod.

John Cotton, the lecturer and vicar of the town, went over the whole course of scripture thrice in his twenty years there and provided leadership in discussion with preachers from other places. In addition there was also a Thursday lecture, and sermons on Wednesdays, Fridays, and Saturday afternoons. Attendance at these naturally brought the godly together regularly and encouraged a brotherliness or good neighbourliness between pastor and flock and between individual members of congregations which was sometimes expressed more formally. At Boston, and in a few other places, this was done by covenanting. Cotton wrote in 1648, 'There were some scores of godly persons in Boston in Lincolnshire . . . who can witness, that we entered into a covenant with the Lord, and with one another, to follow after the Lord in the purity of his worship . . .', and it is suggested that this took place in 1615. By the time of writing Cotton was in Massachusetts, with some of that selfsame flock from Lincolnshire, having resigned the vicarage during the Laudian regime.[12]

III

Cotton's ministry at Boston showed many of the characteristics later identified with congregationalism, and it is now time to turn to some of the more radical corporations frequently in confrontation with the hierarchy. Imogen Luxton has provided details of the vigorous Lollard tradition at Coventry which can be traced back to the mid-fifteenth century. The concern of this sizable group with lay access to the Bible and their devotion to biblical learning foreshadowed later developments and, although primarily artisan in character, the Lollards did include some of the governing families of the city. The connection between this tradition and the radical puritanism of Elizabeth's and James's reign is suggestive, but Lollardy coexisted in Coventry with a vigorous devotional life within the framework of the pre-Reformation church. During the months of January to June each year the citizenry of Coventry enjoyed ceremonial of a religious or semi-religious character culminating in the Corpus Christi plays which attracted a 'very great confluence of people thither from far and near'. The strength of puritanism later may have derived as much from this orthodox tradition of lay participation as from the Lollard precedent.[13] Another midland town with close commercial and social connections with Coventry probably had the most continuous tradition of radical puritanism among provincial towns betweeen 1570 and 1625. In 1604, when talking of puritanism, a hostile critic John Lambe described Northampton as 'the chief fountain of that humour', and some account of events there illustrates the part played by towns in the spread of puritanism and the tensions that ensued between the corporation and the hierarchy.

The puritan tradition was initiated by a fellow exile of Thomas Lever, Percival Wiburn, who, on 5 June 1571, established the order of Northampton with the permission of the mayor and of the bishop. The order sought to graft the religious life of the town on to the civic institutions after the fashion of Geneva. The official Book of Common Prayer was to be used, but sermons were to be an integral part of any service, where psalm-singing was also encouraged. The importance of preaching was underlined by the order that parish services on Sunday were to finish by 9 a.m. in order to allow the inhabitants to congregate at one church to hear a sermon. Attendance at this sermon was compulsory unless one was being preached at the parish church. Further sermons were preached on Tuesdays and on

Thursdays, the latter being followed by disciplining of faults. This took place before the mayor, assisted by the preacher and others who appointed sworn men in each parish to present faults 'so the bishop's authority and the mayor's joined together, being assisted with other men in the commission of peace, ill life is corrected, God's glory set forth and the people brought to good obedience'. In addition to the correction of offences, the corporation assumed responsibility for the furtherance of the gospel and, among activities later to be recorded at Boston in 1614, made provision for examining the youth on Calvin's catechism after Sunday service in the presence of older members of the congregation. The order anticipated many experiments later adopted by puritan corporations but was quickly suppressed by Bishop Scambler, who may not have been aware of its full implications when he gave permission for its establishment. Nevertheless, despite swift action, the bishop could not destroy the local influence of the order. The corporation continued to enforce attendance at sermons and at services and, in 1582, the mayor went as far as imprisoning one persistent absentee. The legal authority for this was doubtful and a judgement at assizes went against the mayor, whose legal expenses were reimbursed by the corporation. Other corporations, such as Lincoln and Leicester, also established bye-laws enforcing attendance at sermons by inhabitants, but their legal authority would not have extended to imprisoning offenders without the issue of a *significavit,* authorising such action, from the church courts. Although in some conflict with the spiritual courts, such bye-laws were not necessarily attempts to subvert the jurisdiction of these courts, but rather an attempt to meet a spiritual responsibility. Indeed bye-laws dealing with ecclesiastical affairs had existed before the reign of Elizabeth at Norwich and Lincoln, where they were designed to bolster the authority of the courts spiritual.

The order also marked the foundation of an exercise in the town providing regular preaching on Saturdays, when four ministers spoke. It was this exercise which established the puritan tradition in surrounding villages and sustained the puritans in the town after the suppression of the order. The success of the exercise was such that the visitation of 1573 uncovered nonconformity in the locality on such a scale that the first provincial crisis of national significance ensued and five clerics were deprived in 1574. For a few years the puritans in the town lost control of the official church and had to rely on unbeneficed clergy and local sympathisers to minister to them. By the end of the 1570s the puritans had recovered control and placed their candidates in the two crown livings of All Saints and St Giles. In addition seven of the assembly, the governing body in the town, were appointed assessors for the wages of a preacher and teacher at All Saints.

For the rest of the period the puritans never lost control of ecclesiastical affairs in the town for long, but they were not without internal tensions. In 1579 a property dispute between various members of the ruling oligarchy resulted in the formation of two opposing groups, one led by Henry Sharpe, the bookbinder later to be involved in the Marprelate scandal, and the other by William Jennings, vicar of All Saints, who was accused of having some of the books of the separatist writer Robert Harrison in 1581. The feud attracted the attention of the Privy Council which ordered the removal of Jennings to a living in Devon, but he remained in the town until 1583 when he was a lessee of some corporation property. If this was a dispute between rival puritan groups, it appears from the leading figures that both were on the radical wing but, during the 1580s, a more obvious tension appeared between the radical Presbyterians and the more moderate puritans in the town. This provided the background to the activities of the *classis,* a clerical group committed to the establishment of a national church on Presbyterian lines, which met in the town. Edmund Snape, curate at St Peter's, was the organising secretary of the midland *classes* and the leader of the clerical group, but John Johnson, vicar of All Saints, was the most influential puritan figure in the town. Johnson worked closely with the corporation, who made him a freeman in 1585 and in 1588 raised a subscription from leading townsmen to settle his debts. Snape and Johnson probably differed in the extent of their support for the official Presbyterian policy of the *classes* but, even without this, Johnson's pre-eminent position in local affairs was likely to clash with Snape's clerical leadership, although the latter was not without friends among the townsmen. The occasion of the rupture may have been Johnson's indebtedness, for the *classis* censured him and he fell out with his colleagues and turned queen's evidence at the subsequent trial of the *classes* leaders.

The corporation responded to the breakup of the *classes* by organising a petition on behalf of the imprisoned Snape, by securing a new living for the deprived Johnson at Yelvertoft, and by refusing the freedom of the town to Richard Awner who was nominated by

that arch-enemy of the *classes*, Bishop Bancroft. Awner was made to
pay for the privilege although the corporation was in two minds: the
aldermen were prepared to accept Bancroft's nominee, albeit
grudgingly, but the commoners would have no truck with it. Whether
they were more radical or not is uncertain, but puritans of every
status in the town again sought spiritual comfort at Whiston until
their brief eclipse was over with the appointment of Robert Catelin as
vicar of All Saints 'at the request of the townsmen of Northampton,
and one Mr Deacon' on 4 October 1591. Catelin appeared regularly
before the diocesan courts in the 1590s but his ministry was undisturbed. The corporation secured his income by a levy on all
parishioners of All Saints and by contributions from parishioners of
other churches in the town. He was the presiding influence in
religious affairs in the town and, by the beginning of James's reign,
played a prominent role among the group of puritan clergy meeting
again at Northampton. He became the local leader of the opposition
to the enforcement of the Canons of 1604 which led to the deprivation of fifteen puritan clergy of the diocese. Catelin was himself
suspended and locked the bishop out of All Saints church when the
latter tried a show of strength in the town. He was saved from
deprivation by the support of the corporation who appealed
successfully to Robert Cecil to intervene on their minister's behalf.
The mayor and other leaders of the community claimed that 1500
communicants were deprived of services due to Catelin's suspension
and that the Canons were attempting to enforce ceremonies on the
town that had been omitted for forty years. So persistent was the
puritan tradition in Northampton that, when an attempt was made to
impose uniformity, it was the diocesan authorities and not the
puritans who were accused of making innovations. Catelin was
restored and remained in the town until 1613 whence his successors
continued the tradition in the church. The arrival of the Arminian
John Lambe as chancellor of the diocese in 1615 threatened the position of the puritans in the town. He procured grants of the patronage
to the churches of St Giles and St Sepulchre to which he presented
two Arminians, Robert Sibthorpe and Samuel Clarke. By the end of
the reign of James the confrontation between All Saints, where
Jeremiah Lewys continued the puritan pattern of worship including
Sunday afternoon sermons and public catechising, and the other
parish churches where Arminians were installed, provided a
microcosm of the wider conflict to be fought in the 1630s.[14]

IV

Northampton had a persistent puritan tradition with wide support in the town which enabled the corporation to survive successive attempts by the hierarchy to impose uniformity. In ecclesiastical affairs the town was generally in advance of its time, both in the early support given to puritan clergy and in the appearance of Arminianism at the parochial level. A far-sighted visitor to the town at the end of James's reign might have been aware that the religious tension in the town provided a microcosm of pre-revolutionary England. In other provincial towns such as York and the towns of East Sussex the puritans had not been so continually at odds with authority, and did not have as yet to face a challenge from the Arminians in the parishes. Indeed the Arminians had not yet come to dominate the episcopal bench. In this respect, then, Northampton is untypical and it is in other provincial towns that the ambiguity in the relationship between puritans and diocesan authorities needs explanation. Nicholas Tyacke has recently demonstrated that, prior to the success of Arminianism in the reign of Charles I, Calvinistic theology dominated both the defenders of the established church and the puritans and provided common ground between them. The importance of preaching in calling the elect 'from the state of servitude to liberty' was stressed in varying degrees by most Calvinist theologians, conformist or not. Local initiatives in towns need to be considered against this almost universal demand for a preaching ministry and against two other features of the English Reformation; the failure to adapt the institutions of the pre-Reformation church to the demands of Protestantism, and the suppression of the chantries and religious gilds.

As has been suggested, the shortcomings of the parochial structure in many towns meant that some local initiative was necessary to secure a ministry of any description. A multiplicity of poor livings in a large town, or a poorly-endowed chapelry with a growing population, often meant no spiritual provision at all and, in such circumstances, a local corporation was only acting responsibly by encouraging parochial reorganisation or raising a voluntary levy to provide a decent salary for a minister. Laud himself acknowledged that these institutional weaknesses were greatest in the towns and it is hardly surprising that, where corporations provided the remedy, some demand for local control over the character of the ministry followed.

When one takes into account the demand for a better trained, preaching ministry, the problems of serving urban parishes seem to have been increased. What could provide a living for a celibate cleric with essentially sacramental functions could not always attract a married graduate of preaching abilities with an increasingly professional approach to his calling. It was in towns with better-endowed livings that disputes between non-preaching incumbents and lecturers whether beneficed or not arose, as at Barnstaple at the end of the century. In Rutland during the 1580s there was friction between the preachers among the parochial clergy and their non-preaching colleagues, largely because the puritans among the former group insisted that preaching was a necessary function of a legitimate ministry. It was on this issue that the puritans were attacked by some of the hierarchy who disapproved of those congregations which went gadding to sermons and refused the services of a 'dumb minister'. The disagreement was one of degree however, for the great majority of the post-Reformation bishops showed the same enthusiasm as Bishop Curteys of Chichester for a preaching ministry. Indeed episcopal support for prophesyings stemmed from a belief that they would improve the preaching abilities of the parish clergy. The bishops, however, maintained that it was not possible to provide all parishes with preaching clergy in the sixteenth century and refuted the charge that a 'dumb' minister was no minister. Before the 1630s, however, criticism of preaching was not levelled at the activity itself, but at particular examples which were said to lead to faction and to disaffection. It was rare indeed for anyone to voice the view of Laud that 'the altar is the greatest place of God's residence upon the earth, greater than the pulpit'. The great majority of the bishops appointed between 1558 and 1625 acknowledged that provision of a preaching ministry was of central importance and, while some had reservations over particular features of that preaching activity, this concern provided the hierarchy and the puritans with a large area of common ground. A church led, as it was for most of James's reign, from Canterbury by Archbishop Abbot, who had himself been a lecturer in the 1590s, and from York by Archbishop Matthew, whose diary reveals the extent of his preaching in exercises and pulpits throughout his diocese, was a church that had a high regard for preaching. It was this concern for preaching which helps to explain the often ambiguous relationship between the puritans and the hierarchy.[15] The failure of the hierarchy to suppress puritan activity was not only testimony to the weakness of the church courts, it also points to the tacit support which puritan clergy often received from the hierarchy. It was an ambiguity illustrated by the subsequent careers of two puritan clerics who attracted the attentions of the diocesan authorities in the 1580s for the manner in which they organised the exercise based at Oakham in Rutland. Robert Johnson, rector of North Luffenham, later became archdeacon of Leicester without changing his puritan views, but the career of his colleague, Thomas Gibson of Ridlington, ended with deprivation in 1605. The margin between confrontation and compromise was not great.[16]

The institutional weakness of the post-Reformation church, and the widespread support for a preaching ministry, provided scope for local initiative within the framework of the established church. More often than not such initiatives received support from the hierarchy, and the provincial towns of England were not slow to act. It was in this context that the dissolution of the chantries and religious gilds in 1547 was important. In the pre-Reformation church lay initiative has often been identified with the Lollard tradition, and at Coventry one has evidence for both pre-Reformation and post-Reformation radical traditions. Lollardy was, however, beyond the pale of the medieval church and characterised by alienation from the established church. There was, however, considerable scope for lay initiative within the pre-Reformation church, often connected with chantries, religious gilds, pageants, and local shrines. In Lincolnshire the increasing involvement of the laity in religious life, and the importance of gilds in providing means of mutual self-help and communal entertainment have been documented. In towns this lay initiative began to have an increasingly corporate identity from the later fourteenth century, and a few examples must suffice. Chantries established at Scarborough in 1397 and Barnard Castle in 1412 were under the patronage of the commonalty of the towns, and at Newcastle under Lyme a private foundation became wrongly identified with the corporation in the fifteenth century. Chantries in York at about the same time were established under communal patronage by representatives of the whole parish rather than by private individuals, and at Lincoln in 1520 the chaplain to the chantry of St Thomas the Martyr was elected after a poll by the mayor and commoners of the city.[17] This communal activity was best expressed in the religious gilds which multiplied in the later Middle Ages; the churchwardens' accounts of

Ashburton, a small town in Devon, show the varieties of gilds to various saints, many of them supporting chaplains to assist in the parish. Also at Ashburton the inhabitants, through the 'Eight Chief Men' of the parish, played an important part in regulating the religious life of the community. Many gilds were associated with pageantry, not only confined to major towns like York, Chester and Coventry with their cycles of mystery plays. Smaller towns like Braintree, Shrewsbury or Sleaford had plays, interludes, or other entertainment provided by gilds. The gilds also provided additional clergy by way of appointing their own chaplains and paying their salaries. Many Lincolnshire towns benefited from this, and in 1541 the inhabitants of Alton, Southampton, and Carisbrooke in the diocese of Winchester were providing salaries for stipendiary curates. These opportunities for local initiative were swept away by the dissolution of religious gilds and chantries and, temporarily, a vacuum was created in local religious life.[18]

Deprived of the traditional vehicles by which they could influence the religious life of their locality, the laity naturally sought new opportunities. The new stress on preaching and the inability of the established church to cater for that provided such an opportunity. Some of the support for establishing lectureships and purchasing advowsons must have been in response to the traditional claims of the laity to play a part in local religious life and, in some respects, such activity was part of a continuing tradition. It was a continuity which did not escape the notice of one observer, Thomas Wyot, town clerk of Barnstaple, who wrote in 1586, 'On St Luke's day this year there was a trental of sermons at Pilton, so that divers as well men as women rode and went thither, they called it an exercise or holy fast, and there some offered as they did when they went on pilgrimage.' Pilton church, adjacent to the town, had had a local pre-Reformation shrine.[19]

This is not to say that the lectureships, salaries, and patronage acquired and financed by town corporations were simply the chantries and religious gilds writ new. The Reformation changed the balance between the part played by the laity and the normal institutions of the established church. Pre-Reformation lay initiative was, for the most part, confined to *supplementing* the central sacramental life of the church by the provision of ancillary services. In the post-Reformation church it was the *essential work* of securing a preaching ministry which was often left to town corporations. The Reformation was a response to and further underlined the belief that religion was too important to be left solely to the clerks.

This was recognised by the bishops who welcomed such activity. In describing the towns of East Sussex in 1564 Bishop Barlow wrote that they were 'governed with such officers as be faithful favourers of God's word and earnestly given to maintain godly orders'. In such communities lectureships were established and a puritan tradition took root. Some towns were more radical than others and lay initiative did lead to tensions but, at the end of James's reign the church in England was, in Patrick Collinson's words, 'a Church consolidated by local loyalties' and, though threatened, 'still largely intact and sure of its integrity'.[20] It was the failure to harness these local loyalties, also a feature of the political history of the period, and the attempt by the Arminians in the reign of Charles I to suppress lay initiative which in ecclesiastical affairs transformed post-Reformation England into pre-revolutionary England.

As the natural centres for local activity the towns were to feature prominently in that transformation. In 1625, however, the motive behind religious initiative by the majority of town corporations was to build the true English Reformation on the admittedly imperfect foundations of the established church. The Laudian attempt to erect a very different edifice on that same foundation was yet to lead many corporations to abandon their endeavours.

Glossary

adiaphora	Matters indifferent: points of ritual and organisation not central to Protestant dogma.
advowson	The right of appointing a clergyman to a parish or other ecclesiastical benefice.
appropriation	A benefice annexed to a religious body, usually a monastery, which then had responsibility for the cure of souls and drew the great tithes and other emoluments of the living.
common services and annates	Payments made to the papacy and the papal curia of the first year's revenue of certain benefices.
de iure	By right or law.
elevation	Promotion to a bishopric.
glebe	Land for the maintenance of the parish priest. The terrier was a land survey.
grantee	Person to whom property was granted or sold.
impropriation	A benefice annexed to a layman (the lay rector) after the Reformation.
in commendam	A benefice so held was technically in trust. It was usually used to supplement the income of a bishop or even a layman who was bound to provide for the cure of souls.
modus decimandi	A voluntary composition between priest and people for the payment of tithe.
ordinary	An ecclesiastic who had the right to exercise jurisdiction – the bishop and the archdeacon were the most prominent.
peculiar	A geographical part of the diocese but not belonging to the diocesan's jurisdiction.
prebendary	The holder of the prebend or share in the endowment of a cathedral.
pro hac vice	for this time.
procurations	Payments to the ordinary at visitation by the parish clergy in lieu of hospitality.
simony	Specifically traffic in ecclesiastical preferment. Some doubt as to whether *indirect* purchase of preferment was technically simony at law.
survivalists	Those who clung to the old ways of late medieval Catholicism rather than the enthusiastic Counter-Reformation recusants.
synodals	Payments to the bishop by the parish priests originally at the annual synod or diocesan meeting.
temporalities	Lands and other property held by the clergy of the King by secular service.
tithe, personal	Tithe on the profits of labour, wages, trade and other non-agrarian activities.
tithe, predial	Tithe of the fruits of the ground.
translation	Preferment from one bishopric to another (usually more important).

List of Abbreviations

(for Bibliographical Notes, and Notes and References)

JOURNALS

AHR	*Agricultural History Review*
BIHR	*Bulletin of the Institute of Historical Research*
ECHR	*Economic History Review*
EHR	*English Historical Review*
HJ	*Historical Journal*
HT	*History Today*
JBS	*Journal of British Studies*
JEH	*Journal of Ecclesiastical History*
LQR	*Law Quarterly Review*
MH	*Midland History*
P & P	*Past and Present*
TRHS	*Transactions of the Royal Historical Society*
TBGAS	*Transactions of the Bristol and Gloucester Archaeological Society*
TCHS	*Transactions of the Congregational History Society*
YAJ	*Yorkshire Archaeological Journal*

OTHER WORKS AND PUBLISHING BODIES

AAS	*Archaeological and Architectural Society*
APC	*Acts of the Privy Council*
AS	Archaeological Society
CJ	*Commons' Journals*
CPR	*Calendar of Patent Rolls*
CSPD	*Calendar of State Papers, Domestic*
CSP Ven.	*Calendar of State Papers, Venetian*
CYS	Canterbury and York Society
DNB	*Dictionary of National Biography*
Foster	J. Foster, *Alumni Oxonienses* (1891–2)
HMC	Historical Manuscripts Commission
LP	*Letters and Papers of Henry VIII*
RS	Record Series
SP	*State Papers*
SPD	*State Papers, Domestic*
SR	*Statutes of the Realm*
VCH	*Victoria County History*
VE	*Valor Ecclesiasticus*
Venn	J. & J. A. Venn, *Alumni Cantabrigienses* (1922–7)

LIBRARIES AND RECORD OFFICES

BCRO	Bristol County Record Office
BM	British Library, British Museum
Bodl.	Bodleian Library, Oxford
CRO	Cheshire County Record Office
CUL	Cambridge University Library
EDR	Ely Diocesan Records
GDR	Gloucester Diocesan Records
HCRO	Hampshire County Record Office
ITL	Inner Temple Library
LJRO	Lichfield Joint Record Office
LPL	Lambeth Palace Library
LRO	Lincoln Record Office
NLW	National Library of Wales
NNRO	Norfolk and Norwich Record Office
NRO	Northamptonshire Record Office
PCC	Prerogative Court of Canterbury
PDR	Peterborough Diocesan Records
PRO	Public Record Office
SRO	Stafford County Record Office
UDPD	University of Durham Paleographical Department
WRO	Worcester Record Office
YorkBIHR	Borthwick Institute of Historical Research, York
YML	York Minster Library

Bibliographical Notes

Note: Place of publication is London unless otherwise stated.

1. CHURCHMEN AND THE ROYAL SUPREMACY

In *Episcopacy and the Royal Supremacy in the Church of England in the XVI Century* (1960), E. T. Davies has considered the theological implications of the working of the royal supremacy in the Tudor period. There is no one work which concentrates upon the royal supremacy from a historical viewpoint for the whole of the century covered by this chapter but in larger works various historians have recently discussed the supremacy for particular reigns. The several acts of supremacy together with valuable commentaries are given in G. R. Elton, *The Tudor Constitution* (1960) and J. P. Kenyon, *The Stuart Constitution* (1966). J. J. Scarisbrick, *Henry VIII* (1968) treats the Henrician supremacy in some depth and D. M. Loades, *The Oxford Martyrs* (1970) provides an important examination of the royal supremacy under Henry VIII, Edward VI and Mary. Claire Cross has written in more detail about the Elizabethan supremacy in *The Royal Supremacy in the Elizabethan Church* (1969). The significant recent article by N. R. N. Tyacke, 'Puritanism, Arminianism and Counter-Revolution', in *The Origins of the English Civil War*, ed. C. S. R. Russell (1973) calls into question older interpretations of the ecclesiastical history of the reign of James I, particularly that of R. G. Usher, *The Reconstruction of the English Church*, 2 vols (1910) and also to some extent that of S. B. Babbage, *Puritanism and Richard Bancroft* (1962). Other books which include material of value are W. A. Clebsch, *England's Earliest Protestants 1520–1535* (1964); L. B. Smith, *Tudor Prelates and Politics 1536–1558* (Princeton 1953); A. G. Dickens, *The English Reformation* (1964); P. Collinson, *The Elizabethan Puritan Movement* (1967); and W. M. Lamont, *Godly Rule* (1969).

Useful articles which touch upon the royal supremacy are: J. J. Scarisbrick, 'The Pardon of the Clergy, 1531', in HJ xii (1956) 22–39; M. Kelly, 'The Submission of the Clergy', in TRHS, 5th ser., xv (1965) 97–119; M. Bowker, 'The Supremacy and the Episcopate: the Struggle for Control, 1534–1540', in HJ, xviii (1975) 227–43; W. D. J. Cargill Thompson, 'Anthony Marten and the Elizabethan Debate on Episcopacy', in *Essays in Modern English Church History in Memory of Norman Sykes*, eds C. V. Bennett and J. D. Walsh (1966) pp. 44–75; W. D. J. Cargill Thompson, 'Sir Francis Knollys' Campaign against the *Jure Divino* Theory of Episcopacy', in *The Dissenting Tradition: Essays for Leland H. Carlson*, eds C. R. Cole and M. E. Moody (Ohio 1975) pp. 39–77; and O. Chadwick, 'Richard Bancroft's Submission' in JEH, iii (1952) 58–73.

The writings of sixteenth- and early seventeenth-century churchmen are readily available in Victorian or more modern editions and some of the most revealing on the royal supremacy include: *Doctrinal Treatises . . . by William Tyndale*, ed. H. Walter (Parker Soc. 1848); *Obedience in Church and State: Three Political Tracts by Stephen Gardiner*, ed. P. Janelle (1930); *Miscellaneous Writings and Letters of Thomas Cranmer*, ed. J. E. Cox (Parker Soc. 1846); *Sermons and Remains of Hugh Latimer*, ed. G. E. Corrie (Parker Soc. 1845); *Zurich Letters*, ed. H. Robinson (Parker Soc. 1842); *Correspondence of Matthew Parker*, eds J. Bruce and T. T. Perowne (Parker Soc. 1853); *The Works of John Jewel*, ed. J. Ayre, 4 vols (Parker Soc. 1845–50); *The Remains of Edmund Grindal*, ed. W. Nicholson (Parker Soc. 1843); *The Correspondence of John Cosin*, ed. G. Ornsby (Surtees Soc., lii, 1869).

Queen Elizabeth gave some indication of her attitude to the royal supremacy in *Letters of Queen Elizabeth and James VI*, ed. J. Bruce (Camden Soc., 1st ser., xlvi, 1849).

2. POPULAR REACTIONS TO THE REFORMATION

Regional studies of the Reformation lean heavily on local and diocesan archives, which have been intensively exploited only in the last thirty years. Some of the *Diocesan Histories* published by the S.P.C.K. in the 1880s and 90s are still valuable, however. Nor should the early large-scale histories and collections of documents be neglected: Foxe's *Acts and Monuments*; Burnet's *History of the Reformation*; and Strype's *Ecclesiastical Memorials* print valuable local documents and draw upon sources no longer extant. There are also in print valuable eyewitness accounts of the Reformation at a local level, such as *Narratives of the Days of the Reformation*, ed. J. G. Nichols (Camden Soc., lxxvii, 1859); *Chronicle of the Grey Friars of London*, ed. J. G. Nichols (Camden Soc., liii, 1852); and 'Robert Parkyn's Narrative of the Reformation', ed. A. G. Dickens in EHR, lxii (1947).

The first major regional study to use diocesan material extensively, though at second hand, was A. L. Rowse, *Tudor Cornwall* (1941; 2nd edn 1969). Its central theme is the Reformation changes and, despite a frank anti-Catholic bias, it remains an excellent account. Meanwhile A. G. Dickens was beginning a series of important northern studies including 'Some Popular Reactions to the Edwardian Reformation in Yorkshire', in YAJ, xxxiv (1938–9); 'Sedition and Conspiracy in Yorkshire During the Later Years of Henry VIII', in YAJ xxxiv (1938–9); 'The First Stages of Romanist Recusancy in Yorkshire, 1560–1590', in YAJ, xxxv (1940–3); and *The Marian Reaction in the Diocese of York* (St Anthony's Hall Publications, Nos. 11–12, 1957). Much of this was summed up and extended in his *Lollards and Protestants in the Diocess of York 1509–1558* (1959), a major book which revised traditional concepts both of the Tudor north and of Lollard survival. J. A. F. Thompson, *The Later Lollards 1414–1520* (1965) has since questioned some of Dickens's distinctions between Lollards and Protestants in the north. J. S. Purvis, *Tudor Parish Documents of the Diocese of York* (1948) is a valuable collection of documents from the York diocesan archives.

Since the pioneer works of Rowse and Dickens, serious local studies have proliferated, though some important ones take the form of theses as yet unpublished. For example P. Tyler, 'The Ecclesiastical Commission for the Province of York, 1561–1641' (Oxford D.Phil. thesis, 1965); see also Select List (below) for details of theses by R. A. Houlbrooke (on Norwich, 1972) and S. J. Lander (on Chichester, 1974).

Among recent published studies, Christopher Haigh's *The Last Days of the Lancashire Monasteries and the Pilgrimage of Grace* (Chetham Soc., 3rd ser., xvii, 1969) and *Reformation and Resistance in Tudor Lancashire* (1975) are outstanding. Others include H. C. Porter, *Reformation and Reaction in Tudor Cambridge* (1958); J. E. Oxley, *The Reformation in Essex to the Death of Mary* (1965); R. B. Manning, *Religion and Society in Elizabethan Sussex* (1969), D. M. Palliser, *The Reformation in York, 1534–1553* (Borthwick Paper, No. 40, 1971); and R. A. Houlbrooke, 'Persecution of Heresy and Protestantism in the Diocese of Norwich under Henry VIII', in *Norfolk Archaeology*, xxxv (1973). There are three important studies by K. G. Powell: 'The Beginnings of Protestantism in Gloucestershire', in TBGAS, xc (1971); 'The Social Background to the Reformation in Gloucestershire', *ibid.*, xcii (1973); and *The Marian Martyrs and the Reformation in Bristol* (Bristol Branch of the Historical Association, Local History Pamphlet No. 31, 1972). A. J. Willis, *Church Life in Kent* (1975) appeared too recently to be consulted. In addition, recent studies of the religious revolts are important, as is G. R. Elton's *Policy and Police: The Enforcement of the Reformation in the Age of Thomas Cromwell* (1972). Finally, there are some local studies on a broader canvas which include valuable sections on religion: they include R. B. Smith, *Land and Politics in the England of Henry VIII: the West Riding of Yorkshire 1530–46* (1970);

A. Hassell Smith, *County and Court: Government and Politics in Norfolk, 1558–1603* (1974); and M. Spufford, *Contrasting Communities: English Villagers in the Sixteenth and Seventeenth Centuries* (1974).

3.   THE REFORMATION AND POPULAR CULTURE

K. Thomas, *Religion and the Decline of Magic* (1971) is the main secondary work on popular culture in the period, drawing together in a comprehensive work information from a wide range of sources, including material in local archives. Apart from studies of single segments of society such as M. L. Campbell, *The English Yeoman under Elizabeth and the Early Stuarts* (new edn 1967) and P. Heath, *The English Parish Clergy on the Eve of the Reformation* (1969) which survey the whole way of life including the mental life of the yeomen and parish clergy respectively, other secondary works containing information on popular culture are mainly regional or local studies. In particular A. G. Dickens, *Lollards and Protestants in the Diocese of York* (1959); C. Haigh, *Reformation and Resistance in Tudor Lancashire* (1975); J. E. Oxley, *The Reformation in Essex* (1965) and, for the post-Reformation period, R. C. Richardson, *Puritanism in North-West England* (1972) may be highly recommended. K. G. Powell, 'The Beginnings of Protestantism in Gloucestershire', in TBGAS, xc (1971) 141–57, sheds interesting light on popular religious attitudes there.

M. James, *Family, Lineage and Civil Society: A Study of Society, Politics and Mentality in the Durham Region 1500–1640* (1974) contains a scholarly account of cultural transition in Durham. The economy, social structure, facilities for elementary schooling and the religious beliefs of three contrasting villages in Cambridgeshire are the subjects of M. Spufford, *Contrasting Communities: English Villagers in the Sixteenth and Seventeenth Centuries* (1974). 'Village Sampling' is also embodied in A. Macfarlane, *Witchcraft in Tudor and Stuart England: A Regional and Comparative Study* (1970) which breaks new ground in its treatment of witchcraft within an anthropological context.

The approach of 'village sampling' is compared with that of '*histoire totale*' in a useful review article by K. Wrightson, 'Villages, Villagers and Village Studies', in HJ, xviii (1975) 632–9, which reviews both Margart Spufford's book and D. G. Hey, *An English Rural Community: Myddle under the Tudors and Stuarts* (1974) which adopts the approach of *histoire totale*. The review concludes that this approach of *histoire totale* is appropriate only to well-documented localities whereas Dr Hey was heavily dependent upon one source. It also emphasises the value of setting local developments within a regional perspective as Margaret Spufford does in her book. A. D. Dyer, *The City of Worcester in the Sixteenth Century* (Leicester 1973) is a good example of the *histoire totale* approach to a community which was of sufficient size and was sufficiently well-documented to yield valuable information on the whole way of life, including social and cultural aspects.

Recommended works on education and literacy are J. Simon, *Education and Society in Tudor England* (1966); N. Orme, *English Schools in the Middle Ages* (1973); J. W. Adamson, 'The Extent of Literacy in England in the Fifteenth and Sixteenth Centuries', in *The Library*, 4th ser., x (1930) 163–93; D. Cressy, 'Occupations, Migrations and Literacy in East London, 1580–1640', in *Local Population Studies*, v (1970) 53–60; and H. S. Bennett, *English Books and Readers* (3 vols, 1952, 1965 and 1970) which contains valuable details of provincial collections of books.

4.   THE PROTESTANT EPISCOPATE

The most useful recent writings on the Elizabethan bishops have been P. Collinson's 'Episcopacy and Reform in the Later Sixteenth Century', in *Studies in Church History;*

III, ed. G. J. Cuming (1966), which is concerned with the extent to which puritan reform could be accommodated within the framework of an episcopal church, and R. B. Manning's 'The Crisis of Episcopal Authority During the Reign of Elizabeth I', in JBS, xi (1971), which is largely devoted to the development of diocesan ecclesiastical commissions as a means of buttressing episcopal authority. Patrick Collinson's *The Elizabethan Puritan Movement* (1967) contains much information about the shaping of the episcopate, while R. B. Manning's *Religion and Society in Elizabethan Sussex* (1969) is the local study which best illustrates the difficulties which a reforming bishop faced in his diocese. Other valuable local studies which have appeared recently are Rosemary O'Day's 'Thomas Bentham: A Case Study in the Problems of the Early Elizabethan Episcopate', in JEH, xxiii (1972); and the same author's 'The Reformation of the Ministry', in *Continuity and Change: Personnel and Administration of the Church in England, 1500–1642*, eds Rosemary O'Day and Felicity Heal (1976); and Christopher Haigh's *Reformation and Resistance in Tudor Lancashire* (1974). For the machinery of episcopal visitation see H. G. Owen, 'The Episcopal Visitation: its Limits and Limitations in Elizabethan London', in JEH, xi (1960). F. O. White's *Lives of the Elizabethan Bishops of the Anglican Church* (1898) is an invaluable mine of information to which this chapter is heavily indebted; it is often superior in both its accuracy and its perspicacity to the lives written for the DNB. The first and last Elizabethan archbishops are covered by V. J. K. Brook's *A Life of Archbishop Parker* (1962); the same author's *Whitgift and the English Church* (1957); and P. M. Dawley's *John Whitgift and the English Reformation* (1954). Patrick Collinson's biography of Edmund Grindal should appear before long.

One of the most readable contemporary statements of the episcopal point of view is Thomas Cooper's *An Admonition to the People of England*, ed. E. Arber (English Scholar's Library xv, 1883). *Visitation Articles and Injunctions of the Period of the Reformation: 1536–75*, eds W. H. Frere and W. P. M. Kennedy (Alcuin Club Collections, i–iii, 1908–10) and W. P. M. Kennedy, *Elizabethan Episcopal Administration: An Essay in Sociology and Politics* (Alcuin Club Collections, xxv–xxvii, 1924) together with *A Collection of Original Letters from the Bishops to the Privy Council, 1564*, ed. M. Bateson in *Miscellany IX* (Camden Soc., new ser., liii, 1895) and the letters from the bishops to Grindal edited by S. E. Lehmberg in *The Historical Magazine of the Protestant Episcopal Church*, xxxiv (1965) are probably the most readily digestible items in a considerable corpus of editions of correspondence and administrative records.

A considerable amount of interesting information and argument is contained in as yet unpublished dissertations. For these see general listing of theses (pp. 186–7 below).

5. ECONOMIC PROBLEMS OF THE CLERGY

The standard work on the finances of the church is Christopher Hill, *Economic Problems of the Church from Archbishop Whitgift to the Long Parliament* (1956). This is an outstanding investigation of the whole range of problems faced by the church but its focus is on the Laudian period and for the sixteenth century its information is sometimes misleading. General accounts of the church in the sixteenth century add little to Hill. There is a brief chapter on the secular church as landlord by Joyce Youings in *The Agrarian History of England and Wales: IV, 1500–1640*, ed. Joan Thirsk (1967). A good discussion on Marian policy towards church finance is R. H. Pogson, 'Revival and Reform in Mary Tudor's Church: a question of money', in JEH, xxv (1974) 249–65. W. P. Haugaard, *Elizabeth and the English Reformation* (1968) provides an account of Elizabethan policy which is occasionally a useful antidote to Hill's gloom but is far too generous to the virgin Queen. There is far too little information on the taxation of the clergy but two articles that are worthwhile are: J. J. Scarisbrick, 'Clerical Taxation in England 1485–1547', in JEH, xi (1960) 41–54, and Felicity Heal, 'Clerical Tax Collection under the Tudors', in *Continuity and Change: Personnel and Administration of the Church in England, 1500–1642*, eds Rosemary O'Day and Felicity Heal (1976).

The finances of the bishops have been given considerable attention in recent years. Phyllis Hembry's *The Bishops of Bath and Wells, 1540–1640* (1967) is the most detailed investigation of one diocese but there are a number of articles on various sees. For example, F. du Boulay, 'Archbishop Cranmer and the Canterbury Temporalities', in EHR, lxvii (1952) 19–36; Claire Cross, 'The Economic Problems of the See of York', in AHR, xviii, supplement (1970) 64–81; Felicity Heal, 'The Tudors and Church Lands: the case of Ely', in ECHR, 2nd ser., xxvi (1973) 198–217; Rosemary O'Day, 'Cumulative Debt: The Bishops of Coventry and Lichfield and their Economic Problems *c.* 1540–1640', in MH, iii (1976) 76–90. A general essay, 'The Plunder of the Church', which attempts to set recent research on the economic problems of the church in context, appears in Rosemary O'Day, *Economy and Community: Economic and Social History of Pre-industrial England, 1500–1700* (1975) pp. 102–21.

Discussion of the finances of the parish clergy is usually included in general studies of their situation. The most systematic studies of the pre-Reformation period are those of Peter Heath, *The English Parish Clergy on the Eve of the Reformation* (1969) and *Medieval Clerical Accounts* (St Anthony's Hall Publication, No. 26, 1964). Also of great value are Margaret Bowker, *The Secular Clergy of the Diocese of Lincoln, 1495–1520* (1968) and Christopher Haigh, *Reformation and Resistance in Tudor Lancashire* (1975). The latter contains invaluable data on clergy of all ranks throughout the Reformation period. On the later sixteenth century much evidence still remains to be published. There is a useful article on Kent by Michael Zell, 'The Personnel of the Clergy in Kent during the Reformation', in EHR, lxxxix (1974) 513–33 and three important dissertations (for details see Select List, below): D. M. Barratt (on Oxford, Worcester and Gloucester, 1950); S. J. Lander (on Chichester, 1974); and M. R. O'Day (on Patronage and Recruitment, 1972). All three theses stress the importance of glebe and the subject is given more detailed treatment in D. M. Barratt, *Ecclesiastical Terriers of Warwickshire Parishes* (Dugdale Soc. 1955).

Finally there are the cathedral chapters, whose finances have been little studied for the sixteenth century. There is some information in A. Hamilton Thompson, *The Cathedral Churches of England* (1925). Margaret Bowker studies the prebendaries of Lincoln in *Secular Clergy* and there is a valuable recent dissertation on Durham by David Marcombe, 'The Dean and Chapter of Durham, 1558–1603' (Durham Ph.D. thesis, 1973).

6. THE DISPOSAL OF MONASTIC AND CHANTRY LANDS

The limitations of many of the works listed below are noted in the chapter. It is perhaps best to read first J. A. Youings, *The Dissoluation of the Monasteries* (1971) which gives the most recent summary of scholarly findings and includes illustrative documents. G. W. O. Woodward, *The Dissolution of the Monasteries* (1968) is also readable and has selected documents but is a less scholarly work with no footnotes. A. G. Dickens, *The English Reformation* (1964) and M. D. Knowles, *The Religious Orders in England:* Vol III (1959) though covering wider issues have important sections on the disposal of monastic lands.

The best local studies in print are J. A. Youings, 'The Terms of the Disposal of the Devon Monastic Lands 1536–58', in EHR, lxix (1954) and *Devon Monastic Lands: Particulars for Grants* (Devon and Cornwall Record Soc., new ser. i, 1955), which should be read in conjunction with J. E. Kew, 'The Disposal of Crown Lands and the Devon Land Market 1536–58', in AHR, xviii (1970). Other notable local studies include W. A. J. Archbold, *The Somerset Religious Houses* (Cambridge Historical Essays, 1892), now a rather scarce book; T. H. Swales, 'The Redistribution of the Monastic Lands in Norfolk ...', in *Norfolk Archaeology*, xxiv (1966), rather concentrated reading and poorly documented; and G. A. J. Hodgett, 'The Dissolution of the Religious Houses in Lincolnshire ...', in *Lincs. AAS Reports and Papers*, new ser. iv, i (1951). The *Victoria County Histories* for many counties also follow through the disposal of some of the monastic sites. A Savine, *English Monasteries on the Eve of the Dissolution* (Oxford Studies in Social and Legal History, ed. P. Vinogradoff, 1909); S. B. Liljegren, *The Fall of the Monasteries and Social Changes in England* (Leipsig 1924); F. C. Dietz, *English Government Finance 1485–1588* (Urbana 1920), must all be read with caution in the light of later research. The work of still earlier writers is often interesting, but an important piece of introductory reading is Margaret Aston, 'English Ruins and English History: the Dissolution and the Sense of the Past', in *Journal of the Warburg and Courtauld Institutes*, xxxvi (1973).

On the disposal of the chantry lands the only detailed appraisal in print is W. K. Jordan, *Edward VI*: Vol. I, *The Young King* (1968) and Vol. II, *The Threshold of Power* (1970) but, whilst the conclusions may be sound, the statistics are suspect. A lively local study is H. J. Hanham, 'The Suppression of the Chantries in Ashburton', in *Transactions of the Devonshire Association* (1967). Many of the conclusions of H. J. Habakkuk, 'The Market for Monastic Property 1539–1603', in *echr*, 2nd ser., x (1958), hold good for the chantries also.

The dissolutions may be seen in a wider context through some of the essays in *The Agrarian History of England and Wales: IV, 1500–1640*, ed. Joan Thirsk (1967), and something of the administrative turmoil may be understood from a reading of W. C. Richardson, *History of the Court of Augmentations* (Baton Rouge 1961).

7. ECCLESIASTICAL PATRONAGE

Rather surprisingly there is very little in print directly on the subject of ecclesiastical patronage, particularly as related to patronage of the parochial as opposed to the higher clergy. For general background the interested reader should consult: Margaret Bowker, *The Secular Clergy in the Diocese of Lincoln, 1495–1520* (1968); Christopher Haigh, *Reformation and Resistance in Tudor Lancashire* (1975); A. Hamilton Thompson, *The English Clergy and their Organization in the Later Middle Ages* (1966); Peter Heath, *English Parish Clergy on the Eve of the Reformation* (1969); Roger B. Manning, *Religion and Society in Elizabethan Sussex* (1969); R. C. Richardson, *Puritanism in North-West England* (1972). Articles in print which deal specifically with patronage include: Claire Cross, 'Noble Patronage in the Elizabethan Church', in *hj*, iii (1960); A. P. Kautz, 'The Selection of Jacobean Bishops', in *Early Stuart Studies: Essays in Honour of D. H. Willson*, ed. H. S. Reinmuth (Minneapolis 1970); H. R. Trevor-Roper, 'King James and his Bishops', in *ht* (1955) and Rosemary O'Day, 'The Ecclesiastical Patronage of the Lord Keeper, 1558–1642', in *trhs*, 5th ser., xxiii (1973); and 'The Law of Patronage in the Early Modern Church of England', in *jeh*, xxvi (1975).

Some of the more important discussions of patronage, however, appear in unpublished dissertations which are well worth acquiring through inter-library loan services. The following are of especial interest (see Select List below for details): R. Donaldson (on Durham, 1955); D. M. Barratt (on Oxford, Worcester and Gloucester, 1950); R. Christopher (on Surrey Clergy, 1975); J. I. Daeley (on Parker's Administration, 1967); M. R. O'Day (on Patronage and Recruitment, 1972); H. G. Owen (on London Clergy, 1957); W. J. Sheils (Puritans in Peterborough, 1974); and M. L. Zell (Church and Gentry in Kent, 1974).

Those seeking a definition of patronage would do well to consult Wallace MacCaffrey, 'Place and Patronage in Elizabethan Politics', in *Elizabethan Government and Society: Essays Presented to Sir John Neale*, eds S. T. Bindoff, Joel Hurstfield and C. H. Williams (1961). General discussions of the problems facing those who 'controlled' the church in England include Joel Hurstfield's 'Church and State, 1558–1612: The Task of the Cecils', reprinted in *Freedom, Corruption and Government in Elizabethan England* (1973); Patrick Collinson's *The Elizabethan Puritan Movement* (1967) and W. P. Haugaard, *Elizabeth and the English Reformation* (1968).

8.   RELIGION IN PROVINCIAL TOWNS: INNOVATION AND TRADITION

The debate originated with R. H. Tawney, *Religion and the Rise of Capitalism* (1926) and was continued by C. Hill in *Economic Problems of the Church from Archbishop Whitgift to the Long Parliament* (1956), *Society and Puritanism in Pre-Revolutionary England* (1964) and 'The Puritans and the Dark Corners of the Land', in TRHS, xiii (1963). Christopher Hill's work provoked further studies, notably P. S. Seaver, *The Puritan Lectureships, the Politics of Religious Dissent, 1560–1640* (Stanford, Calif. 1970); R. C. Richardson, *Puritanism in North-West England* (1972); and M. H. Curtis, 'The Alienated Intellectuals of Early Stuiart England', in *P & P*, xxiii (1962) which stands as the most pronounced statement of the opposition between puritan lecturers and the establishment. In contrast the common ground between these groups has been stressed in recent articles by N. R. N. Tyacke, 'Puritanism, Arminianism and Counter-Revolution', in *The Origins of the English Civil War*, ed. C. S. R. Russell (1973) and by Patrick Collinson, 'Lectures by Combination: Structures and Characteristics of Church Life in 17th-Century England', in BIHR, xlviii (1975), and 'Towards a Broader Understanding of the early Dissenting Tradition', in *The Dissenting Tradition: Essays for Leland H. Carlson*, eds C. R. Cole and M. E. Moody (Ohio 1975). Much of the approach of my chapter derives from these last three articles and from Patrick Collinson's *The Elizabethan Puritan Movement* (1967).

Two general books can be mentioned for urban history: *Perspectives in Urban History*, ed. A. Everitt (1973); and *Crisis and Order in English Towns, 1500–1700*, eds P. Clark and P. Slack (1972), particularly the essays by Slack and Phythian-Adams in the latter. Alan Everitt's article, 'The Marketing of Agricultural Produce', in *The Agrarian History of England and Wales*: IV, *1500–1640*, ed. Joan Thirsk (1967) is also important. Individual towns where the Reformation has received extended treatment include Exeter: W. T. MacCaffrey, *Exeter 1540–1650* (Cambridge, Mass. 1958 and 1976) and York: D. M. Palliser, *The Reformation in York, 1534–1553* (1971) and 'The Unions of Parishes in York, 1547–86', in YAJ, xlvi (1974). Two areas which have received close attention are Lancashire, where R. C. Richardson's work is supplemented by C. Haigh, *Reformation and Resistance in Tudor Lancashire* (1975), and Sussex, treated by R. B. Manning, *Religion and Society in Elizabethan Sussex* (1969) and A. J. Fletcher, *A County Community at Peace and War, Sussex 1600–1660* (1975). Finally, Paul Seaver's book has a valuable appendix showing printed borough records of interest, and there are plenty of nuggets to be dug out of the postwar volumes of the *Victoria County History*.

SELECT LIST OF THESES

Barratt, D. M. 'Conditions of the Parish Clergy from the Reformation to 1660 in the Dioceses of Oxford, Worcester and Gloucester' (Oxford D.Phil., 1950)

Berlatsky, J. A. 'The Social Structure of the Elizabethan Episcopacy' (Northwestern Ph.D., 1970)

Block, J. S. 'Church and Commonwealth: Ecclesiastical Patronage During Thomas Cromwell's Ministry, 1535–1540' (University of California, Los Angeles, Ph.D., 1973)

Christophers, R. 'The Social and Educational Background of the Surrey Clergy, 1520–1620' (London Ph.D., 1975)

Daeley, J. I. 'The Episcopal Administration of Matthew Parker Archbishop of Canterbury, 1559–1575' (London Ph.D., 1967)

Donaldson, R. 'Patronage and the Church: A Study in the Social Structure of the Secular Clergy in the Diocese of Durham, 1311–1540' (Edinburgh Ph.D., 1955)

Heal, F. M. 'The Bishops of Ely and their Diocese During the Reformation Period: c. 1515–1600' (Cambridge Ph.D., 1972)

Houlbrooke, R. A. 'Church Courts and People in the Diocese of Norwich, 1519–70' (Cambridge Ph.D., 1970)

Lander, S. J. 'The Diocese of Chichester, 1508–58' (Cambridge Ph.D., 1974)

Marcombe, D. 'The Dean and Chapter of Durham, 1558–1603' (Durham Ph.D., 1973)

Mullins, E. L. C. 'The Effect of the Marian and Elizabethan Religious Settlements upon the Clergy of the City of London, 1553–1560' (London M.A., 1948)

O'Day, M. R. 'Clerical Patronage and Recruitment in England During the Elizabethan and Early Stuart Periods . . .' (London Ph.D., 1972; to be published as *The English Clergy: The Emergence and Consolidation of a Profession*)

Owen, H. G. 'The London Parish Clergy in the Reign of Elizabeth I' (London Ph.D., 1957)

Sheils, W. J. 'The Puritans in Church and Politics in the Diocese of Peterborough, 1570–1610' (London Ph.D., 1974)

Shipps, K. W. 'Lay Patronage of East Anglian Puritan Clerics in Pre-Revolutionary England' (Yale Ph.D., 1971)

Steig, M. F. 'The Parochial Clergy of the Diocese of Bath and Wells, 1625–85' (University of California, Berkeley, Ph.D., 1970)

Zell, M. L. 'Church and Gentry in Reformation Kent, 1533–53' (University of California, Los Angeles, Ph.D., 1974)

Notes and References

For abbreviations used here, see pages 178–9 above.

INTRODUCTION   *Felicity Heal* and *Rosemary O'Day*

1. R. Hooker, *Of the Laws of Ecclesiastical Polity*, Book viii (New York 1931) p. 166.
2. Ibid., p. 165.
3. See, for example, C. Phythian-Adams, 'Ceremony and the Citizen: the Communal Year at Coventry, 1450–1550', in *Crisis and Order in English Towns, 1500–1700*, eds P. Clark and P. Slack (1972) pp. 57–85.
4. K. V. Thomas, *Religion and the Decline of Magic* (1971).
5. P. Heath, *English Parish Clergy on the Eve of the Reformation* (1969); M. Bowker, *The Secular Clergy in the Diocese of Lincoln 1495–1520* (1968).
6. W. Haller, *The Rise of Puritanism* (New York 1938).
7. See, for example, S. J. Lander, 'The Church Courts and the Reformation in the Diocese of Chichester', in *Continuity and Change: Personnel and Administration of the Church in England, 1500–1642*, eds M. R. O'Day and F. Heal (1976).
8. BM Lansdowne MS. vi, fo. 87.
9. W. K. Jordan, *Philanthropy in England, 1480–1660* (1959).
10. C. Hill, *Economic Problems of the Church from Archbishop Whitgift to the Long Parliament* (1956).
11. LP, xiv, i, 402.
12. N. R. N. Tyacke, 'Puritanism, Arminianism and Counter-Revolution', in *The Origins of the English Civil War*, ed. C. S. R. Russell (1973).

1.   CHURCHMEN AND THE ROYAL SUPREMACY   *Claire Cross*

1. W. Tyndale, *The Obedience of a Christian Man* (1528) in *Doctrinal Treatises . . . by William Tyndale*, ed. H. Walter (Parker Soc. 1848) p. 334.
2. G. R. Elton, *The Tudor Constitution* (1960) pp. 330, 355; J. J. Scarisbrick, *Henry VIII* (1968) p. 299.
3. S. Gardiner, *The Oration of True Obedience* (1535) in *Obedience in Church and State*, ed. P. Janelle (1930) pp. 91, 93; compare R. Hooker, *Of the Laws of Ecclesiastical Polity* (1666), Book viii, pp. 448–9; repr. New York 1931, pp. 448–9.
4. *Miscellaneous Writings and Letters of Thomas Cranmer*, ed. J. E. Cox (Parker Soc. 1846) p. 98.
5. Ibid., p. 116.
6. *Sermons and Remains of Hugh Latimer*, ed. G. E. Corrie (Parker Soc. 1845) p. 158.
7. J. Foxe, *Acts and Monuments* (1684) iii, p. 548.
8. *Miscellaneous Writings . . . of Thomas Cranmer*, ed. Cox, p. 563.
9. SR, iv, pt i, pp. 355–8.
10. *The Zurich Letters*, ed. H. Robinson (Parker Soc. 1842) p. 33; J. Jewel, *The Defence of the Apology* (1567) in *The Works of John Jewel* (Parker Soc. 1850) iv, p. 974.
11. *Correspondence of Matthew Parker*, eds. J. Bruce and T. T. Perowne (Parker Soc. 1853) p. 94.

12. Ibid., pp. 156–7.

13. *The Remains of Edmund Grindal*, ed. W. Nicholson (Parker Soc. 1843) pp. 387–90.

14. J. Strype, *Whitgift* (1718) p. 293 and Appendix, pp. 129–30.

15. Quoted in W. D. J. Cargill Thompson, 'Anthony Marten and the Elizabethan Debate on Episcopacy', in *Essays in Modern English Church History in Memory of Norman Sykes*, eds C. V. Bennett and J. D. Walsh (1966) p. 44.

16. R. Hooker, *Ecclesiastical Polity*, p. 481.

17. Strype, *Whitgift*, p. 461; Trinity College Cambridge MS. B/14/9, fo. 117; *Correspondence of John Cosin*, ed. G. Ornsby (Surtees Soc., lii, 1869) i, p. 56.

18. Quoted in N. R. N. Tyacke, 'Puritanism, Arminianism, and Counter-Revolution', in *The Origins of the English Civil War*, ed. C. S. R. Russell (1973) pp. 123–4.

2. POPULAR REACTIONS TO THE REFORMATION

D. M. Palliser

1. T. Fuller, *The Worthies of England*, ed. J. Freeman (1952) p. 23.

2. M. D. Knowles, *The Religious Orders in England*: Vol. III: *The Tudor Age* (1959) p. 436.

3. HMC 12th Report, Appendix, part ix, p. 534; C. Haigh, *Reformation and Resistance in Tudor Lancashire* (1975) p. 220.

4. A. G. Dickens, *The English Reformation* (1964) p. 69; and *Lollards and Protestants in the Diocese of York* (1959) p. 48; C. Haigh, *Reformation and Resistance*, pp. 159–77.

5. For the Pilgrimage see M. H. and R. Dodds, *The Pilgrimage of Grace, 1536–37, and the Exeter Conspiracy, 1538*, 2 vols (1915), a full narrative from a sympathetic standpoint. The social and economic interpretation was advanced by R. R. Reid, *The King's Council in the North* (1921); see also A. G. Dickens, *Lollards and Protestants* and 'Secular and Religious Motivation in the Pilgrimage of Grace', in *Studies in Church History*: IV, ed. G. J. Cuming (1967) pp. 39–64. Covert gentry leadership is cogently argued in R. B. Smith, *Land and Politics in the England of Henry VIII . . .* (1970) ch. 5, and in M. James, 'Obedience and Dissent in Henrician England: the Lincolnshire Rebellion 1536', in P & P xlviii (1970) 3–78. A reassertion of the religious element is contained in Haigh, *Last Days of the Lancashire Monasteries . . .* (1969) *passim*; Palliser, *The Reformation in York 1534–1553* (Borthwick Paper, No. 40, 1971) pp. 7–12; and J. J. Scarisbrick, *Henry VIII* (1968) pp. 339–46.

6. *Ballads from Manuscripts*, ed. F. J. Furnivall (Ballad Soc. 1868–72) pp. 304–6.

7. Dickens, *English Reformation*, pp. 190, 193; *Narratives of the Days of the Reformation*, ed. J. G. Nichols (Camden Soc., lviii, 1852) pp. 349–51; R. A. Houlbrooke, 'Persecution of Heresy and Protestantism in the Diocese of Norwich under Henry VIII', in *Norfolk Archaeology*, xxxv (1973) 319.

8. M. Spufford, *Contrasting Communities . . .* (1974) pp. 320–44.

9. Ibid., pp. 334–41; Dickens, *Lollards and Protestants*, pp. 171–2; Palliser, *Reformation in York*, pp. 19–21, 28, 32; K. G. Powell, 'Beginnings of Protestantism in Gloucestershire', in TBGAS, xc (1971) 144; J. Strype, *Ecclesiastical Memorials*: I (1721) pp. 316–19 and Appendix, pp. 249–52.

10. J. Phillips, *The Reformation of Images: The Destruction of Art in England, 1535–1660* (University of California Press, Los Angeles 1973) pp. 8, 187.

11. Dickens, *The Marian Reaction in the Diocese of York* (St Anthony's Hall Publication, No. 11, 1957) pp. 15–19 and *English Reformation*, p. 245; Houlbrooke, 'Persecution of Heresy', 317; Spufford, *Contrasting Communities*, p. 244; R. B. Walker, 'Reformation and Reaction in the County of Lincoln, 1547–58', in Lincs. AAS, ix (1961) 57; Haigh, *Reformation and Resistance*, p. 181.

12. D. M. Loades, *Two Tudor Conspiracies* (1965) pp. 12–127; map opposite p. 284.

13. *York Civic Records*, ed. A. Raine, 8 vols (York ASRS, 1939–53), v, p. 92; P. F. Tytler, *England under the Reigns of Edward VI and Mary* (1839) ii, p. 309 (translated).

14. C. H. Garrett, *The Marian Exiles* (1938).

15. For doubts about the Bristol martyrs see K. G. Powell, *The Marian Martyrs and the Reformation in Bristol* (Bristol HA, 1972).

16. Spufford, *Contrasting Communities*, p. 248n.

17. Strype, *Ecclesiastical Memorials*, iii, Appendix, p. 248; Dickens, *English Reformation*, pp. 272–7; D. M. Loades, 'The Enforcement of Reaction, 1553–1558', in JEH, xvi (1965) 62.

18. Hayward's Annals of the *First Four Years of the Reign of Queen Elizabeth*, ed. J. Bruce (Camden Soc., vii, 1840) p. 28; *The Zurich Letters*, ed. H. Robinson (Parker Soc. 1842) i, p. 44.

19. P. McGrath, *Papists and Puritans under Elizabeth I* (1967) p. 47; *York Civic Records*, vi, 42.

20. *A collection of Original Letters from the Bishops to the Privy Council, 1564*, ed. M. Bateson in *Miscellany IX* (Camden Soc., new ser., liii, 1895), separate pagination.

21. J. S. Purvis, *Tudor Parish Documents . . .* (1948) pp. 15–34; R. B. Manning, *Religion and Society in Elizabethan Sussex* (1969) pp. 42–6; C. Cross, *The Royal Supremacy in the Elizabethan Church* (1969) p. 100; P. Collinson, *The Elizabethan Puritan Movement* (1967) pp. 84–91.

22. *The Remains of Edmund Grindal*, ed. W. Nicholson (Parker Soc., 1843) p. 326.

23. R. Welford, *History of Newcastle and Gateshead*, iii (1887) p. 33; J. Hunter, *Hallamshire*, 2nd edn (1869) p. 82; York BIHR, PROB reg. xxiv, fo. 49; Haigh, *Reformation and Resistance*, pp. 220–1.

24. T. M. Parker, *The English Reformation to 1558* (1950) p. 24.

25. Haigh, *Reformation and Resistance*, p. vii.

26. Cross, *Royal Supremacy*, pp. 95–114; *Reformation and Resistance*, entries indexed under Stanley, Edward.

27. Powell, *Marian Martyrs*, pp. 8–9; Spufford, *Contrasting Communities*, pp. 244–5.

28. G. R. Elton, *Policy and Police* (1972) pp. 162–4; McGrath, *Papists and Puritans*, p. 81; CSP Ven., v. 345; *Chronicle of the Grey Friars of London*, ed. J. G. Nichols (Camden Soc., liii, 1852), pp. 67, 89.

29. *Narratives of the Reformation*, pp. 71–84, 315–16.

30. A. L. Rowse, *Tudor Cornwall*, 2nd edn (1969) p. 262; J. Hooker, *The Description of the Citie of Excester* (Devon and Cornwall RS 1919) pp. 62–3, 67–8, 71.

31. *Tudor Economic Documents*, ed. R. H. Tawney and E. Power (1924) i, pp. 20–1, 28.

32. W. K. Jordan, *Edward VI: The Young King* (1968) p. 150; Rowse, *Tudor Cornwall*, p. 318; Loades, *Two Tudor Conspiracies*, pp. 44–5; Dickens, *Lollards and Protestants*, p. 99; Spufford, *Contrasting Communities*, pp. 246–8.

33. Elton, *Policy and Police*, pp. 20–1, 85–90; Palliser, *Tudor York* (forthcoming).

34. J. H. Gleason, *The Justices of the Peace in England, 1558–1640* (1969) pp. 68–72; R. B. Manning, 'Elizabethan Recusancy Commissions', in HJ, xv (1972) 25; A. Hassell Smith, *County and Court . . .* (1974) pp. 206–8, 226–8; Manning, *Religion and Society*, pp. 61–125.

35. L. Stone, *The Crisis of the Aristocracy 1558–1641* (1965) p. 741; Manning, *Religion and Society*, p. 259; J. T. Cliffe, *The Yorkshire Gentry from the Reformation to the Civil War* (1969) p. 169.

36. K. R. Wark, *Elizabethan Recusancy in Cheshire* (Chetham Soc., 3rd ser., xix, 1971) pp. 16–17.

37. M. R. O'Day, 'Thomas Bentham', in JEH, xxiii (1972) 145; J. C. H. Aveling, *Catholic Recusancy in the City of York 1558–1791* (Catholic RS Monograph ser., 2, 1970) p. 20; Haigh, *Reformation and Resistance*, p. 210.

38. W. T. MacCaffrey, *Exeter 1540–1640 . . .* 1st edn (Cambridge, Mass. 1958) pp. 191–2.

39. W. H. Jones, *Diocesan Histories: Salisbury* (1880) p. 194.

40. Spufford, *Contrasting Communities*, pp. 244, 249; A. G. Dickens, 'Robert Parkyn's Narrative of the Reformation', in EHR, lxii (1947) 58–83; Haigh, *Reformation and Resistance*, pp. 212, 217–18.

41. Spufford, *Contrasting Communities*, pp. 306–15.

42. Dickens, *Lollards and Protestants*, p. 247; R. J. Knecht, 'The Early Reformation in England and France', in *History*, lvii (1972) 7.

43. Haigh, *Reformation and Resistance*, p. 139.

44. A. G. Dickens, 'The First Stages of Romanist Recusancy in Yorkshire', in YAJ, xxxv (1940–3) 180–1, and *Marian Reaction*, ii, p. 14.

45. Such wills have been observed between 1549 and 1586; the latest noted in York BIHR, PROB reg. xxiii, fo. 223.

3. THE REFORMATION AND POPULAR CULTURE *Imogen Luxton*

(The writer would like to thank Professor A. G. Dickens for reading this chapter in draft.)

1. A. G. Dickens, 'Aspects of Intellectual Transition among the English Parish Clergy of the Reformation Period: A Regional Example', in *Archiv für Reformationsgeschichte*, xl (1952) 51–70; 'The Writers of Tudor Yorkshire', in TRHS, 5th ser., xiii (1963) 49–76.

2. Margaret Bowker's review of K. Thomas, *Religion and the Decline of Magic* (1971), in HJ, xv (1972) 363–6; E. P. Thompson, 'Anthropology and the Discipline of Historical Context', in MH, i (1972) 41–55.

3. Bodl. MS. Lat. misc. c66. The texts of the poems are printed in R. Hope Robbins, 'The Poems of Humfrey Newton, Esquire 1466–1536', in *Publications of the Modern Language Association of America*, lxv (1950) 249–81.

4. PCC 31 Dyngeley: Will of John Wistowe of Stotteford, Staffordshire, dated 1 Feb 1539, proved 14 Oct 1539. Wistowe bequeathed 6s 8d and a velvet jacket to the wardens of the Corpus Christi play at Tamworth.

5. L. Powlick, 'The Staging of the Chester Cycle; An Alternate Theory', in *Theatre Survey*, xii (1971) 119–50.

6. A. H. Nelson, 'Some Configurations of Staging in Medieval English Drama', in *Medieval English Drama*, eds J. Taylor and A. H. Nelson (Chicago 1972) pp. 116–47; A. H. Nelson, *The Medieval English Stage Corpus Christi Pageants and Plays* (Chicago 1974).

7. W. Dugdale, *Antiquities of Warwickshire* 2 vols (1730) i, p. 183.

8. *Life of Master John Shaw in Yorkshire Diaries and Autobiographies in the seventeenth and eighteenth centuries*, ed. H. J. Morehouse (Surtees Soc., lxv, 1875) pp. 138–9.

9. Charles Phythian-Adams, 'Ceremony and the Citizen: The Communal Year at Coventry, 1450–1550', in *Crisis and Order in English Towns, 1500–1700*, eds P. Clark and P. Slack (1972) pp. 57–85.

10. *The Holy Lyfe and History of Saynt Werburge*, ed. E. Hawkins (Chetham Soc., xv, 1848) p. 209.

11. SP I/22/1285.

12. LP xiii ii 1243, fo. 516.

13. Bodl. MS. Lat. misc. c66, fos 21–21v.

14. J. Gairdner, 'Bishop Hooper's Visitation of Gloucester in 1551', in EHR, xix (1904) 98–121; F. D. Price, 'Gloucester Diocese under Bishop Hooper', in TBGAS, lx (1939) 51–151.

15. *Narratives of the Days of the Reformation*, ed. J. G. Nichols (Camden Soc., lxxvii, 1859) p. 335.

16. F. G. Emmison, *Elizabethan Life: Morals and the Church Courts* (1973).

17. J. Foxe, *Acts and Monuments* (1839) viii, p. 123.

18. WRO, B.A.2764/802, fo. 107.

19. Ibid., fo. 117.

20. Ibid., fo. 110v.

21. *Registrum Ricardi Mayew*, ed. A. T. Bannister, (CYS, xxvii, 1921) pp. 109–10.

22. For a detailed study of the Coventry group see I. Luxton, 'The Lichfield Court Book: A Postscript', in BIHR, xliv (1971) 120–5.

23. T. More, *The Defence of the Second Reason agaynst Tindall* (*The Seconde Parte of the Confutation of Tyndale, made in the Yere of Our Lorde 1533*), in *The Workes* (1557) p. 727.

24. BM Cleopatra MS. Eiv, fo. 56: Commissioners at Bristol to Cromwell.

25. R. Ricart, *The Maire of Bristowe is Kalendar*, ed. L. T. Smith (Camden Soc., new ser., v, 1872) p. 55.

26. LPL, Register of Archbishop Thomas Cranmer, fo. 68.

27. *The Zurich Letters*, ed. H. Robinson (Parker Soc., 1842) i, pp. 86–7: Thomas Lever to Bullinger, 10 July 1560.

28. T. Becon, 'The Jewel of Joy' in *The Catechism of Thomas Becon with other pieces written by him in the Reign of King Edward the Sixth*, ed. J. Ayre (Parker Soc., iii, 1844) p. 426.

29. H. Bullinger, *A Most Godly and Learned Discourse of the Woorthynesse, Authorities, and Sufficiencie of the Holy Scripture . . .*, translated by John Tomkys (1579).

30. Extracts from the register of Sir Thomas Butler, Vicar of Much Wenlock, are printed in *The Cambrian Journal*, 2nd ser., lv (1861), 82–98.

31. LP, xii, ii, 587, fo. 218.

32. Ed. F. R. Raines in *Miscellany V* (Chetham Soc., xcvi, 1875) pp. 1–48.

33. NLW MS. 4919D, fos 85–6; cited in M. R. O'Day, 'Thomas Bentham: a Case Study in the Problems of the Early Elizabethan Episcopate', in JEH, xxiii (1972), 137–59.

34. WRO, B.A. 2764/802, fos 109–10.

35. GDR, iv, fos 34–5; cited in F. D. Price, 'Gloucester Diocese under Bishop Hooper', in TBGAS, lx (1939) 140.

36. BM Add. MS. 29,780, fo. 131; BM Harleian MS. 2057, fo. 29.

37. Extracts from *Fearful News of Thunder and Lightening with Terrible Effects, which Almighty God Sent on a Place Called Olveston, in the County of Gloucester, the 28th of November 1605*, are printed in *Gloucestershire Notes and Queries*, iii (1885–7) 137–8.

38. WRO, Prob. 112/1610.

39. BM Add. MS. 30,076. The will of Richard Dobbs is in CRO, WS 1621.

40. R. Edgeworth, *Sermons Very Fruitfull, Godly and Learned, Preached and Sette Foorthe by Maister Roger Edgeworth* (1557) fo. 43v.

41. WRO, B.A. 2764/802, fo. 137.

42. J. Foxe, *Acts and Monuments* (1839) viii, pp. 163–70.

43. William Hinde, *A Faithfull Remonstrance of the Holy Life and Happy Death of John Bruen of Bruen Stapleford in the County of Chester, Esquire* (1641) pp. 56–7.

44. BM Harleian MS. 1927, fo. 17v.

45. A. D. Dyer, *The City of Worcester in the Sixteenth Century* (Leicester 1973) p. 250.

46. A. Roger, 'Roger Ward's Shrewsbury Stock: An Inventory of 1585', in *The Library*, 5th ser., xiii (1958) 247–68.

47. PCC 3 Bolein; will of Thomas Parker, Wednesbury, dated 11 Jan 1602, proved 28 Jan 1602.

48. Margaret Spufford, 'The Schooling of the Peasantry in Cambridgeshire, 1570–1700', in *Land, Church and People: Essays presented to Professor H. P. R. Finberg*, ed. Joan Thirsk (AHR Supplement, 1970) 112–47.

49. BRO: will dated 1 Dec 1574, proved 9 Dec 1574.

50. SRO, D 1057, fos 82v, 107 (Congreve family commonplace book).

4. THE PROTESTANT EPISCOPATE   Ralph Houlbrooke

1. A Discourse of the Common Weal of this Realm of England, ed. E. Lamond (1893) p. 133.

2. F. D. Price, 'Gloucester Diocese under Bishop Hooper', in TBGAS, lx (1939) 51–151.

3. Documentary Annals of the Reformed Church in England, ed. E. Cardwell (1844) i, pp. 180, 193–4; R. H. Pogson, 'Reginald Pole and the Priorities of Government in Mary Tudor's Church', in HJ, xviii (1975) 3–20.

4. Correspondence of Matthew Parker, eds J. Bruce and T. T. Perowne (Parker Soc., xxxiii, 1853) p. 356; The Zurich Letters, ed. H. Robinson (Parker Soc. 1842) p. 51.

5. F. Heal, 'The Bishops and the Act of Exchange of 1559', in HJ, xvii (1974) 227–46.

6. Correspondence of Parker, p. 378.

7. F. O. White, Lives of the Elizabethan Bishops of the Anglican Church (1898) p. 260.

8. Correspondence of Parker, p. 360.

9. P. Collinson, The Elizabethan Puritan Movement (1967) pp. 62–3.

10. J. Harington, Nugae Antiquae, ed. T. Park (1804) ii, pp. 45, 206–9; White, Lives, p. 413.

11. Conyers Read, Lord Burghley and Queen Elizabeth (1960) p. 303.

12. J. Strype, Annals of the Reformation . . . during Queen Elizabeth's Happy Reign (1824) ii (2), pp. 600–1; White, Lives, pp. 290, 338–42; A. G. R. Smith, The Government of Elizabethan England (1967) p. 65.

13. M. R. O'Day, 'Clerical Patronage and Recruitment in England during the Elizabethan and Early Stuart Periods . . .' (London Ph.D. thesis, 1972), fos 24–38; Lincoln Episcopal Records temp. Thomas Cooper, 1571–84, ed. C. W. Foster (Lincoln RS 1912) ii, pp. 82, 87; White, Lives, pp. 262–3, 387–8; C. Haigh, Reformation and Resistance in Tudor Lancashire (1975) p. 239; F. M. Heal, 'The Bishops of Ely and their Diocese During the Reformation Period: c. 1515–1600' (Cambridge Ph.D. thesis, 1972) fo. 125.

14. Tudor Parish Documents of the Diocese of York, ed. J. S. Purvis (1948) pp. 98–101; Foster, Lincoln Episcopal Records, p. 138; CUL MS. Ee ii 34, fos 61v, 63v–4; J. W. Blench, Preaching in England in the Late Fifteenth and Sixteenth Centuries; a Study of English Sermons, 1450–c.1600 (1964) p. 301; T. Cooper, An Admonition to the People of England, ed. E. Arber (English Scholar's Library, xv, 1883) p. 110.

15. The Letter Book of John Parkhurst, ed. R. A. Houlbrooke (Norfolk RS, xliii, 1974–5) pp. 35–7, 43–4; M. R. O'Day, 'Thomas Bentham: a Case Study in the Problems of the Early Elizabethan Episcopate', in JEH, xxiii (1972) 155; R. B. Manning, Religion and Society in Elizabethan Sussex (1969) p. 64; H. G. Owen, 'The London Parish Clergy in the Reign of Elizabeth I' (London Ph.D. thesis, 1957) fos 250–1; Harington, Nugae Antiquae, ii, pp. 183–4.

16. S. E. Lehmberg, 'Archbishop Grindal and the Prophesyings', in Historical Magazine of the Protestant Episcopal Church, xxxiv (1965) 97–128; HRCO, C.B. 39, fos 148, 152, 157V; CUL MS. Ee ii 34, fo. 106; J. Strype, The History of the Life and Acts of the Most Reverend Father in God, Edmund Grindal (1821) p. 260; Strype, Annals, ii (2), pp. 611–12.

17. Strype, Grindal, p. 444; Purvis, Tudor Parish Documents, p. 96; Haigh, Reformation and Resistance, pp. 301–2; Collinson, Elizabethan Puritan Movement, pp. 209–10.

18. Purvis, Tudor Parish Documents, pp. 109–25; Heal, 'The Bishops of Ely', 133–4; R. A. Houlbrooke, 'Church Courts and People in the Diocese of Norwich, 1519–70' (Cambridge Ph.D. thesis, 1970) fo. 335.

19. *Correspondence of Parker*, p. 126; *The Registrum Vagum of Anthony Harison*, ed. T. F. Barton (Norfolk RS, xxxiii, 1963–4) p. 273; NNRO, HAR 3, fos 384–5.

20. H. G. Owen, 'The Episcopal Visitation: Its Limits and Limitations in Elizabethan London', in JEH, xi (1960) 179–85; Cardwell, *Documentary Annals*, ii, pp. 43–4; A. L. Rowse, *Tudor Cornwall* (1941) p. 337: *Bishop Redman's Visitation*, ed. J. F. Williams (Norfolk RS, xviii, 1946).

21. J. Strype, *Ecclesiastical Memorials* (1882) ii(2) pp. 41–2; *Visitation Articles and Injunctions of the Period of the Reformation,* eds W. H. Frere and W. P. M. Kennedy (Alcuin Club Collections 1910) iii, p. 163; White, *Lives*, pp. 160–1; Cardwell, *Documentary Annals,* ii, pp. 42–4; NNRO, HAR 3, fo. 385; Quoted in DNB under Matthew, Tobie.

22. A. Whiteman, 'The Church of England 1542–1837', in VCH *Wilts.*, iii (1956) p. 34; HRCO, C.B. 29, C.B. 31, C.B. 35; Heal, 'Bishops of Ely', 116–17; Houlbrooke, *Parkhurst*, pp. 31–2; Barton, *Registrum Vagum*, pp. 87–8; A. Hassell Smith, *County and Court: Government and Politics in Norfolk, 1558–1603* (1974), ch. 10; Strype, *Annals*, iii(1), pp. 131–8; iii(2) pp. 202–11; F. D. Price, 'The Abuses of Excommunication and the Decline of Ecclesiastical Discipline under Queen Elizabeth', in EHR, lvii (1942) 106–15; 'Bishop Bullingham and Chancellor Blackleech: a Diocese Divided', in TBGAS, xci (1972) 175–198; CUL MS. Ee ii 34, fo. 189; UDPD, Diocesan Records, xviii, 2; Haigh, Reformation and Resistance, pp. 232–3; Collinson, *Elizabethan Puritan Movement*, pp. 450–1.

23. *A Collection of Original Letters from the Bishops to the Privy Council, 1564*, ed. M. Bateson, in *Miscellany IX* (Camden Soc. new ser., liii, 1895); White, *Lives*, pp. 99–101; Manning, *Religion and Society*, pp. 84–90.

24. R. B. Manning, 'The Crisis of Episcopal Authority During the Reign of Elizabeth I', in JBS, xi (1971) 1–25; Haigh, *Reformation and Resistance*, pp. 223; Rowse, *Tudor Cornwall*, p. 334.

25. CUL MS. Ee ii 34, fos 97v–8.

26. J. Strype, *Historical Collections of the Life and Acts of the Right Reverend Father in God, John Aylmer* (1821) p. 83; A. H. Smith, *op. cit.*, p. 104.

27. *Harrison's Description of England*, ed. F. J. Furnivall (New Shakspere Soc. 1877) p. 16: Cardwell, *Documentary Annals*, ii, pp. 43–5; *The Injunctions and other Ecclesiastical Proceedings of Richard Barnes, Bishop of Durham* (Surtees Soc., xxii, 1850) pp. 81–2. Information on individual bishops is in White, *Lives, passim*. See ibid., pp. 339–40 for story about Matthew.

5.   ECONOMIC PROBLEMS OF THE CLERGY   *Felicity Heal*

1. *Councils and Synods*, eds F. Powicke and C. R. Cheney (1964) pp. 27, 64, 128, 461.

2. *The Works of Thomas Becon*, ed. J. Ayre (Parker Soc., 1844) ii, p. 325.

3. F. du Boulay, 'Charitable Subsidies granted to the Archbishop of Canterbury, 1300–1489', in BIHR, xxiii (1950) 157–8.

4. M. Bowker, *The Secular Clergy in the Diocese of Lincoln: 1495–1520* (1968) pp. 144–5; M. Zell, 'The Personnel of the Clergy in Kent during the Reformation', in EHR, lxxxix (1974) 522; C. Haigh, *Reformation and Resistance in Tudor Lancashire* (1975) pp. 34–5; P. Heath, *Medieval Clerical Accounts* (1964) p. 15.

5. P. Heath, *The English Parish Clergy on the Eve of the Reformation* (1969) pp. 23–4.

6. Bowker, *The Secular Clergy*, pp. 90–91; Zell, 'The Personnel of the Clergy', 532; Haigh, *Reformation and Resistance*, p. 27.

7. C. Hill, *Economic Problems of the Church from Archbishop Whitgift to the Long Parliament* (1956) p. 190. The detailed *Valor* for dioceses such as Bath and Wells and Lincoln always draws a careful distinction between tithe accruing to the appropriator and the vicar.

8. Heath, *Clerical Accounts*, p. 24; Haigh, *Reformation and Resistance*, p. 23.

9. S. J. Lander, 'The Diocese of Chichester, 1508–1558' (Cambridge Ph.D. thesis, 1974) fo. 257; D. M. Barratt, *Ecclesiastical Terriers of Warwickshire* (1955) *passim*.

10. D. M. Palliser, *The Reformation in York* (Borthwick Paper, No. 40, 1971) p. 3.

11. F. Godwin, *A Catalogue of the Bishops of England* (1615) p. 280; A. Hamilton Thompson, *The Cathedral Churches of England* (1925) p. 176.

12. Exeter Cathedral Muniments, MS. 3690.

13. Haigh, *Reformation and Resistance*, pp. 238–9; H. G. Owen, 'Parochial Curates in Elizabethan London', in JEH, x (1959) 69.

14. BM Harleian MS. 584, fo. 196.

15. *Synodalia*, ed. E. Cardwell (1842) i, pp. 507–8.

16. CSPD, Charles I, vol. cxci, 48.

17. Lander, thesis, fo. 267.

18. Hill, *Economic Problems*, p. 111; E. Phelps Brown and S. Hopkins, 'Seven Centuries of the Prices of Consumables, Compared with Builders' Wage Rates', in *Economica*, new ser., xxiii (1956) 312–13.

19. Bodl. Tanner MS. 79, fo. 21.

20. BM Lansdowne MS. xx, fo. 73; CSPD, Elizabeth, vol. CCLXXVII.

21. D. Marcombe, 'The Dean and Chapter of Durham, 1558–1603' (Durham Ph.D. thesis, 1973) 117–35.

22. C. Haigh, 'The Finances of the Bishops of Chester', in *Continuity and Change . . .*, eds M. R. O'Day and F. Heal (1976).

23. William Harrison, *A Description of England*, ed. G. Edelen (New York 1968) p. 30.

24. LP, xiv, i, 402.

25. SPD 11/151/868(15); SPD 12/27/47; R. H. Pogson, 'Revival and Reform in Mary Tudor's Church', in JEH, xxv (1974) 249–65.

26. Inner Temple, Petyt MS. 538/54/fo. 49v.

27. *Select Sixteenth Century Causes in Tithe*, ed. J. S. Purvis (Yorks. AS, cxiv, 1949) p. viii.

28. *Tudor Treatises*, ed. A. G. Dickens (Yorks. ASRS, v. 1959) p. 125.

29. BM Lansdowne MS. 79/42.

30. Corpus Christi College, Cambridge MS. 581.

31. CUL Mm/1/42, fo. 326.

32. Harrison, *A Description of England*, p. 28; *The Diary of the Rev. Ralph Josselin* (Camden Soc. 1908) pp. 10–11.

33. M. R. O'Day, 'The Reformation of the Ministry', in *Continuity and Change, passim*.

6. THE DISPOSAL OF MONASTIC AND CHANTRY LANDS

Christopher Kitching

1. *Valor Ecclesiasticus*, 6 vols (1810–34).

2. T. H. Swales, 'The Redistribution of Monastic Lands in Norfolk at the Dissolution', in *Norfolk Archaeology*, xxxiv (1966) 17.

3. H. A. L. Fisher, *The History of England from the Accession of Henry VII to the Death of Henry VIII* (1919) Appendix II, p. 499; among the commentators see especially K. Pickthorne, *Early Tudor Government, Henry VIII* (1934) pp. 372–86.

4. A. G. Dickens, *The English Reformation* (1964) p. 158; J. A. Youings, 'Landlords in England: the Church', in *The Agrarian History of England and Wales: IV, 1500–1640*, ed. Joan Thirsk (1967) pp. 306–56, and *The Dissolution of the Monasteries* (1971); G. A. J. Hodgett, 'The Dissolution of the Religious Houses in Lincolnshire and the Changing Structure of Society, in *Lincs*. AAS *Reports and Papers*, new ser., iv, i (1951) 83–99.

5. J. E. Kew, 'The Disposal of Crown Lands and the Devon Land Market 1536–58', in AHR, xviii (1970); and Swales, 'Redistribution of Monastic Lands', 30.

6. Dickens, *English Reformation*, p. 157; Sybil Jack, 'Monastic Lands in Leicestershire and their Administration on the Eve of the Dissolution', in *Transactions of the Leicestershire Archaeological and Historical Society*, xli (1965–6) 9–40.

7. G. Baskerville, *English Monks and the Suppression of the Monasteries* (1937) pp. 57–8.

8. J. A. Youings, *Devon Monastic Lands: Particulars for Grants* (Devon and Cornwall Record Soc., new ser., i, 1955) p. xxiv.

9. R. H. Tawney, 'The Rise of the Gentry', in ECHR, 2nd ser., xi (1941) 23.

10. E.g. R. B. Outhwaite, 'Who Bought Crown Lands? The Pattern of Purchases 1589–1603', in BIHR, xliv (1971) 18–23.

11. F. M. L. Thompson, 'The Social Distribution of Landed Property in England since the Sixteenth Century', in ECHR, 2nd ser., xix (1966) 505.

12. F. C. Dietz, *English Government Finance 1485–1558* (University of Illinois Studies in Social Sciences, ix, 3, Urbana 1920) pp. 137ff.

13. Youings, *The Dissolution of the Monasteries* (1971) p. 17.

14. PRO Ministers' Accounts (SC6) and Receivers' Accounts (LR6).

15. Youings, *Particulars*, p. viii.

16. PRO LR6/154, 156–9, 161–84 and LR9 *passim*.

17. C. J. Kitching, 'The Quest for Concealed Lands in the Reign of Elizabeth I', in TRHS, 5th ser., xxiv (1974) 63–78.

18. See PRO *Lists and Index, Supplementary*, ii (Kraus 1967) pp. 365, 393.

19. PRO E135/454 covers Lincs., Notts., Derbys., and Chesh. in the reign of Jas I; SC11/957 is a roll of monastic rents in London in the reign of Chas II.

20. G. R. Batho, 'Syon House: the first 200 Years', in *London and Middlesex Archaeological Society Transactions*, xix (1956); Sister Jane Mary, 'A History of Burnham Abbey' (typescript available from the abbey). Other examples are noted in G. R. Batho, 'Landlords in England: the Crown', in *The Agrarian History of England and Wales*: IV, *1500–1640*, ed. Joan Thirsk (1967) p. 263.

21. PRO *Deputy Keeper's Report*, 38 (1877).

22. PRO E134/7 Eliz. Trinity/1, and 7 & 8 Eliz. Michaelmas/1 : Exchequer, Depositions before Special Commissions.

23. Youings, 'Landlords in England', *passim*.

24. W. K. Jordan, *Edward VI: The Threshold of Power* (1970) p. 191; Dr. Alan Kreider discusses this point in a forthcoming study of the background to the dissolution of the monasteries.

25. Jordan, *Threshold of Power*, p. 198.

26. See A. F. Leach, *English Schools at the Reformation* (1896) and J. Simon, *Education and Society in Tudor England* (1966) for the two main views in this debate.

27. W. K. Jordan, *Philanthropy in England, 1480–1660* (1959).

28. PRO SP10/15 fo. 18; E315/258.

29. PRO LR2/65.

30. Richardson, *Puritanism in North-West England* (1972) pp. 8, 173.

31. LPL MS. 695, fo. 31.

32. A. Bell, *Tudor Foundation* (Chalfont St Giles 1974) pp. 10–11.

33. Hatfield Cecil MS. 144, fos 60–70.

34. PRO E318/1971–73.

35. J. Hurstfield, 'Greenwich Tenures of Edward VI', in LQR, lxv (1949) 72ff.

36. PRO E315/68 records the early sales.

37. E. Lodge, *Illustrations of British History* (1838) i, 149.

38. CPR, iii, 386.

39. *Calendar of Treasury Books*, ed. W. A. Shaw (1904) i, 68.

40. PRO E315/343; E315/68 fo. 503v.

41. W. K. Jordan, *Edward VI: The Young King* (1968), p. 110.
42. C. J. Kitching, 'Studies in the Redistribution of Collegiate and Chantry Property in the Diocese and County of York at the Dissolution' (Durham Ph.D. thesis, 1970).
43. This statement is based upon examination of a sample of counties: PRO SC6/Mary/32 (Bucks.), 74 (Devon), 88 (Durham), 94 (Essex), 205 (Norfolk) and 264 (Staffs.).
44. PRO LR6/113/5 (Kent) and LR6/104/4 (Somerset) for example.
45. BCRO, DDCC/139/65, fo. 16.
46. PRO LR2/65, fo. 30v; SC6/Phil. & Mary/30.

7. ECCLESIASTICAL PATRONAGE Rosemary O'Day

1. W. M. Lamont, *Godly Rule* (1969) p. 57.
2. P. Collinson, *The Elizabethan Puritan Movement* (1967) pp. 59–68; 201, 271; cf. R. A. Houlbrooke, 'The Protestant Episcopate', 84–6, for a more detailed account of patronage at this level.
3. H. R. Trevor-Roper, 'King James and his Bishops', in HT (1955) *passim*.
4. A. P. Kautz, 'The Selection of Jacobean Bishops', in *Early Stuart Studies: Essays in Honour of D. H. Willson*, ed. H. S. Reinmuch (Minneapolis 1970) pp. 152–79.
5. M. Bowker, *The Secular Clergy in the Diocese of Lincoln, 1495–1520* (1968) p. 67.
6. R. Christophers, 'The Social and Educational Background of the Surrey Clergy, 1520–1620' (London Ph.D. thesis, 1975) fo. 191.
7. LJRO B/V/1/2.
8. See M. R. O'Day, 'THE Ecclesiastical Patronage of the Lord Keeper, 1558–1642', in TRHS, 5th ser., xxiii (1973) *passim*.
9. BM Lansdowne MS. 443; Bodleian Tanner MS. 179.
10. LJRO B/C/3/12: Office v. Thomas Hodgkinson, 3 July 1623.
11. Melbourne Hall, Coke MSS, Bundle 43, *passim*.
12. M. R. O'Day, 'Immanuel Bourne: A Defence of the Ministerial Order', in JEH, xxviii (1976) 101–14.
13. R. B. Outhwaite, 'Who Bought Crown Lands? The Pattern of Purchases 1589–1603', in BIHR, xliv (1971) 18–23.
14. W. J. Sheils, 'The Puritans in Church and Politics in the Diocese of Peterborough, 1570–1610' (London Ph.D. thesis, 1974) esp. fos 50–70.
15. H. G. Owen, 'The London Parish Clergy in the Reign of Elizabeth I' (London Ph.D. thesis, 1957) *passim*.
16. See M. R. O'Day, 'Clerical Patronage and Recruitment in England during the Elizabethan and Early Stuart Periods' (London Ph.D. thesis, 1972) 196–221.
17. Owen, thesis, *passim*.
18. See D. M. Barratt, 'Conditions of the Parish Clergy from the Reformation to 1660 . . .' (Oxford D.Phil. thesis, 1950) *passim*; and O'Day, thesis, 73–103.
19. But see W. J. Sheils, 'Religion in Provincial Towns: Innovation and Tradition', pp. 162–3, for an alternative or complementary view.

8. RELIGION IN PROVINCIAL TOWNS: INNOVATION AND
TRADITION W. J. Sheils

1. See bibliographical note. For Baxter see G. F. Nuttall, *Richard Baxter* (1965).
2. Perspectives in Urban History, ed. A. Everitt (1973) pp. 5–9; *The Agrarian History*

of England and Wales: IV, *1500–1640*, ed. Joan Thirsk (1967) pp. 478–86: M. C. Cross, *The Puritan Earl* (1966) pp. 124–30; J. E. Neale, *The Elizabethan House of Commons* (1949).

   3. P. Slack, 'Poverty and Politics in Salisbury, 1597–1666', in *Crisis and Order in English Towns, 1500–1700*, eds P. Clark and P. Slack (1972 pp. 178–92; P. Slack, 'Religious Protest and Urban Authority: the case of Henry Sherfield, iconoclast, 1633', in *Schism, Heresy and Religious Protest*, ed. D. Baker (1972); P. Collinson, *The Elizabethan Puritan Movement* (1967) pp. 141–3.

   4. C. Hill, *Economic Problems of the Church from Archbishop Whitgift to the Long Parliament* (1956) p. 57; VCH *Gloucestershire*, xi (1976) pp. 81, 136–7; VCH *Wiltshire*, x (1975) pp. 285–6; see below n.14.

   5. D. M. Palliser, 'The unions of Parishes at York 1547–1586', in YAJ, xlvi (1975) 87–102; see article by F. M. Heal.

   6. YML MSS, WC, fos 77–8; R. C. Richardson, *Puritanism in North-West England* (1972) pp. 13–17; J. Newton, 'The Yorkshire Puritan Movement, 1603–40', in TCHS, xix (1960–4) 3–17; C. Hill, *Economic Problems*, p. 57; C. Hill, *Society and Puritanism in Pre-Revolutionary England* (1964) p. 59; Cross, *The Puritan Earl*, pp. 256–7.

   7. Hill, *Economic Problems*, p. 142; W. J. Sheils, 'A Survey of the Diocese of Gloucester, 1603', in *An Ecclesiastical Miscellany* (BGAS, RS, 1976) pp. 61–102; G. Hart, *A History of Cheltenham* (1965) pp. 94–101; VCH *Gloucestershire*, viii (1968) p. 155.

   8. *The Zurich Letters*, ed. H. Robinson (Parker Soc. 1842) i, pp. 86–7. *Reprint of the Barnstaple Records*, eds J. R. Chanter and T. Wainwright (1900) ii, pp. 99–100; J. W. F. Hill, *Tudor and Stuart Lincoln* (1956) pp. 101, 110; R. B. Manning, *Religion and Society in Elizabethan Sussex* (1969) pp. 76–8; A. J. Fletcher, *A County Community at Peace and War* (1967) p. 71.

   9. P. S. Seaver, *The Puritan Lectureships* . . . (Stanford, Calif. 1970) Appendix A; Hill, *Society and Puritanism*, pp. 98–9, 102–5; see n.12 below.

   10. P. Collinson, 'Lectures by Combination . . .', in BIHR, xlviii (1975) 198–9; Richardson, *Puritanism*, pp. 65–9; BIHR York MSS, v. 1594/CB, fo. 167; Collinson, *Career of John Cotton* (Princeton 1962).

   11. PRO, SP 12/150/42(1); Fletcher, *A County Community*, pp. 70–1; Cross, *The Puritan Earl*, pp. 115–42.

   12. P. Collinson, 'Towards a Broader Understanding of the Early Dissenting Tradition', in *The Dissenting Tradition*, eds C. R. Cole and M. E. Moody (Ohio 1975) pp. 12–15; E. Venables, 'The Primary Visitation of the Diocese of Lincoln by Bishop Neile, 1614', in Association of Architects Society Reports, xvi (1881) 41; L. Ziff, *The Career of John Cotton* (Princeton 1962).

   13. See chapter by I. Luxton and her bibliographical note; also C. Phythian-Adams, 'Ceremony and the Citizen: the Communal Year at Coventry, 1450–1550', in *Crisis and Order in English Towns*, pp. 57–85.

   14. W. J. Sheils, 'The Puritans in Church and Politics in the Diocese of Peterborough, 1570–1610' (London Ph.D. thesis, 1974), fos 206–27; *The Records of the Borough of Northampton*, eds C. A. Markham and J. C. Cox, (1898) ii, pp. 385–91, 396–8; J. W. F. Hill, *Tudor and Stuart Lincoln*, p. 99; *Depositions Taken Before the Mayor and Aldermen of Norwich, 1549–1567*, ed. W. Rye (1905) pp. 23, 48–9.

   15. N. R. N. Tyacke, 'Puritanism, Arminianism and Counter-Revolution', in *The Origins of the English Civil War*, ed. C. S. R. Russell (1973) pp. 119–43; Collinson, 'Lectures by Combination', 199 n.4, 213; Manning, *Religion and Society*, pp. 76–8; Fletcher, *A County Community*, pp. 76–93; R. A. Marchant, *The Puritans and the Church Courts in the Diocese of York, 1560–1642* (1960) p. 65.

   16. Sheils, thesis, fos 94, 101–2, 104–6, 159.

   17. D. M. Owen, *Church and Society in Medieval Lincolnshire* (1971) pp. 110–12, 126–31; *A Calendar of the Register of Archbishop Robert Waldby, 1397*, ed. D. M. Smith (1974) pp. 19–20; *Bishop Langley's Register*, ed. R. L. Storey (Surtees Soc. 1957) ii,

pp. 6–7; VCH *Staffordshire*, viii (1963) pp. 18–19; R. B. Dobson, 'The Foundations of Perpetual Chantries by the Citizens of Medieval York', in *Studies in Church History*, ed. G. J. Cuming (Leiden 1967) iv, p. 37; K. L. Wood-Legh, *Perpetual Chantries in Britain* (1965) p. 158.

18. *Churchwardens' Accounts of Ashburton, 1479–1580*, ed. A. Hanham (Devon and Cornwall RS, 1970) Introduction; M. D. Anderson, *Drama and Imagery in English Medieval Churches* (1963) *passim*; Owen, *Church and Society*, p. 130; *Registrata Stephani Gardiner et Johannis Ponet*, ed. H. Chitty (CYS, 1930) pp. 177, 179, 181.

19. J. R. Chanter, *Sketches of the Literary History of Barnstaple . . . to which is appended the Diary of Philip Wyot, Town Clerk of Barnstaple from 1586 to 1608* (Barnstaple, no date) p. 92.

20. Manning, *Religion and Society*, p. 243; P. Collinson, 'Lectures by Combination', 212.

Notes on Contributors

CLAIRE CROSS, Senior Lecturer in History, University of York. M.A., Ph.D. Cambridge. Author of numerous articles in academic journals and essay volumes and of *The Puritan Earl* and *The Royal Supremacy in the Elizabethan Church*.

FELICITY HEAL, formerly Research Fellow in History, Newnham College, Cambridge. M.A., Ph.D. Cambridge. Author of numerous articles and co-editor of *Continuity and Change: Personnel and Administration of the Church in England, 1500–1642*. Is currently completing a monograph on the Bishops' Lands.

RALPH HOULBROOKE, Lecturer in History, University of Reading. M.A., D. Phil. Oxford. Author of articles in learned journals and editor of the letters of John Parkhurst, bihsop of Norwich. Is currently preparing a monograph on the church courts in the sixteenth century.

CHRISTOPHER KITCHING, Assistant Keeper, Public Record Office. B.A., Ph.D. Durham. Author of numerous articles and editions. Winner of Alexander Prize, 1973.

IMOGEN LUXTON, B.A. Durham. She was a research student at the Institute of Historical Research 1969–71. She then entered the Civil Service and is now a Principal in the Department of Education and Science.

ROSEMARY O'DAY, Lecturer in History, The Open University. B.A. York, Ph.D. London. Author of articles in academic journals and of *Economy and Community: Economic and Social History of Pre-industrial England*. Co-editor of *Continuity and Change*. Is currently completing a monograph on the clerical profession and a work on early modern education.

D. M. PALLISER, Lecturer in Economic History, University of Birmingham. M.A., D.Phil. Oxford. Has written numerous articles and contributions to essay volumes. Author of *The Reformation in York, 1534–1553*. Is currently preparing a monograph on York.

W. J. SHEILS, Senior Archivist, Borthwick Institute of Historical Research, University of York. B.A. York, Ph.D. London. Has contributed to a previous essay volume and to the Victoria County History of Gloucestershire. Is currently preparing a monograph on Northamptonshire Puritans.

Index